THE 'EX POST FACTO'
GOVERNMENT
GUN
GRAB

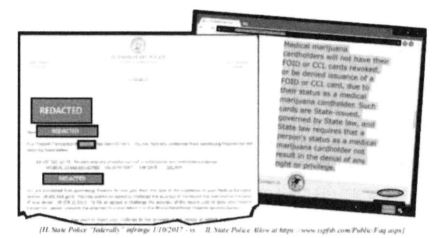

[Il. State Police "federally" infringe 1/10/2017 - vs   Il. State Police Allow at https://www.ispfsb.com/Public/Faq.aspx]

An Exposé of Obama's 'After-the-Fact' 'Bill of Attainder' Cover-Up-Conspiracy Timed to Un-Constitutionally Target America's 'Bill of Rights' During President Trump's Administration.

* * * * * * * * * * * * *

By Detective Matthew P. Kulesza, P.I.
[Il. License # 115-002274]

'Unauthorized' Foreword by JFK

'The Ex-Post-Facto Government Gun Grab' © 2018 by Matthew P. Kulesza

Acknowledgments.

To my mother and father. We miss you dearly, with fond, loving memories forever in our hearts. I can never fully express my appreciation for our Faith in Christ and our Patriotism for America you have granted unto me. The respect for others and ourselves are lessons I continue to share with others. I will trust in our Lord Jesus Christ as I Patriotically serve those in need. Thank you, so very much, Mom and Dad. Love you.

To my family, I could not have done this without your support. I feel very fortunate to have such a close, loving family. As I have matured over the years, I have gained a greater appreciation for all we have shared and taught one another about God, Faith, our Heritage, Math, Science, the Arts, Cheerleading, Photography, Friendship, Family and our world. Thank you for being there and for always watching out for kin. I love you.

I would like to thank my four, 8th grade US History teachers at Barrington Public School District 220. Our class was truly blessed to have such a terrific host of Patriots for our American History studies. Since my eight-grade, I now travel with two pieces of literature from our shared History... and the other one is the King James Version of The Holy Bible.

I would also like to thank all those Americans who have spoken out in defense of the US Constitution and our *'Bill of Rights'* at times of great opposition. Adam Baldwin, Thomas E. Bearden, John Carpenter, Clint Eastwood, Laura Magdalene Eisenhower, R. Lee Ermy, Dr. Steven Greer, Maurice A. Hargraves, Dr. Suzanna Gratia Hupp, Alex Jones, James Earl Jones, Ice T, Chuck Norris, Kris Paronto, Dolly Parton, Julia Roberts, Dr. Carol Rosin, Kurt Russell, Steven Seagal, Tom Selleck, Gary Sinise, (God in a Nutshell) Trey Smith, Suzanne Sommers, Howard Stern, Oliver Stone, Denzel Washington, Bruce Willis and James Woods are just a few of the countless many who've spoken in defense of our American Freedom, Liberty and Independence. Thank you all, so very much.

Thank you to Humphrey Bogart, for showing us all how it's done.

Thank you to James Cagney, a true American family-man who found the time to entertain us on the Silver Screen.

I would like to thank best-selling author Tom Clancy, for his defense of our Constitutional Rights, in print, and at the movies.

I would like to thank the late, FBI SAIC, Ted Gunderson, for having the courage to speak the truth. Prayers are extended to your family.

To Dashiell Hammett, thanks for writing one of the greatest detective novels of all time. Though exposing some of the wicked vermin, *'The Maltese Falcon'* can be quite an elusive bird, to put one's hands on.

To Russell David Johnson, thank you for your service and your sacrifices; *'We'* will cherish the entertaining memories on the screen, knowing you were so much more than just our castaway *'Professor'*.

To Reverend Dr. Martin Luther King, Jr., thank you for keeping the Dream alive as you held our American Flag high. We're a better world.

Lee Marvin, thanks for your service and the memories shared on the Silver Screen. America always loves a *'Dozen Dirty Patriots'*.

I would like to extend my prayers to the Family of American Film Legend, Walter Matthau. We are all huge fans as he never failed to entertain. I especially thank the Matthau Family for one of our all-time favorites, *'Hopscotch'*. Honestly, I am not sure if my mother was laughing more from your father, or from watching my father and I laugh and snicker all the way through. It is truly a film we could never watch enough. To the Matthau Family and cast, thank you; *'a te fortuna non mancherà'*!

Thank you to Rich Mullins for staying the course and never losing sight. The world was fortunate to have been entertained by such a talented *'Ragamuffin'* who brought the *'Good Word'* to so many.

To US Treasury Agent Eliot Ness, thank you for standing up to corruption at every level, private and public, during Prohibition and after.

Alan Pinkerton, thanks for keeping him alive whenever you were at his side. We would've had a different world without your service.

Roddy Piper, thanks for running out of bubble-gum.

Elvis Presley, thank you for your music, your films and your service. Not many chart-topping artists would serve their country the way you did for our United States.

To General H. Norman Schwarzkopf, thank you for your service and for sharing some laughs with our Dad.

Thank you to Mickey Spillane, for bringing us a glimpse into the world of a *'Private Eye'*.

This *'Pilgrim'* would like to thank *'The Duke'*. If an explanation is needed, you're probably not an American from an elder generation.

I thank the private investigators and private security contractors I have worked with over the better part of two decades and will continue to do so in the future. It is an honor to work with professionals from many different branches of the American military, law enforcement, and private sector. You have all served America honorably.

Thanks to the American men and women, past and present, who have honorably served our country in uniform, including members of the law enforcement community who uphold our US Constitution in the shadow of conflicting orders, risking it all in these tempestuous times.

I would like to thank President Donald J. Trump, for always acting in America's best interest. You surprised the heck out of a lot of People - me included. I would also like to extend my best wishes to the First Family with prayers for a safer and more prosperous future as *'We the People'* Make America Great Again and then Keep America Great.

I thank our Lord and Savior, Jesus Christ and our Heavenly Father, for everything. Thank you for granting us mercy though your sacrifice.

I would like to thank all American Patriots, past, present and future, from America's Founders to the hard-working citizens in America today. I give thanks to all who persist through my run-on sentences, poor grammar and spelling lgitches. I do wish I had more time to provide a thorough edit. The *'anonymous detective',* who has provided some of the redacted documents presented herein, felt it more important to hasten the delivery of this information to the American People.

Thanks for reading.

This presentation is dedicated to, *'We the People'*.

God Bless the United States of America.

THE 'EX POST FACTO' GOVERNMENT GUN GRAB

By Detective Matthew P. Kulesza, P.I.

[IL Private Detective License # 115-002274]

'Unauthorized' Foreword by JFK

Table of Contents.

Chapter 1 – The Evidence...1

Chapter 2 - The Facts...33

Chapter 3 – The Modus Operandi...110

Chapter 4 – The Remedies..206

Chapter 5 – America's Private Eyes..235

Foreword.

[President John F. Kennedy spoke to a gathering of publishers, editors and journalists at a New York City hotel on April 27, 1961. After his introductions to the crowd, the President began his three-part speech addressing the concerns for White House and government-insider intelligence leaks to the press which caused dangerous disruptions in the peaceful endeavors of our Republic during already tumultuous times. We revisit President Kennedy's speech after he warmed-up the crowd with his trademark charm.]

'Unauthorized' Foreword.

"The President and the Press."

President John Fitzgerald Kennedy - April 27, 1961

".... 'My topic tonight is a more sober one of concern to publishers as well as editors.

I want to talk about our common responsibilities in the face of a common danger. The events of recent weeks may have helped to illuminate that challenge for some; but the dimensions of its threat have loomed large on the horizon for many years. Whatever our hopes may be for the future--for reducing this threat or living with it--there is no escaping either the gravity or the totality of its challenge to our survival and to our security--a challenge that confronts us in unaccustomed ways in every sphere of human activity.

This deadly challenge imposes upon our society two requirements of direct concern both to the press and to the President--two requirements that may seem almost contradictory in tone, but which must be reconciled and fulfilled if we are to meet this national peril. I refer, first, to the need for a far greater public information; and, second, to the need for far greater official secrecy.

(I)

The very word "secrecy" is repugnant in a free and open society; and we are as a people inherently and historically opposed to secret societies, to secret oaths and to secret proceedings. We decided long ago that the dangers of excessive and unwarranted concealment of pertinent facts far outweighed the dangers which are cited to justify it. Even today, there is little value in opposing the threat of a closed society by imitating its arbitrary restrictions. Even today, there is little value in insuring the survival of our nation if our traditions do not survive with it. And there is very grave danger that an announced need for increased security will be seized upon by those anxious to expand its meaning to the very limits of official censorship and concealment. That I do not intend to permit to the extent that it is in my control. And no official of my Administration, whether his rank is high or low, civilian or military, should interpret my words here tonight as an excuse to censor the news, to stifle dissent, to cover up our mistakes or to withhold from the press and the public the facts they deserve to know.

But I do ask every publisher, every editor, and every newsman in the nation to reexamine his own standards, and to recognize the nature of our country's peril. In time of war, the government and the press have customarily joined in an effort based largely on self-discipline, to prevent unauthorized disclosures to the enemy. In time of "clear and present danger," the courts have held that even the privileged rights of the First Amendment must yield to the public's need for national security.

Today no war has been declared--and however fierce the struggle may be, it may never be declared in the traditional fashion. Our way of life is under attack. Those who make themselves our enemy are advancing around the globe. The survival of our friends is in danger. And yet no war has been declared, no borders have been crossed by marching troops, no missiles have been fired.

If the press is awaiting a declaration of war before it imposes the self-discipline of combat conditions, then I can only say that no war ever posed a greater threat to our security. If you are awaiting a finding of "clear and present danger," then I can only say that the danger has never been more clear and its presence has never been more imminent.

It requires a change in outlook, a change in tactics, a change in missions--by the government, by the people, by every businessman or labor leader, and by every newspaper. For we are opposed around the world by a monolithic and ruthless conspiracy that relies primarily on covert means for expanding its sphere of influence--on infiltration instead of invasion, on subversion instead of elections, on intimidation instead of free choice, on guerrillas by night instead of armies by day. It is a system which has conscripted vast human and material resources into the building of a tightly knit, highly efficient machine that combines military, diplomatic, intelligence, economic, scientific and political operations.

Its preparations are concealed, not published. Its mistakes are buried, not headlined. Its dissenters are silenced, not praised. No expenditure is questioned, no rumor is printed, no secret is revealed. It conducts the Cold War, in short, with a war-time discipline no democracy would ever hope or wish to match.

Nevertheless, every democracy recognizes the necessary restraints of national security--and the question remains whether those restraints need to be more strictly observed if we are to oppose this kind of attack as well as outright invasion.

For the facts of the matter are that this nation's foes have openly boasted of acquiring through our newspapers information they would otherwise hire agents to acquire through theft, bribery or espionage; that details of this nation's covert preparations to counter the enemy's covert operations have been available to every newspaper reader, friend and foe alike; that the size, the strength, the location and the nature of our forces and weapons, and our plans and strategy for their use, have all been pinpointed in the press and other news media to a degree sufficient to satisfy any foreign power; and that, in at least in one case, the publication of details concerning a secret mechanism whereby satellites were followed required its alteration at the expense of considerable time and money.

The newspapers which printed these stories were loyal, patriotic, responsible and well-meaning. Had we been engaged in open warfare, they undoubtedly would not have published such items. But in the absence of open warfare, they recognized only the tests of journalism and not the tests of national security. And my question tonight is whether additional tests should not now be adopted.

The question is for you alone to answer. No public official should answer it for you. No governmental plan should impose its restraints against your will. But I would be failing in my duty to the nation, in considering all of the responsibilities that we now bear and all of the means at hand to meet those responsibilities, if I did not commend this problem to your attention, and urge its thoughtful consideration.

On many earlier occasions, I have said--and your newspapers have constantly said--that these are times that appeal to every citizen's sense of sacrifice and self-discipline. They call out to every citizen to weigh his rights and comforts against his obligations to the common good. I cannot now believe that those citizens who serve in the newspaper business consider themselves exempt from that appeal.

I have no intention of establishing a new Office of War Information to govern the flow of news. I am not suggesting any new forms of censorship or any new types of security classifications. I have no easy answer to the dilemma that I have posed, and would not seek to impose it if I had one. But I am asking the members of the newspaper profession and the industry in this country to reexamine their own responsibilities, to consider the degree and the nature of the present *danger, and to heed the duty of self-restraint which that danger imposes upon us all.*

Every newspaper now asks itself, with respect to every story: "Is it news?" All I suggest is that you add the question: "Is it in the interest of the national security?" And I hope that every group in America--unions and businessmen and public officials at every level-- will ask the same question of their endeavors, and subject their actions to the same exacting tests.

And should the press of America consider and recommend the voluntary assumption of specific new steps or machinery, I can assure you that we will cooperate whole-heartedly with those recommendations.

Perhaps there will be no recommendations. Perhaps there is no answer to the dilemma faced by a free and open society in a cold and secret war. In times of peace, any discussion of this subject, and any action that results, are both painful and without precedent. But this is a time of peace and peril which knows no precedent in history.

(II)

It is the unprecedented nature of this challenge that also gives rise to your second obligation--an obligation which I share. And that is our obligation to inform and alert the American people--to make certain that they possess all the facts that they need, and understand them as well--the perils, the prospects, the purposes of our program and the choices that we face.

No President should fear public scrutiny of his program. For from that scrutiny comes understanding; and from that understanding comes support or opposition. And both are necessary. I am not asking your newspapers to support the Administration, but I am asking your help in the tremendous task of informing and alerting the American people. For I have complete confidence in the response and dedication of our citizens whenever they are fully informed.

I not only could not stifle controversy among your readers--I welcome it. This Administration intends to be candid about its errors; for as a wise man once said: "An error does not become a mistake until you refuse to correct it." We intend to accept full responsibility for our errors; and we expect you to point them out when we miss them.

Without debate, without criticism, no Administration and no country can succeed--and no republic can survive. That is why the Athenian lawmaker Solon decreed it a crime for any citizen to shrink from controversy. And that is why our press was protected by the First Amendment-- the only business in America specifically protected by the Constitution- -not primarily to amuse and entertain, not to emphasize the trivial and the sentimental, not to simply "give the public what it wants"--but to inform, to arouse, to reflect, to state our dangers and our opportunities, to indicate our crises and our choices, to lead, mold, educate and sometimes even anger public opinion.

This means greater coverage and analysis of international news--for it is no longer far away and foreign but close at hand and local. It means greater attention to improved understanding of the news as well as improved transmission. And it means, finally, that government at all levels, must meet its obligation to provide you with the fullest possible information outside the narrowest limits of national security--and we intend to do it.

(III)

It was early in the Seventeenth Century that Francis Bacon remarked on three recent inventions already transforming the world: the compass, gunpowder and the printing press. Now the links between the nations first forged by the compass have made us all citizens of the world, the hopes and threats of one becoming the hopes and threats of us all. In that one world's efforts to live together, the evolution of gunpowder to its ultimate limit has warned mankind of the terrible consequences of failure.

And so it is to the printing press--to the recorder of man's deeds, the keeper of his conscience, the courier of his news--that we look for strength and assistance, confident that with your help man will be what he was born to be: free and independent."

JFK - April 27, 1961

=======

Chapter 1

<u>The Evidence.</u>

The Constitution of the United States ´ was adopted into law by America's original 13 States over 227 years ago. After years of debate following the American Revolutionary War, our Founding Fathers secured our *'Bill of Rights'* in our Constitution's First Ten Amendments, providing safeguards to ensure our Freedoms, our Liberties, and our United States to exist for America's future generations.

Though tyrannical powers continually threaten our American Liberty, *'We the People'* believed our Constitution to be impervious to attacks from tyrants, foreign and domestic. We were wrong.

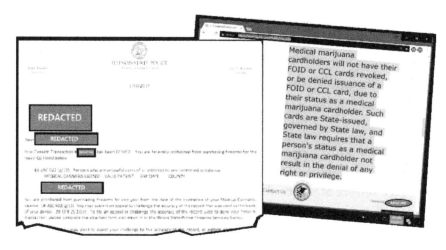

[IL State Police infringement letter 01/10/2017 Vs. IL State Police invite at ISP-Public-FAQ webpage: https://www.ispfsb.com/Public/Faq.aspx *]*

Amendment I

Congress shall make no law respecting an establishment of religion, or prohibiting the free exercise thereof; or abridging the freedom of speech, or of the press; or the right of the people peaceably to assemble, and to petition the Government for a redress of grievances.

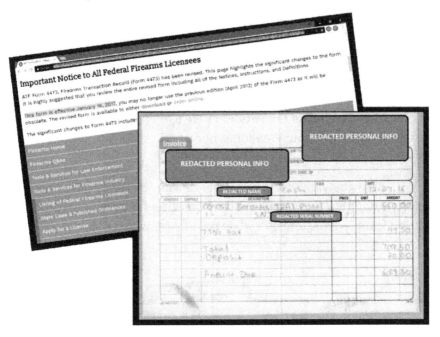

[Actual down-payment 12/27/2016 -vs- Obama's 'new rule' 01/16/2017 at ATF webpage: https://www.atf.gov/firearms/atf-form-4473-firearms-transaction-record-revisions]

   The State of Illinois continues to deceive Americans, infringing on their Rights with an Obama-era un-Constitutional '*Ex-Post-Facto,*' 'After-the-Facts' seizure of personal property and family businesses. The State of Illinois falsely invites medical marijuana patients to exercise their 2nd Amendment before classifying them as felonious narcotic users through the FBI-NCIS law enforcement databases. The Obama *'executive order'* results in denying every American's Constitutional Rights.

Under Obama, Americans lost our Rights to, *"freedom of speech, or of the press; or the right of the people peaceably to assemble, and to petition the Government for a redress of grievances. (1st), 'to be secure in their persons, houses, papers, and effects, against unreasonable searches and seizures', (4th)"* and to *"...'due process of law; nor shall private property be taken for public use, without just compensation (5th)."* Now, the tyrannical powers are coming for every American's 2nd Amendment Right with an *'ex post facto Law'*.

Amendment II

A well regulated Militia, being necessary to the security of a free State, the right of the people to keep and bear Arms, shall not be infringed.

One private detective and his family have faced the brunt of these government attacks against our American *'Bill of Rights'*. I have the scoop on this Obama-era *'Ex-Post-Facto Government Gun Grab'*, and the continuing cover-up, timed to land its blame upon President Trump's administration as the covert agenda increasingly unfolds into America's undetermined future.

--- August 31, 2018 ---

Illinois State Police deadline for the detective to surrender his 'Compassionate Use' medical treatments.

Now the *'Countdown-Clock'* is ticking for a detective and his family owned and operated business, as well as America's *'Bill of Rights'* as the impossible burden of nothing less than *'time-travel'* will be able to meet the new compliance set forth under Obama's un-Constitutional *"Bill of Attainder"* and *'after-the-fact'*, *"ex post facto Law"*, lest *'We the People'* are enlightened, in time, to address the ongoing government cover-up and concealments within our United States.

Will President Trump act with his signature, ending Obama's un-Constitutional siege upon our American *'Bill of Rights'?* These continuing government attacks on *'The Constitution of the United States'* set dangerous precedents for *'We the People'* as Constitutionally protected medical records of law-abiding Americans are seized and held to criminal scrutiny by state, federal and even international law enforcement agencies, including Obama's FBI NCIS, without any knowledge of the American People.

Amendment IV

The right of the people to be secure in their persons, houses, papers, and effects, against unreasonable searches and seizures, shall not be violated, and no Warrants shall issue, but upon probable cause, supported by Oath or affirmation, and particularly describing the place to be searched, and the persons or things to be seized.

The Obama-era impossible *'ex post facto Law,"* has given the detective until August 31, 2018 to surrender his legally-protected medical treatment before his un-Constitutionally in-validated Firearm Owner's Identification card will face denied renewal thereby setting a precedent for all America.

Amendment V

No person shall be held to answer for a capital, or otherwise infamous crime, unless on a presentment or indictment of a Grand Jury, except in cases arising in the land or naval forces, or in the Militia, when in actual service in time of War or public danger; nor shall any person be subject for the same offence to be twice put in jeopardy of life or limb; nor shall be compelled in any criminal case to be a witness against himself, nor be deprived of life, liberty, or property, without due process of law; nor shall private property be taken for public use, without just compensation.

Obama's un-Constitutional *'ex post facto Law'* created his *'Bill of Attainder'*, with an *'executive order'*, holding law-abiding Americans to criminal scrutiny, denying them their *'Bill of Rights'*, only after pillaging through America's Constitutionally protected medical records. Now that the detective's family business has been burdened with the impossible, Obama's *'Ex-Post-Facto Government Gun Grab'*, turns to the rest of our country as it advances forward, setting aim on American healthcare and our *'Bill of Rights'*, unless President Trump ends this un-Constitutional siege which has quietly seized the detective's defined firearm license-status under a continued government cover-up to the public.

During Barack Obama's tenure, Americans lost our First Amendment *"...right of the people peaceably to assemble, and to petition the Government for a redress of grievances."* as men in police uniforms attacked Standing Rock *'Water Protectors'* for defending their land, and our nation's water, from what was later determined a questionable court seizure that, *"... 'deprived 'property without due process of law', and 'without just compensation'.*

National Security contractor Eric Snowden, Private Chelsea Manning and even foreign publisher Julian Assange were all hunted, *"...abridging the freedom of speech, or of the press',"* with the precedents established under Barack Obama for law enforcement to further threaten our First Amendment as People of good conscience expose government corruption.

America watched in horror as a nurse was dragged from her emergency room and arrested by police for defending an unconscious patient's *'right of the people to be secure in their persons, houses papers, and effects, against unreasonable searches and seizures'* in 2017. The nurse may have helped if the police were charging the patient with a crime and stated what they were looking for exactly. But the police could not arrest the unconscious patient as they lacked *"probable cause, supported by Oath or affirmation, and particularly describing the place to be searched, and the persons or things to be seized."*

We saw our 4th Amendment Rights wither under these Obama-era precedents. Though some argue a different President was in office as the nurse was dragged from an ER by police, the evidence contained in this presentation will demonstrate an un-Constitutional government cover-up by Obama-era law enforcement tactics, seeping into every state and every community's police department while acting on the behalf of political agendas, reaching beyond the White House all the way to the United Nations (UN) disarmament treaties. This un-Constitutional agenda is set to meet its sunset-date deep inside President Trump's first term as Americans discover they no longer have access to our *'Bill of Rights'*.

The documentation presented herein is not intended to be legal or medical advice, nor to cast accusations at any one specific individual or government body. The information is presented to enlighten the American People of documented evidence, facts and, methods to conceal the truth of the Obama-era cover-up that continues its stealth into Donald Trump's Presidency. And perhaps most importantly, to inform the American People of the changes in our Constitutional Rights that occurred with absolutely zero elected representatives of *'We the People'* involved in Barack Obama's *'Ex-Post-Facto Government Gun Grab'*.

===

"All tyranny needs to gain a foothold is for people of good conscience to remain silent."

Thomas Jefferson

My name is Matthew P. Kulesza. I am one of approximately 900 remaining private detectives in the world who is licensed to provide investigative and armed protective services in the State of Illinois. My Illinois private detective license number is 115-002274; my Illinois Firearm Control Card number is 229-076810. Over the course of 2016 and 2017, during America's transition from Barack Obama's administration to Donald Trump's Presidency, I came into possession of very alarming information documenting an un-Constitutional 'after-the-fact' *'ex post facto'* attack on the American People's *'Bill of Rights'*, and an ongoing government cover-up to conceal the truth to the public. Millions of law-abiding Americans, left in the dark, are stripped of their Rights while Obama's law enforcement directives falsely classify medical marijuana patients as felonious narcotic users within the FBI's NCIS (Federal Bureau of Investigation's National Criminal Investigative Service) database system. These un-Constitutional changes were implemented gradually, over time as they continue to be quietly carried out at state and federal levels into America's new Presidential administration.

Various documentation included in this presentation demonstrating the government's ongoing, un-Constitutional attack on our *'Bill of Rights',* belong to that of an Illinois private detective. To protect the confidentiality of the detective's family while defending every American's Right to have their private medical records protected under our state and federal laws including our 4th Amendment, *"'right of the people to be secure in their persons, houses, papers, and effects',"* as well as protecting the innocent families and business harmed by these un-Constitutional conflicting law enforcement directives, I have made redactions and cropped-out identifying information of private individuals and entities on various documents included herein. To maintain the detective's anonymity, I will refer to him as *"the detective",* or variations thereof, throughout this presentation.

As Americans are distracted by *"Fake News"* from mainstream media misreporting facts while pertinent stories suffer from media-blackout, most Americans remained oblivious to what was happening behind our government's closed doors. Some Americans remain in denial of the truth as it was never shown to them before.

Before we explore the events of this ongoing government siege, we will examine the definitions of some of the laws and Constitutional Rights that are being denied to law-abiding Americans in this un-Constitutional, Obama-Era *'Ex-Post-Facto Government Gun Grab'.*

=======

Our United States Constitution is the supreme governing law for Americans. No State can override its laws, or the Rights of the People set forth within our Constitution. Adversely, the federal government cannot deny the States any powers or Rights not specified by our US Constitution. Marijuana is not denied by our Founding Document; *'Arms'* are mentioned directly. We will now examine Sections 9. through 10. in Article I. of our United States Constitution.

'The Constitution of the United States'

Article I. Section 9.

" ' No Bill of Attainder or ex post facto Law shall be passed.'..."

Article. I. Section. 10.

"No State shall... ' pass any Bill of Attainder, ex post facto Law, or Law impairing the Obligation of Contracts..."

How are the *'Bill of Attainder'* and an *'ex post facto Law'* defined?

A *'Bill of Attainder'* is a legislative action holding a person or a group of people to punishments of a crime without a trial.

An *'ex post facto Law'* (Latin for *'after the facts'*) is a law which retroactively changes the consequences of actions, relationships or rules of evidence that were legal before the law was enacted.

========

America's *'Bill of Rights'* were ratified into *'The Constitution of the United States'* on December 15, 1791. After years of debate, our Founders knew the corruption of power can infiltrate into any government body. Our Founding Fathers solidified our *'Bill of Rights'* in our First Ten Amendments, protecting Americans and our country for future generations. Tyrannical threats need deny *'Equal Access to Justice',* to only one American to set this dangerous precedent for all.

'The Constitution of the United States' - 'Bill of Rights'

Amendment I

Congress shall make no law respecting an establishment of religion, or prohibiting the free exercise thereof; or abridging the freedom of speech, or of the press; or the right of the people peaceably to assemble, and to petition the Government for a redress of grievances.

Amendment II

A well regulated Militia, being necessary to the security of a free State, the right of the people to keep and bear Arms, shall not be infringed.

Amendment III

No Soldier shall, in time of peace be quartered in any house, without the consent of the Owner, nor in time of war, but in a manner to be prescribed by law.

Amendment IV

The right of the people to be secure in their persons, houses, papers, and effects, against unreasonable searches and seizures, shall not be violated, and no Warrants shall issue, but upon probable cause, supported by Oath or affirmation, and particularly describing the place to be searched, and the persons or things to be seized.

Amendment V

No person shall be held to answer for a capital, or otherwise infamous crime, unless on a presentment or indictment of a Grand Jury, except in cases arising in the land or naval forces, or in the Militia, when in actual service in time of War or public danger; nor shall any person be subject for the same offence to be twice put in jeopardy of life or limb; nor shall be compelled in any criminal case to be a witness against himself, nor be deprived of life, liberty, or property, without due process of law; nor shall private property be taken for public use, without just compensation.

Amendment VI

In all criminal prosecutions, the accused shall enjoy the right to a speedy and public trial, by an impartial jury of the State and district wherein the crime shall have been committed, which district shall have been previously ascertained by law, and to be informed of the nature and cause of the accusation; to be confronted with the witnesses against him; to have compulsory process for obtaining witnesses in his favor, and to have the Assistance of Counsel for his defence.

Amendment VII

In Suits at common law, where the value in controversy shall exceed twenty dollars, the right of trial by jury shall be preserved, and no fact tried by a jury, shall be otherwise re-examined in any Court of the United States, than according to the rules of the common law.

Amendment VIII

Excessive bail shall not be required, nor excessive fines imposed, nor cruel and unusual punishments inflicted.

Amendment IX

The enumeration in the Constitution, of certain rights, shall not be construed to deny or disparage others retained by the people.

Amendment X

The powers not delegated to the United States by the Constitution, nor prohibited by it to the States, are reserved to the States respectively, or to the people.

=======

Barack Obama's ongoing changes are not only un-Constitutional, but also in violation of the laws of the State of Illinois as the *'Controlled Substance Act of 1970' (CSA)* is not, *"... delegated to the United States by the Constitution, nor prohibited by it to the States... "*. So, the marijuana laws, *"... are reserved to the States respectively, or to the people."* (10*th*)

Since 2003, the United States government has owned the US Patent on medical applications of marijuana. The citation follows:

"United States Patent   6,630,507

Hampson , et al.   October 7, 2003

'Cannabinoids as antioxidants and neuroprotectants - Abstract

Cannabinoids have been found to have antioxidant properties, unrelated to NMDA receptor antagonism. This new found property makes cannabinoids useful in the treatment and prophylaxis of wide variety of oxidation associated diseases, such as ischemic, age-related, inflammatory and autoimmune diseases. The cannabinoids are found to have particular application as neuroprotectants, for example in limiting neurological damage following ischemic insults, such as stroke and trauma, or in the treatment of neurodegenerative diseases, such as Alzheimer's disease, Parkinson's disease and HIV dementia. Nonpsychoactive cannabinoids, such as cannabidoil, are particularly advantageous to use because they avoid toxicity that is encountered with psychoactive cannabinoids at high doses useful in the method of the present invention. A particular disclosed class of cannabinoids useful as neuroprotective antioxidants is formula (I) wherein the R group is independently selected from the group consisting of H, CH.sub.3, and COCH.sub.3. ##STR1##"

[http://patft.uspto.gov/netacgi/nph-Parser?Sect1=PTO1&Sect2=HITOFF&d=PALL&p=1&u=/netahtml/PTO/srchnum.htm&r=1&f=G&l=50&s1=6630507.PN.&OS=PN/6630507&RS=PN/6630507]

In addition to our American *'Bill of Rights'*, Illinois residents were granted protections by elected state lawmakers in 2013 as the governor signed into law the *'Illinois Compassionate Use of Medical Cannabis Pilot Program [Law] Act'*. The State of Illinois added more protections for Illinois residents during the summer of 2016, before Obama's un-Constitutional infringements prompted the Illinois State Police to *'federally'* deny a fully compliant private detective his Constitutional Rights along with that of all Americans. We will examine more of the Illinois Civil Statute *'Public Act 099-00519 - 410 ILCS 130/'* and its Administrative Code, *'Title 77: Public Health, Chapter 1, Subchapter u, Part 946'* throughout the presentation.

The Illinois State laws governing medical marijuana, specifically addressing a patient's rights, demonstrate solid, legal protections enacted by the state lawmakers. The State of Illinois jumps in on Obama's *'Ex-Post-Facto Government Gun Grab'* as they include a *'hold-harmless'* clause buried into their laws to indemnify the state; but that in and of itself does not exempt those individuals participating or enforcing state and federal laws, from legally upholding medical patient confidentiality. The following laws demonstrate the Illinois legal protections provided to all patients participating in the state's medical marijuana program:

=======

"(410 ILCS 130/1)

(Section scheduled to be repealed on July 1, 2020)

Sec. 1. Short title. This Act may be cited as the Compassionate Use of Medical Cannabis Pilot Program Act.

(Source: P.A. 98-122, eff. 1-1-14.)

(410 ILCS 130/5)

(Section scheduled to be repealed on July 1, 2020)

Sec. 5. Findings..."

"... (f) States are not required to enforce federal law or prosecute people for engaging in activities prohibited by federal law. Therefore, compliance with this Act does not put the State of Illinois in violation of federal law.

(g) State law should make a distinction between the medical and non-medical uses of cannabis. Hence, the purpose of this Act is to protect patients with debilitating medical conditions, as well as their physicians and providers, from arrest and prosecution, criminal and other penalties, and property forfeiture if the patients engage in the medical use of cannabis.

(Source: P.A. 98-122, eff. 1-1-14; 99-519, eff. 6-30-16.)

(410 ILCS 130/7)

(Section scheduled to be repealed on July 1, 2020)

Sec. 7. Lawful user and lawful products. For the purposes of this Act and to clarify the legislative findings on the lawful use of cannabis:

(1) A cardholder under this Act shall not be considered an unlawful user or addicted to narcotics solely as a result of his or her qualifying patient or designated caregiver status.

(2) All medical cannabis products purchased by a qualifying patient at a licensed dispensing organization shall be lawful products and a distinction shall be made between medical and non-medical uses of cannabis as a result of the qualifying patient's cardholder status under the authorized use granted under State law.

(Source: P.A. 99-519, eff. 6-30-16.)"

[Illinois Compassionate Use of Medical Cannabis Pilot Program (Law)' citation at: http://www.ilga.gov/legislation/publicacts/99/PDF/099-0519.pdf]

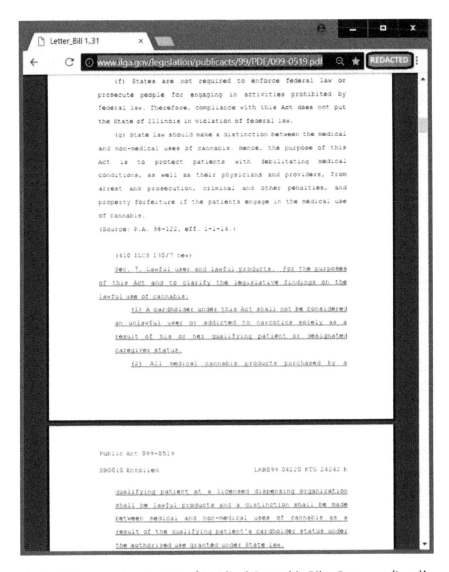

[Illinois Compassionate Use of Medical Cannabis Pilot Program (Law)':
http://www.ilga.gov/legislation/publicacts/99/PDF/099-0519.pdf]

"..."

"... (410 ILCS 130/25)

(Section scheduled to be repealed on July 1, 2020)

Sec. 25. Immunities and presumptions related to the medical use of cannabis.

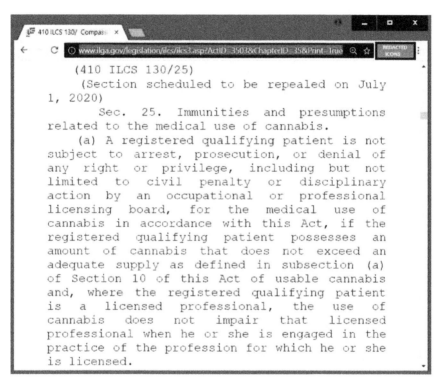

[http://www.ilga.gov/legislation/ilcs/ilcs3.asp?ActID=3503&ChapterID=35&Print=True]

(a) A registered qualifying patient is not subject to arrest, prosecution, or denial of any right or privilege, including but not limited to civil penalty or disciplinary action by an occupational or professional licensing board, for the medical use of cannabis in accordance with this Act, if the registered qualifying patient possesses an amount of cannabis that does not exceed an adequate supply as defined in subsection (a) of Section 10 of this Act

of usable cannabis and, where the registered qualifying patient is a licensed professional, the use of cannabis does not impair that licensed professional when he or she is engaged in the practice of the profession for which he or she is licensed.'..."

"..."

"... (n) Nothing in this Act shall preclude local or state law enforcement agencies from searching a registered dispensing organization where there is probable cause to believe that the criminal laws of this State have been violated and the search is conducted in conformity with the Illinois Constitution, the Constitution of the United States, and all State statutes.

(o) No individual employed by the State of Illinois shall be subject to criminal or civil penalties for taking any action in accordance with the provisions of this Act, when the actions are within the scope of his or her employment. Representation and indemnification of State employees shall be provided to State employees as set forth in Section 2 of the State Employee Indemnification Act.'..."

"... (Source: P.A. 98-122, eff. 1-1-14; 99-96, eff. 7-22-15.)'..."

"..."

"... (410 ILCS 130/40)

(Section scheduled to be repealed on July 1, 2020)

Sec. 40. Discrimination prohibited..."

"... (2) For the purposes of medical care, including organ transplants, a registered qualifying patient's authorized use of cannabis in accordance with this Act is considered the equivalent of the authorized use of any other medication used at the direction of a physician, and may not constitute the use of an illicit substance or otherwise disqualify a qualifying patient from needed medical care.'..."

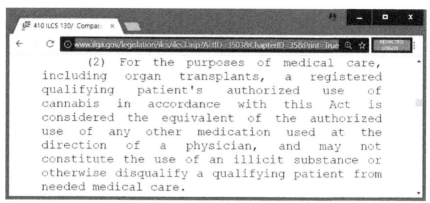

(2) For the purposes of medical care, including organ transplants, a registered qualifying patient's authorized use of cannabis in accordance with this Act is considered the equivalent of the authorized use of any other medication used at the direction of a physician, and may not constitute the use of an illicit substance or otherwise disqualify a qualifying patient from needed medical care.

[http://www.ilga.gov/legislation/ilcs/ilcs3.asp?ActID=3503&ChapterID=35&Print=True]

"... (410 ILCS 130/60)' (Section scheduled to be repealed on July 1, 2020)

Sec. 60. Issuance of registry identification cards..."

"... (e) Upon the approval of the registration and issuance of a registry card under this Section, the Department of Public Health shall electronically forward the registered qualifying patient's identification card information to the Prescription Monitoring Program established under the Illinois Controlled Substances Act and certify that the individual is permitted to engage in the medical use of cannabis. For the purposes of patient care, the Prescription Monitoring Program shall make a notation on the person's prescription record stating that the person is a registered qualifying patient who is entitled to the lawful medical use of cannabis. If the person no longer holds a valid registry card, the Department of Public Health shall notify the Prescription Monitoring Program and Department of Human Services to remove the notation from the person's record. The Department of Human Services and the Prescription Monitoring Program shall establish a system by which the information may be shared electronically. This confidential list may not be combined or linked in any manner with any other list or database except as provided in this Section.'..."

[http://www.ilga.gov/legislation/ilcs/ilcs3.asp?ActID=3503&ChapterID=0&Print=True]

=======

"ILLINOIS ADMINISTRATIVE CODE

TITLE 77: PUBLIC HEALTH

CHAPTER I: DEPARTMENT OF PUBLIC HEALTH

SUBCHAPTER u: MISCELLANEOUS PROGRAMS AND SERVICES

PART 946 COMPASSIONATE USE OF MEDICAL CANNABIS PATIENT REGISTRY

The General Assembly's Illinois Administrative Code database includes only those rulemakings that have been permanently adopted. This menu will point out the Sections on which an emergency rule (valid for a maximum of 150 days, usually until replaced by a permanent rulemaking) exists. The emergency rulemaking is linked through the notation that follows the Section heading in the menu.

SUBPART A: GENERAL PROVISIONS ..."

"...Section 946.40 Limitations and Penalties'..."

"...Section 946.60 Confidentiality' ..."

"... SUBPART B: QUALIFYING PATIENTS AND DESIGNATED CAREGIVERS..."

"... Section 946.220 Fingerprint-Based Criminal History Records Check'..."

"... Section 946.230 General Provisions'..."

"... SUBPART E: ENFORCEMENT

Section 946.500 Circuit Court Review

AUTHORITY: Implementing and authorized by the Compassionate Use of Medical Cannabis Pilot Program Act (410 ILCS 130).

SOURCE: Adopted at 38 Ill. Reg. 17367, effective July 29, 2014; emergency amendment at 39 Ill. Reg. 444, effective December 22, 2014, for a maximum of 150 days; amended at 39 Ill. Reg. 7712, effective May 15, 2015; emergency amendment at 40 Ill. Reg. 10992, effective August 1, 2016, for a maximum of 150 days; emergency amendment to emergency rule at 40 Ill. Reg. 13732, effective September 16, 2016, for the remainder of the 150 days; amended at 40 Ill. Reg. 16753, effective December 15, 2016.'..."

"..."

[ftp://www.ilga.gov/jcar/admincode/077/07700946sections.html]

"... [SUBPART A: GENERAL PROVISIONS]

TITLE 77: PUBLIC HEALTH

CHAPTER I: DEPARTMENT OF PUBLIC HEALTH

SUBCHAPTER u: MISCELLANEOUS PROGRAMS AND SERVICES

PART 946 COMPASSIONATE USE OF MEDICAL CANNABIS PATIENT REGISTRY

SECTION 946.40 LIMITATIONS AND PENALTIES..."

"... h)   Nothing in the Act shall prevent a private business from restricting or prohibiting the medical use of cannabis on its property.'..."

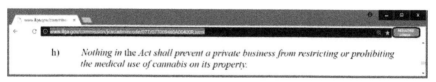

h)   Nothing in the Act shall prevent a private business from restricting or prohibiting the medical use of cannabis on its property.

[http://www.ilga.gov/commission/jcar/admincode/077/077009460A00 400R.html]

"..."

"... k) Any person, including an employee or official of the Department of Public Health, Department of Financial and Professional Regulation, or Department of Agriculture or another State agency or local government, is guilty of a Class B misdemeanor with a $1,000 fine for breaching the confidentiality of information obtained under the Act (Section 145(c) of the Act) and Sections 946.270 and 946.275 of this Part.'..."

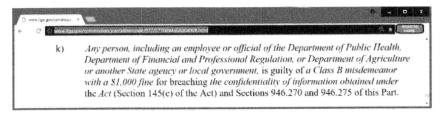

[*ftp://www.ilga.gov/jcar/admincode/077/077009460A00400R.html*]

"... [SUBPART A: GENERAL PROVISIONS]

TITLE 77: PUBLIC HEALTH

CHAPTER I: DEPARTMENT OF PUBLIC HEALTH

SUBCHAPTER u: MISCELLANEOUS PROGRAMS AND SERVICES

PART 946 COMPASSIONATE USE OF MEDICAL CANNABIS PATIENT REGISTRY

SECTION 946.60 CONFIDENTIALITY

Section 946.60 Confidentiality

a) The following information received and records kept by the Department for purposes of administering this Part are subject to all applicable federal privacy laws, are confidential, are exempt from the Illinois Freedom of Information Act, and are not subject to disclosure to any individual or public or private entity, except as necessary for authorized employees of the Department to perform official duties of the Department pursuant to this Part:

1) Applications or renewals, their contents and supporting information submitted by qualifying patients and designated caregivers, including information regarding designated caregivers and physicians;

2) The individual names and other information identifying persons to whom the Department has issued registry identification cards; and

3) All medical records provided to the Department in connection with an application for a registry identification card.

b) Department hard drives or other data recording media that are no longer in use and that contain cardholder information will be destroyed.

c) Data subject to this Section shall not be combined or linked in any manner with any other list or database and shall not be used for any purpose not provided by this Part or the Act. (Section 150(a) of the Act)

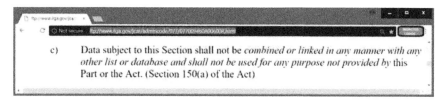

[ftp://www.ilga.gov/jcar/admincode/077/077009460A00600R.html]

d) Any dispensing information required to be kept under Section 135 or 150 of the Act or under this Part will identify cardholders by their registry identification numbers and not contain names or other personally identifying information.

e) The Department of Agriculture, the Department of Financial and Professional Regulation and the Illinois State Police may verify registry identification cards. Law enforcement personnel shall have access to the Department's on-line verification system to verify application date and application status of qualifying patients who have submitted an application for a registry identification card.

f) This Section does not preclude the following notifications:

1) Department employees may notify law enforcement if information submitted to the Department is suspected to be falsified or fraudulent.

2) The Department may notify State or local law enforcement about alleged criminal violations of this Part.

3) The Department will notify the Department of Financial and Professional Regulation if there is reasonable cause to believe that a physician has:

A) Issued a written certification without a bona-fide physician-patient relationship; or

B) Issued a written certification to a person who was not under the physician's care for the debilitating medical condition; or

C) Failed to abide by the acceptable and prevailing standard of care when evaluating a patient's medical condition.'..."

g) The Department will share, disclose, and forward patient information as required by Section 60(e) of the Act.

(Source: Amended at 40 Ill. Reg. 16753, effective December 15, 2016)'..."

[ftp://www.ilga.gov/jcar/admincode/077/077009460A00600R.html]

"... [SUBPART B: QUALIFYING PATIENTS & DESIGNATED CAREGIVERS]

TITLE 77: PUBLIC HEALTH

CHAPTER I: DEPARTMENT OF PUBLIC HEALTH

SUBCHAPTER u: MISCELLANEOUS PROGRAMS AND SERVICES

PART 946 COMPASSIONATE USE OF MEDICAL CANNABIS PATIENT REGISTRY

SECTION 946.220 FINGERPRINT-BASED CRIMINAL HISTORY RECORDS CHECK

Section 946.220 Fingerprint-Based Criminal History Records Check

No person convicted of an excluded offense shall be eligible to receive a registry identification card.

a)   The Illinois State Police (ISP) will act as the Department's agent for purposes of receiving electronic fingerprints and conducting background checks of each qualifying patient and designated caregiver, if applicable, applying for a registry identification card.

1) The ISP will conduct background checks for conviction information contained within ISP and Federal Bureau of Investigation (FBI) criminal history databases to the extent allowed by law.

2) For verification of any statutorily imposed duty to conduct background checks pursuant to the Act, ISP will transmit the results of the background check to the Department.

3)   The electronic background checks will be submitted as outlined in the Illinois Uniform Conviction Information Act or ISP rules at 20 Ill. Adm. Code 1265.30 (Electronic Transmission of Fingerprints).'..."

"...(Source: Amended at 40 Ill. Reg. 16753, effective December 15, 2016)"

[ftp://www.ilga.gov/JCAR/AdminCode/077/077009460B02200R.html]

"... [SUBPART B: QUALIFYING PATIENTS & DESIGNATED CAREGIVERS]

TITLE 77: PUBLIC HEALTH

CHAPTER I: DEPARTMENT OF PUBLIC HEALTH

SUBCHAPTER u: MISCELLANEOUS PROGRAMS AND SERVICES

PART 946 COMPASSIONATE USE OF MEDICAL CANNABIS PATIENT REGISTRY

SECTION 946.230 GENERAL PROVISIONS

Section 946.230 General Provisions,..."

"... d) The Department will require each applicant for a registry identification card to include a signed statement that specifies that the applicant attests that all information submitted as part of the application is true and accurate to the best of the applicant's knowledge and, at minimum, certifies that the applicant has actual notice that, notwithstanding any State law:

1) Cannabis is a prohibited Schedule I controlled substance under federal law;

2) Participation in the program is permitted only to the extent provided by the strict requirements of the Act and this Part;

3) Any activity not sanctioned by the Act or this Part may be in violation of State law;

4) Growing, distributing or possessing cannabis in any capacity, except through a federally approved research program, is a violation of federal law;

5) Use of medical cannabis may affect an individual's ability to receive federal or state licensure in other areas;

6) Use of medical cannabis, in tandem with other conduct, may be in violation of State or federal law;

7) Participation in the program does not authorize any person to violate federal or State law and, other than as specified in Section 25 of the Act, does not provide any immunity from or affirmative defense to arrest or prosecution under federal or State law; and

8) Applicants shall indemnify, hold harmless, and defend the State of Illinois for any and all civil or criminal penalties resulting from participation in the program.'..." "..."

"... (Source: Amended at 39 Ill. Reg. 7712, effective May 15, 2015)'..."

[ftp://www.ilga.gov/jcar/admincode/077/077009460B02300R.html]

"...[SUBPART E: ENFORCEMENT]

TITLE 77: PUBLIC HEALTH

CHAPTER I: DEPARTMENT OF PUBLIC HEALTH

SUBCHAPTER u: MISCELLANEOUS PROGRAMS AND SERVICES

PART 946 COMPASSIONATE USE OF MEDICAL CANNABIS PATIENT REGISTRY

SECTION 946.500 CIRCUIT COURT REVIEW

Section 946.500 Circuit Court Review..."

"... d) All final administrative decisions of the Department of Public Health are subject to direct judicial review under the provisions of the Administrative Review Law and the rules adopted under that Law. The term "administrative decision" is defined as in Section 3-101 of the Code of Civil Procedure. (Section 155 of the Act)

e) If any final Department action is appealed in Circuit Court pursuant to this Section, the record on review shall include the following:

1) The application or petition submitted;

2) Any written documentation considered by the Department in making its final decision with respect to the application or petition.

3) Any written correspondence between the Department and the person submitting the application or petition, provided that the correspondence either played a material role in the final decision rendered by the Department; made a material argument to the Department with respect to the application or petition; or would be helpful to the Circuit Court in reviewing the matter because the correspondence provides helpful procedural background.

f) If the materials in the record on review contain any confidential information as defined in Section 946.60, either the information shall be redacted, as appropriate, or the entirety or portions of the record on review shall be filed under seal so as to retain the confidentiality of, without limitation, patient medical records or Departmental documents or data.

(Source: Amended at 40 Ill. Reg. 16753, effective December 15, 2016)"

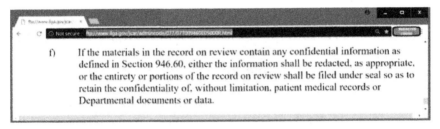

[ftp://www.ilga.gov/jcar/admincode/077/077009460E05000R.html]

=======

" Constitution of the State of Illinois
Adopted at special election on December 15, 1970
PREAMBLE

We, the People of the State of Illinois – grateful to Almighty God for the civil, political and religious liberty which He has permitted us to enjoy and seeking His blessing upon our endeavors – in order to provide for the health, safety and welfare of the people; maintain a representative and orderly government; eliminate poverty and inequality; assure legal, social and economic justice; provide opportunity for the fullest development of the individual; insure domestic tranquility; provide for the common defense; and secure the blessings of freedom and liberty to ourselves and our posterity – do ordain and establish this Constitution for the State of Illinois. (Source: Illinois Constitution.)

ARTICLE I

BILL OF RIGHTS

SECTION 1. INHERENT AND INALIENABLE RIGHTS

All men are by nature free and independent and have certain inherent and inalienable rights among which are life, liberty and the pursuit of happiness. To secure these rights and the protection of property, governments are instituted among men, deriving their just powers from the consent of the governed.

(Source: Illinois Constitution.)

SECTION 2. DUE PROCESS AND EQUAL PROTECTION

No person shall be deprived of life, liberty or property without due process of law nor be denied the equal protection of the laws.

(Source: Illinois Constitution.)'…"

"… SECTION 4. FREEDOM OF SPEECH

All persons may speak, write and publish freely, being responsible for the abuse of that liberty. In trials for libel, both civil and criminal, the truth, when published with good motives and for justifiable ends, shall be a sufficient defense.

(Source: Illinois Constitution.)

SECTION 5. RIGHT TO ASSEMBLE AND PETITION

The people have the right to assemble in a peaceable manner, to consult for the common good, to make known their opinions to their representatives and to apply for redress of grievances.

(Source: Illinois Constitution.)

SECTION 6. SEARCHES, SEIZURES, PRIVACY AND INTERCEPTIONS

The people shall have the right to be secure in their persons, houses, papers and other possessions against unreasonable searches, seizures, invasions of privacy or interceptions of communications by eavesdropping devices or other means. No warrant shall issue without probable cause, supported by affidavit particularly describing the place to be searched and the persons or things to be seized.

(Source: Illinois Constitution.)

SECTION 7. INDICTMENT AND PRELIMINARY HEARING

No person shall be held to answer for a criminal offense unless on indictment of a grand jury, except in cases in which the punishment is by fine or by imprisonment other than in the penitentiary, in cases of impeachment, and in cases arising in the militia when in actual service in time of war or public danger. The General Assembly by law may abolish the grand jury or further limit its use. No person shall be held to answer for a crime punishable by death or by imprisonment in the penitentiary unless either the initial charge has been brought by indictment of a grand jury or the person has been given a prompt preliminary hearing to establish probable cause. *(Source: Illinois Constitution.)'..."*

"... SECTION 10. SELF-INCRIMINATION AND DOUBLE JEOPARDY

No person shall be compelled in a criminal case to give evidence against himself nor be twice put in jeopardy for the same offense.

(Source: Illinois Constitution.)'..."

"... SECTION 12. RIGHT TO REMEDY AND JUSTICE

Every person shall find a certain remedy in the laws for all injuries and wrongs which he receives to his person, privacy, property or reputation. He shall obtain justice by law, freely, completely, and promptly.

(Source: Illinois Constitution.) "..."

"... SECTION 16. EX POST FACTO LAWS AND IMPAIRING CONTRACTS

No ex post facto law, or law impairing the obligation of contracts or making an irrevocable grant of special privileges or immunities, shall be passed.

(Source: Illinois Constitution.) "..."

"... SECTION 20. INDIVIDUAL DIGNITY

To promote individual dignity, communications that portray criminality, depravity or lack of virtue in, or that incite violence, hatred, abuse or hostility toward, a person or group of persons by reason of or by reference to religious, racial, ethnic, national or regional affiliation are condemned.

(Source: Illinois Constitution.)

SECTION 21. QUARTERING OF SOLDIERS

No soldier in time of peace shall be quartered in a house without the consent of the owner; nor in time of war except as provided by law.

(Source: Illinois Constitution.)

SECTION 22. RIGHT TO ARMS

Subject only to the police power, the right of the individual citizen to keep and bear arms shall not be infringed.

(Source: Illinois Constitution.)..."

Constitution of the State of Illinois

[http://www.ilga.gov/commission/lrb/conmain.htm]

Constitution of the State of Illinois – entire single document:

[http://www.ilga.gov/commission/lrb/conent.htm]

Illinois Bill of Rights

[http://www.ilga.gov/commission/lrb/con1.htm]

1970 Illinois Constitution – Annotated for Legislators - 4ᵗʰ Edition:

[http://www.ilga.gov/commission/lru/ilconstitution.pdf]

=======

Before long, the detective would see his family's business bank account closed, his legal insurance coverage dropped without explanation after 14 years of on-time payments, his health insurance suppressed for over seven months through the state's exchange website and the defined legal status of his family business license seized with an ongoing government cover-up to conceal the truth from the American public. And yet the government continues its violations of our Rights.

The State of Illinois violated Section 1. of the *Illinois Bill of Rights'* for the detective by disrupting his *'inalienable rights'*.

Section 2. was violated as the State denied *'due process'* and *'equal protection'* to the detective.

Section 5. was violated as the detective has still not been able to petition the government for his grievances, especially in light of the Section 6. violation of the detective's private medical records seized along with a business license.

Section 7. demonstrated Illinois' *'Bill of Attainder'* as the State won't indict medical marijuana users when they are *'Lawful'* yet, use the same laws to deny *'due process'*.

Section 10. was violated by the Illinois State Police as they presented a *'Denial Appeal'* requiring the detective to self-incriminate in answering their *'Appeal'* questions without legally afforded redaction.

Section 12., has been denied to the detective as his only remedy was to publish this redacted information via my detective agency in hopes his Section 4. protection to free speech remains in-tact.

Section 16. is the other namesake of this presentation; holding *'Lawful'* Citizens to an *'ex post facto Law'*, impairing the detective's obligation of contracts.

Section 20. demonstrates the assassination of all medical marijuana cardholders' dignity – the detective is one of many casualties.

Section 22. is un-Constitutional in so many ways at a federal level, where does one begin. The Right grants police powers to infringe our United States Constitutional Rights without any *'due process'* as long as *'We the People'* overlook their multiple violations of our laws.

=======

The detective has operated as a special investigator for the government investigating government employees, including police. Those same government departments misled Americans, including the detective, with their website invitations into the commercialized and *"Lawful"* medical marijuana program as they conceal the truth of licenses and seizures. Nothing less than *'time-travel'*, legislation, court precedent or *'Executive Action'* will be able to protect Americans, including the detective and his family, from Obama's continuing siege on our Rights.

=======

We have detected *'The Evidence'.* Now, the precedent has been set for the government to infringe on our *'Bill of Rights'* through the exploitation of America's private medical records, bypassing all elected lawmakers of *'We the People'*. Next, you're invited to examine *'The Facts'* as they became relevant to the detective, leading to Obama's sunset-date for our *'Bill of Rights'* in *'The Ex-Post-Facto Government Gun Grab'*.

Chapter 2

The Facts.

In this section we will examine the facts of this ongoing un-Constitutional *'Ex-Post-Facto Government Gun Grab'* as they became relevant to the detective, quietly setting a precedent for all Americans if allowed to continue into America's future with a sunset-date rapidly counting-down into President Donald J. Trump's administration.

=== October 19, 2009 ===

The detective had built his family business from the ground up as many Americans do. His detective agency started in a limited number of states and grew. Becoming a detective in Illinois wasn't easy; but he accomplished it after a long career of working for other agencies, protecting businesses, properties and families. The years spent working for other agencies, in addition to the education and training, were necessary requirements for aspiring Illinois detectives to qualify for the license exam. A detective's average commute can be brutal; the days can be long. It is not uncommon for detectives to work 15 to 20 hours or more each day. The detective worked a lot of surveillance which requires long hours of uninterrupted sitting in a driver's seat, unable to stand up at all.

October 19, 2009 saw Barack Obama's first DOJ *'executive order'*, on medical marijuana programs in the states. Instructing US Attorneys on procedures for *'Lawful'* programs and patients within the states seemed moot in light of our 10th Amendment.

U.S. Department of Justice

Office of the Deputy Attorney General

The Deputy Attorney General   Washington, D.C. 20530

October 19, 2009

MEMORANDUM FOR SELECTED UNITED STATES ATTORNEYS

FROM   David W. Ogden
              Deputy Attorney General

SUBJECT   Investigations and Prosecutions in States
              Authorizing the Medical Use of Marijuana

This memorandum provides clarification and guidance to federal prosecutors in States that have enacted laws authorizing the medical use of marijuana. These laws vary in their substantive provisions and in the extent of state regulatory oversight, both among the enacting States and among local jurisdictions within those States. Rather than developing different guidelines for every possible variant of state and local law, this memorandum provides uniform guidance to focus federal investigations and prosecutions in these States on core federal enforcement priorities.

The Department of Justice is committed to the enforcement of the Controlled Substances Act in all States. Congress has determined that marijuana is a dangerous drug, and the illegal distribution and sale of marijuana is a serious crime and provides a significant source of revenue to large-scale criminal enterprises, gangs, and cartels. One timely example underscores the importance of our efforts to prosecute significant marijuana traffickers: marijuana distribution in the United States remains the single largest source of revenue for the Mexican cartels.

The Department is also committed to making efficient and rational use of its limited investigative and prosecutorial resources. In general, United States Attorneys are vested with "plenary authority with regard to federal criminal matters" within their districts. USAM 9-2.001. In exercising this authority, United States Attorneys are "invested by statute and delegation from the Attorney General with the broadest discretion in the exercise of such authority." *Id.* This authority should, of course, be exercised consistent with Department priorities and guidance.

The prosecution of significant traffickers of illegal drugs, including marijuana, and the disruption of illegal drug manufacturing and trafficking networks continues to be a core priority in the Department's efforts against narcotics and dangerous drugs, and the Department's investigative and prosecutorial resources should be directed towards these objectives. As a general matter, pursuit of these priorities should not focus federal resources in your States on

[https://www.justice.gov/sites/default/files/opa/legacy/2009/10/19/me dical-marijuana.pdf]

[Pg. 1 of 3 – Obama's 'order' on marijuana – 10/19/2009]

Memorandum for Selected United States Attorneys   Page 2
Subject: Investigations and Prosecutions in States Authorizing the Medical Use of Marijuana

individuals whose actions are in clear and unambiguous compliance with existing state laws
providing for the medical use of marijuana. For example, prosecution of individuals with cancer
or other serious illnesses who use marijuana as part of a recommended treatment regimen
consistent with applicable state law, or those caregivers in clear and unambiguous compliance
with existing state law who provide such individuals with marijuana, is unlikely to be an efficient
use of limited federal resources. On the other hand, prosecution of commercial enterprises that
unlawfully market and sell marijuana for profit continues to be an enforcement priority of the
Department. To be sure, claims of compliance with state or local law may mask operations
inconsistent with the terms, conditions, or purposes of those laws, and federal law enforcement
should not be deterred by such assertions when otherwise pursuing the Department's core
enforcement priorities.

   Typically, when any of the following characteristics is present, the conduct will not be in
clear and unambiguous compliance with applicable state law and may indicate illegal drug
trafficking activity of potential federal interest:

- unlawful possession or unlawful use of firearms;
- violence;
- sales to minors;
- financial and marketing activities inconsistent with the terms, conditions, or purposes of
  state law, including evidence of money laundering activity and/or financial gains or
  excessive amounts of cash inconsistent with purported compliance with state or local law;
- amounts of marijuana inconsistent with purported compliance with state or local law;
- illegal possession or sale of other controlled substances; or
- ties to other criminal enterprises.

   Of course, no State can authorize violations of federal law, and the list of factors above is
not intended to describe exhaustively when a federal prosecution may be warranted.
Accordingly, in prosecutions under the Controlled Substances Act, federal prosecutors are not
expected to charge, prove, or otherwise establish any state law violations. Indeed, this
memorandum does not alter in any way the Department's authority to enforce federal law,
including laws prohibiting the manufacture, production, distribution, possession, or use of
marijuana on federal property. This guidance regarding resource allocation does not "legalize"
marijuana or provide a legal defense to a violation of federal law, nor is it intended to create any
privileges, benefits, or rights, substantive or procedural, enforceable by any individual, party or
witness in any administrative, civil, or criminal matter. Nor does clear and unambiguous
compliance with state law or the absence of one or all of the above factors create a legal defense
to a violation of the Controlled Substances Act. Rather, this memorandum is intended solely as a
guide to the exercise of investigative and prosecutorial discretion.

[https://www.justice.gov/sites/default/files/opa/legacy/2009/10/19/medical-marijuana.pdf]

[Pg. 2 of 3 – Obama's 'order' on marijuana – 10/19/2009]

Memorandum for Selected United States Attorneys   Page 3
Subject: Investigations and Prosecutions in States Authorizing the Medical Use of Marijuana

       Finally, nothing herein precludes investigation or prosecution where there is a reasonable basis to believe that compliance with state law is being invoked as a pretext for the production or distribution of marijuana for purposes not authorized by state law. Nor does this guidance preclude investigation or prosecution, even when there is clear and unambiguous compliance with existing state law, in particular circumstances where investigation or prosecution otherwise serves important federal interests.

       Your offices should continue to review marijuana cases for prosecution on a case-by-case basis, consistent with the guidance on resource allocation and federal priorities set forth herein, the consideration of requests for federal assistance from state and local law enforcement authorities, and the Principles of Federal Prosecution.

cc: All United States Attorneys

      Lanny A. Breuer
      Assistant Attorney General
      Criminal Division

      B. Todd Jones
      United States Attorney
      District of Minnesota
      Chair, Attorney General's Advisory Committee

      Michele M. Leonhart
      Acting Administrator
      Drug Enforcement Administration

      H. Marshall Jarrett
      Director
      Executive Office for United States Attorneys

      Kevin L. Perkins
      Assistant Director
      Criminal Investigative Division
      Federal Bureau of Investigation

[https://www.justice.gov/sites/default/files/opa/legacy/2009/10/19/medical-marijuana.pdf]

[Pg. 3 of 3 – Obama's 'order' on marijuana – 10/19/2009]

The following is a link to Obama's October 19, 2009 Obama's DOJ 'executive order' addressed as a *"MEMORANDUM TO SELECT US ATTORNEYS"*:

https://www.justice.gov/archives/opa/blog/memorandum-selected-united-state-attorneys-investigations-and-prosecutions-states

A paradox presented itself in Obama's *'executive order'* as a firearm suggested to disqualify Americans from medical marijuana; at the same time medical marijuana disqualified Americans from our 2nd Amendment. Round and round, Obama's logic went.

Yet, state laws and our *'Bill of Rights'* protected America's medical patients in their states' legal medical marijuana programs. Our American 4th Amendment protected all of our medical records equally, *'to be secure in our papers, houses and effects'*. Our 10th Amendment exempted the states from Obama's rules and our 5th Amendment protected us from testifying against ourselves, our property from being seized, and guaranteed *'due process'*. Of course, our 2nd Amendment cannot ever be infringed.

=== September 21, 2011 ===

In 2011, Obama was reported to have released another *'executive order'* on marijuana. But the 2011 document was addressed to federal *"Firearm Licensees"*. The one-page document was difficult to find online as I conducted research. I found two links to copies of Obama's *'executive order'* at an online encyclopedia's 12th reference.

One of the links suggested that it would redirect to the *"original document"*, but instead was redirected to a default *"Page Not Found"* webpage at the Bureau of Alcohol, Tobacco and Firearms (ATF) website.

The US DOJ calls this a *"...press/release..."* within their URL domain-text; but I never discovered any release in the press in 2011.

[ATF linked-page located at:
https://www.atf.gov/press/releases/2011/09/092611-atf-open-letter-to-all-ffls-marijuana-for-medicinal-purposes.pdf]

The other webpage accessible from a link at the online encyclopedia did redirect to an internet archive website with a viewable copy. I saved the document as a PDF *'Printable Document File'* and printed it out. Odd thing is, Obama's DOJ letterhead and all the text above the heading didn't print; no date either. Perhaps it was just a printer error? I tried a few times with the same results on a different printer.

The first of the following printed documents is a scanned copy of what printed out. The second document *[on page 40]* demonstrates what the *'copy-and-pasted'* screenshot I cropped and printed to include the *'disappearing-phantom-letterhead'.* The document became more easily accessible at the ATF under our new President Donald Trump during my research. ATF site is up. Yet, an awful lot of work was needed to chase after our *'Bill of Rights',* during Obama's time in charge our US DOJ. Glitches can occur; but they can't explain away our Constitution Rights.

OPEN LETTER TO ALL FEDERAL FIREARMS LICENSEES

The Bureau of Alcohol, Tobacco, Firearms and Explosives (ATF) has received a number of inquiries regarding the use of marijuana for medicinal purposes, and its applicability to Federal firearms laws. The purpose of this open letter is to provide guidance on the issue and to assist you, a Federal firearms licensee, in complying with Federal firearms laws and regulations.

A number of States have passed legislation allowing under State law the use or possession of marijuana for medicinal purposes, and some of these States issue a card authorizing the holder to use or possess marijuana under State law. During a firearms transaction, a potential transferee may advise you that he or she is a user of medical marijuana, or present a medical marijuana card as identification or proof of residency.

As you know, Federal law, 18 U.S.C. § 922(g)(3), prohibits any person who is an "unlawful user of or addicted to any controlled substance (as defined in section 102 of the Controlled Substances Act (21 U.S.C. 802))" from shipping, transporting, receiving or possessing firearms or ammunition. Marijuana is listed in the Controlled Substances Act as a Schedule I controlled substance, and there are no exceptions in Federal law for marijuana purportedly used for medicinal purposes, even if such use is sanctioned by State law. Further, Federal law, 18 U.S.C. § 922(d)(3), makes it unlawful for any person to sell or otherwise dispose of any firearm or ammunition to any person knowing or **having reasonable cause to believe** that such person is an unlawful user of or addicted to a controlled substance. As provided by 27 C.F.R. § 478.11, "an inference of current use may be drawn from evidence of a recent use or possession of a controlled substance or a pattern of use or possession that reasonably covers the present time."

Therefore, any person who uses or is addicted to marijuana, regardless of whether his or her State has passed legislation authorizing marijuana use for medicinal purposes, is an unlawful user of or addicted to a controlled substance, and is prohibited by Federal law from possessing firearms or ammunition. Such persons should answer "yes" to question 11.e. on ATF Form 4473 (August 2008), Firearms Transaction Record, and you may not transfer firearms or ammunition to them. Further, if you are aware that the potential transferee is in possession of a card authorizing the possession and use of marijuana under State law, then you have "reasonable cause to believe" that the person is an unlawful user of a controlled substance. As such, you may not transfer firearms or ammunition to the person, even if the person answered "no" to question 11.e. on ATF Form 4473.

ATF is committed to assisting you in complying with Federal firearms laws. If you have any questions, please contact ATF's Firearms Industry Programs Branch at (202) 648-7190.

Arthur Herbert
Assistant Director
Enforcement Programs and Services

The Federal government does not recognize marijuana as a medicine. The FDA has determined that marijuana has a high potential for abuse, has no currently accepted medical use in treatment in the United States, and lacks an accepted level of safety for use under medical supervision. [remaining footnote text illegible]

[No letterhead or date on <u>printed</u> copy of Obama's DOJ medical marijuana 'executive order' dated September 21, 2011 located at: 'REDACTED' PRIVATE / NON-PUBLIC-DOMAIN NAME OF 'ORGANIZATION' WHICH WILL 'ARCHIVE' URL'S]

U.S. Department of Justice

Bureau of Alcohol, Tobacco,
Firearms and Explosives

Washington DC 20226

September 21, 2011

www.atf.gov

OPEN LETTER TO ALL FEDERAL FIREARMS LICENSEES

The Bureau of Alcohol, Tobacco, Firearms and Explosives (ATF) has received a number of inquiries regarding the use of marijuana for medicinal purposes and its applicability to Federal firearms laws. The purpose of this open letter is to provide guidance on the issue and to assist you, a Federal firearms licensee, in complying with Federal firearms laws and regulations.

A number of States have passed legislation allowing under State law the use or possession of marijuana for medicinal purposes, and some of these States issue a card authorizing the holder to use or possess marijuana under State law. During a firearms transaction, a potential transferee may advise you that he or she is a user of medical marijuana, or present a medical marijuana card as identification or proof of residency.

As you know, Federal law, 18 U.S.C. § 922(g)(3), prohibits any person who is an "unlawful user of or addicted to any controlled substance (as defined in section 302 of the Controlled Substances Act (21 U.S.C. 802))" from shipping, transporting, receiving or possessing firearms or ammunition. Marijuana is listed in the Controlled Substances Act as a Schedule I controlled substance, and there are no exceptions in Federal law for marijuana purportedly used for medicinal purposes, even if such use is sanctioned by State law. Further, Federal law, 18 U.S.C. § 922(d)(3), makes it unlawful for any person to sell or otherwise dispose of any firearm or ammunition to any person knowing or **having reasonable cause to believe** that such person is an unlawful user of or addicted to a controlled substance. As provided by 27 C.F.R. § 478.11, "an inference of current use may be drawn from evidence of a recent use or possession of a controlled substance or a pattern of use or possession that reasonably covers the present time."

Therefore, any person who uses or is addicted to marijuana, regardless of whether his or her State has passed legislation authorizing marijuana use for medicinal purposes, is an unlawful user of or addicted to a controlled substance, and is prohibited by Federal law from possessing firearms or ammunition. Such persons should answer "yes" to question 11.e. on ATF Form 4473 (August 2008), Firearms Transaction Record, and you may not transfer firearms or ammunition to them. Further, if you are aware that the potential transferee is in possession of a card authorizing the possession and use of marijuana under State law, then you have "reasonable cause to believe" that the person is an unlawful user of a controlled substance. As such, you may not transfer firearms or ammunition to the person, even if the person answered "no" to question 11.e. on ATF Form 4473.

ATF is committed to assisting you in complying with Federal firearms laws. If you have any questions, please contact ATF's Firearms Industry Programs Branch at (202) 648-7190.

Arthur Herbert
Assistant Director
Enforcement Programs and Services

The Federal government does not recognize marijuana as a medicine. The FDA has determined that marijuana has a high potential for abuse, has no currently accepted medical use or treatment in the United States, and lacks an accepted level of safety for use under medical supervision. See 66 Fed. Reg. 20037, 20051. This Open Letter will use the terms "medical use" or "for medical purposes" with the understanding that such use is not sanctioned by the Federal agency charged with determining what substances are safe and effective as medicines.

[Letterhead on printed-screenshot - Obama's 9/21/2009 medical marijuana 'executive order' to 'Firearm Licensees' at: (REDACTED URL – See original 'possibly' available at:
https://www.atf.gov/press/releases/2011/09/092611-atf-open-letter-to-all-ffls-marijuana-for-medicinal-purposes.pdf)]

The Obama's DOJ archived document is addressed as an *"OPEN LETTER TO ALL FIREARMS LICENSEES"*. *'We the People of the United States of America'* are not mentioned; only gun-sellers are addressed. The document is at an archived webpage that provides the letterhead to view. The link to the webpage has been omitted from this presentation as it is a private/non-public domain.

=== *'REDACTED URL'* ===

Please note the footer on the previous 2011 Obama DOJ document stating, *"The Federal Government does not recognize marijuana as a medicine...."* If this is indeed the case, I hereby make claim to US Patent Number 6,630,507. Is that how it works? I'm sure it is probably a bit more complicated. But one can see a tremendous amount of irony exists under Obama's *'rules'*. A citation from a government archived webpage follows:

> *"US Patent 6,630,507 - Cannabinoids as Antioxidants and Neuroprotectants"*
>
> *"Cannabinoids have been found to have antioxidant properties, unrelated to NMDA receptor antagonism. This new found property makes cannabinoids useful in the treatment and prophylaxis of wide variety of oxidation associated diseases, such as ischemic, <u>age-related, inflammatory and autoimmune diseases</u>. The cannabinoids are found to have particular application as neuroprotectants, for example in limiting neurological damage following ischemic insults, such as stroke and trauma, or in the treatment of neurodegenerative diseases, such as Alzheimer's disease, Parkinson's disease and HIV dementia.'...".*
>
> *[http://patft.uspto.gov/netacgi/nph-Parser?Sect1=PTO1&Sect2=HITOFF&d=PALL&p=1&u=/netahtml/PTO/srchnum.htm&r=1&f=G&l=50&s1=6630507.PN.&OS=PN/6630507&RS=PN/6630507]*

=== April 2012 ===

Under Barack Obama the federal government's background check form the detective would use in December of 2016, was revised. *'Firearm Transfer Form 4473 (Revised April 2012)'* will be reviewed more throughout this presentation. The form still asked if the firearm transfer applicant is an *"unlawful user"* of marijuana; as the Illinois laws would soon indicate, state approved medical marijuana users are *"Lawful"*.

=== August 01, 2013 ===

Illinois passed *'The Compassionate Use of Medical Cannabis Pilot Program [Law] Act'* (410 ILCS 130/), which assured all medical marijuana applicants and state approved users would not lose nor be denied any rights, or be punished, or be forced to forfeit property to an un-Constitutional *'Bill of Attainder'* or *'ex post facto Law'*.

As one can determine, this Illinois State medical marijuana Law is protected by our Constitution's 10th Amendment as follows:

Amendment X

The powers not delegated to the United States by the Constitution, nor prohibited by it to the States, are reserved to the States respectively, or to the people.

Section *'5. f.-g.'* of the Illinois medical marijuana law, speaks to the patient's Rights being protected from criminal or other punishments under our state laws as well as America's Constitutional protections. Following is a screenshot from the Illinois State Civil Statutes (ILCS) webpage citing the Public Health Law's text; parts *'f-g.'*, of section *'5'*, of the Law speaks to our 10th Amendment:

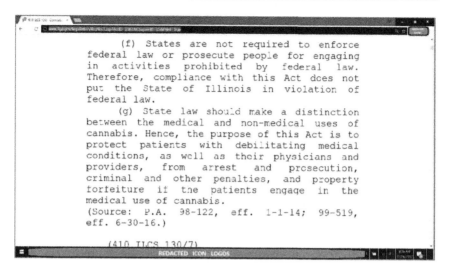

```
        (f)   States   are   not   required   to   enforce
federal  law  or  prosecute  people  for  engaging
in   activities   prohibited   by   federal   law.
Therefore,  compliance  with  this  Act  does  not
put  the  State  of  Illinois  in  violation  of
federal law.
        (g)  State  law  should  make  a  distinction
between  the  medical  and  non-medical  uses  of
cannabis.  Hence,  the  purpose  of  this  Act  is  to
protect   patients   with   debilitating   medical
conditions,  as  well  as  their  physicians  and
providers,    from    arrest    and    prosecution,
criminal  and  other  penalties,  and  property
forfeiture  if  the  patients  engage  in  the
medical use of cannabis.
        (Source:   P.A.   98-122,   eff.   1-1-14;   99-519,
eff. 6-30-16.)

        (410 ILCS 130/7)
```

[The Compassionate Use of Medical Cannabis Pilot Program Act (410 -
130/5, f-g) at:
http://www.ilga.gov/legislation/ilcs/ilcs3.asp?ActID=3503&ChapterID=3
5]

The link to a printer friendly version of the IL law follows:

[http://www.ilga.gov/legislation/ilcs/ilcs3.asp?ActID=3503&ChapterID=
35&Print=True]

=== August 29, 2013 ===

The year 2013 also saw Barack Obama's third DOJ *'executive order'*, on medical marijuana. But the 2013 order is of particular interest as Obama's DOJ no longer speaks of medical marijuana users as in *"...clear and unambiguous compliance..."*. Then Obama's 2013 *'order'* directs the targeting of medical marijuana under investigative discretion of US Attorneys for crimes peripheral to the use of a controlled substance including but not limited to *'marijuana'*. They call it the *'Cole Memo'*.

U.S. Department of Justice

Office of the Deputy Attorney General

The Deputy Attorney General   Washington, D.C. 20530

August 29, 2013

MEMORANDUM FOR ALL UNITED STATES ATTORNEYS

FROM: James M. Cole
            Deputy Attorney General

SUBJECT: Guidance Regarding Marijuana Enforcement

In October 2009 and June 2011, the Department issued guidance to federal prosecutors concerning marijuana enforcement under the Controlled Substances Act (CSA). This memorandum updates that guidance in light of state ballot initiatives that legalize under state law the possession of small amounts of marijuana and provide for the regulation of marijuana production, processing, and sale. The guidance set forth herein applies to all federal enforcement activity, including civil enforcement and criminal investigations and prosecutions, concerning marijuana in all states.

As the Department noted in its previous guidance, Congress has determined that marijuana is a dangerous drug and that the illegal distribution and sale of marijuana is a serious crime that provides a significant source of revenue to large-scale criminal enterprises, gangs, and cartels. The Department of Justice is committed to enforcement of the CSA consistent with those determinations. The Department is also committed to using its limited investigative and prosecutorial resources to address the most significant threats in the most effective, consistent, and rational way. In furtherance of those objectives, as several states enacted laws relating to the use of marijuana for medical purposes, the Department in recent years has focused its efforts on certain enforcement priorities that are particularly important to the federal government:

- Preventing the distribution of marijuana to minors;
- Preventing revenue from the sale of marijuana from going to criminal enterprises, gangs, and cartels;
- Preventing the diversion of marijuana from states where it is legal under state law in some form to other states;
- Preventing state-authorized marijuana activity from being used as a cover or pretext for the trafficking of other illegal drugs or other illegal activity;

[page 1 of 4]

*[https://www.justice.gov/iso/opa/resources/3052013829132756857467
.pdf]*

Memorandum for All United States Attorneys   Page 2
Subject: Guidance Regarding Marijuana Enforcement

- Preventing violence and the use of firearms in the cultivation and distribution of marijuana;
- Preventing drugged driving and the exacerbation of other adverse public health consequences associated with marijuana use;
- Preventing the growing of marijuana on public lands and the attendant public safety and environmental dangers posed by marijuana production on public lands; and
- Preventing marijuana possession or use on federal property.

These priorities will continue to guide the Department's enforcement of the CSA against marijuana-related conduct. Thus, this memorandum serves as guidance to Department attorneys and law enforcement to focus their enforcement resources and efforts, including prosecution, on persons or organizations whose conduct interferes with any one or more of these priorities, regardless of state law.[1]

Outside of these enforcement priorities, the federal government has traditionally relied on states and local law enforcement agencies to address marijuana activity through enforcement of their own narcotics laws. For example, the Department of Justice has not historically devoted resources to prosecuting individuals whose conduct is limited to possession of small amounts of marijuana for personal use on private property. Instead, the Department has left such lower-level or localized activity to state and local authorities and has stepped in to enforce the CSA only when the use, possession, cultivation, or distribution of marijuana has threatened to cause one of the harms identified above.

The enactment of state laws that endeavor to authorize marijuana production, distribution, and possession by establishing a regulatory scheme for these purposes affects this traditional joint federal-state approach to narcotics enforcement. The Department's guidance in this memorandum rests on its expectation that states and local governments that have enacted laws authorizing marijuana-related conduct will implement strong and effective regulatory and enforcement systems that will address the threat those state laws could pose to public safety, public health, and other law enforcement interests. A system adequate to that task must not only contain robust controls and procedures on paper; it must also be effective in practice. Jurisdictions that have implemented systems that provide for regulation of marijuana activity

---

[1] These enforcement priorities are listed in general terms; each encompasses a variety of conduct that may merit civil or criminal enforcement of the CSA. By way of example only, the Department's interest in preventing the distribution of marijuana to minors would call for enforcement not just when an individual or entity sells or transfers marijuana to a minor, but also when marijuana trafficking takes place near an area associated with minors; when marijuana or marijuana-infused products are marketed in a manner to appeal to minors; or when marijuana is being diverted, directly or indirectly, and purposefully or otherwise, to minors.

[page 2 of 4]
[https://www.justice.gov/iso/opa/resources/3052013829132756857467.pdf]

Memorandum for All United States Attorneys   Page 3
Subject: Guidance Regarding Marijuana Enforcement

must provide the necessary resources and demonstrate the willingness to enforce their laws and
regulations in a manner that ensures they do not undermine federal enforcement priorities.

In jurisdictions that have enacted laws legalizing marijuana in some form and that have
also implemented strong and effective regulatory and enforcement systems to control the
cultivation, distribution, sale, and possession of marijuana, conduct in compliance with those
laws and regulations is less likely to threaten the federal priorities set forth above. Indeed, a
robust system may affirmatively address those priorities by, for example, implementing effective
measures to prevent diversion of marijuana outside of the regulated system and to other states,
prohibiting access to marijuana by minors, and replacing an illicit marijuana trade that funds
criminal enterprises with a tightly regulated market in which revenues are tracked and accounted
for. In those circumstances, consistent with the traditional allocation of federal-state efforts in
this area, enforcement of state law by state and local law enforcement and regulatory bodies
should remain the primary means of addressing marijuana-related activity. If state enforcement
efforts are not sufficiently robust to protect against the harms set forth above, the federal
government may seek to challenge the regulatory structure itself in addition to continuing to
bring individual enforcement actions, including criminal prosecutions, focused on those harms.

The Department's previous memoranda specifically addressed the exercise of
prosecutorial discretion in states with laws authorizing marijuana cultivation and distribution for
medical use. In those contexts, the Department advised that it likely was not an efficient use of
federal resources to focus enforcement efforts on seriously ill individuals, or on their individual
caregivers. In doing so, the previous guidance drew a distinction between the seriously ill and
their caregivers, on the one hand, and large-scale, for-profit commercial enterprises, on the other,
and advised that the latter continued to be appropriate targets for federal enforcement and
prosecution. In drawing this distinction, the Department relied on the common-sense judgment
that the size of a marijuana operation was a reasonable proxy for assessing whether marijuana
trafficking implicates the federal enforcement priorities set forth above.

As explained above, however, both the existence of a strong and effective state regulatory
system, and an operation's compliance with such a system, may allay the threat that an
operation's size poses to federal enforcement interests. Accordingly, in exercising prosecutorial
discretion, prosecutors should not consider the size or commercial nature of a marijuana
operation alone as a proxy for assessing whether marijuana trafficking implicates the
Department's enforcement priorities listed above. Rather, prosecutors should continue to review
marijuana cases on a case-by-case basis and weigh all available information and evidence,
including, but not limited to, whether the operation is demonstrably in compliance with a strong
and effective state regulatory system. A marijuana operation's large scale or for-profit nature
may be a relevant consideration for assessing the extent to which it undermines a particular
federal enforcement priority. The primary question in all cases – and in all jurisdictions – should
be whether the conduct at issue implicates one or more of the enforcement priorities listed above.

[page 3 of 4]

*[https://www.justice.gov/iso/opa/resources/3052013829132756857467
.pdf]*

Memorandum for All United States Attorneys   Page 4
Subject: Guidance Regarding Marijuana Enforcement

As with the Department's previous statements on this subject, this memorandum is intended solely as a guide to the exercise of investigative and prosecutorial discretion. This memorandum does not alter in any way the Department's authority to enforce federal law, including federal laws relating to marijuana, regardless of state law. Neither the guidance herein nor any state or local law provides a legal defense to a violation of federal law, including any civil or criminal violation of the CSA. Even in jurisdictions with strong and effective regulatory systems, evidence that particular conduct threatens federal priorities will subject that person or entity to federal enforcement action, based on the circumstances. This memorandum is not intended to, does not, and may not be relied upon to create any rights, substantive or procedural, enforceable at law by any party in any matter civil or criminal. It applies prospectively to the exercise of prosecutorial discretion in future cases and does not provide defendants or subjects of enforcement action with a basis for reconsideration of any pending civil action or criminal prosecution. Finally, nothing herein precludes investigation or prosecution, even in the absence of any one of the factors listed above, in particular circumstances where investigation and prosecution otherwise serves an important federal interest.

cc: Mythili Raman
        Acting Assistant Attorney General, Criminal Division

        Loretta E. Lynch
        United States Attorney
        Eastern District of New York
        Chair, Attorney General's Advisory Committee

        Michele M. Leonhart
        Administrator
        Drug Enforcement Administration

        H. Marshall Jarrett
        Director
        Executive Office for United States Attorneys

        Ronald T. Hosko
        Assistant Director
        Criminal Investigative Division
        Federal Bureau of Investigation

[Page 4 of 4]

*[https://www.justice.gov/iso/opa/resources/3052013829132756857467
.pdf]*

The investigative discretion granted by Obama's *'order'* adds to the 2009 Obama medical marijuana *'executive order'* which indicates infringements stating legal medical marijuana users will *"will not be in clear and unambiguous compliance"* if the patient exercises their 2nd Amendment Constitutional American Right. This creates an un-Constitutional *'Bill of Attainder'* without a trial, yet plenty of punishment.

No law-abiding American citizen should ever need to have their 2nd Amendment infringed, or any of their Rights for that, as they are the laws which keep our United States Free. Without our Liberties, America is left vulnerable, unable to protect our families and our Republic.

Obama's' *'executive orders'* from 2009 through 2013 indicate, if you have a firearm or expect to exercise your 2nd Amendment to protect your family or our country, you are disqualified from the states' medical marijuana programs. At the same time, Obama attempts to disqualify Americans from exercising their 2nd Amendment if they are a patient in their state's medical marijuana program. If allowed to continue, the un-Constitutional *'rules'* will soon affect other healthcare treatments and our National Security, all without our elected representatives involved.

=== February 14, 2014 ===

Valentine's Day - 2014

Barack Obama's DOJ released another *'executive order'* memo on Valentine's Day 2014. The memo didn't address medical marijuana but was *'guidance'* on general marijuana enforcement. The detective would later, in March 2017, have a family-business bank account closed when speaking with the bank president to determine why his ATM-card never worked for the withdrawing of cash. The bank president offered to help and fix the bank's error, but then he changed his mind and instead, all of a sudden, closed the detective's bank account under odd circumstances.

U.S. Department of Justice

Office of the Deputy Attorney General

The Deputy Attorney General   Washington D.C. 20530

February 14, 2014

MEMORANDUM FOR ALL UNITED STATES ATTORNEYS

FROM: James M. Cole
             Deputy Attorney General

SUBJECT: Guidance Regarding Marijuana Related Financial Crimes

On August 29, 2013, the Department issued guidance (August 29 guidance) to federal prosecutors concerning marijuana enforcement under the Controlled Substances Act (CSA). The August 29 guidance reiterated the Department's commitment to enforcing the CSA consistent with Congress' determination that marijuana is a dangerous drug that serves as a significant source of revenue to large-scale criminal enterprises, gangs, and cartels. In furtherance of that commitment, the August 29 guidance instructed Department attorneys and law enforcement to focus on the following eight priorities in enforcing the CSA against marijuana-related conduct:

- Preventing the distribution of marijuana to minors;
- Preventing revenue from the sale of marijuana from going to criminal enterprises, gangs, and cartels;
- Preventing the diversion of marijuana from states where it is legal under state law in some form to other states;
- Preventing state-authorized marijuana activity from being used as a cover or pretext for the trafficking of other illegal drugs or other illegal activity;
- Preventing violence and the use of firearms in the cultivation and distribution of marijuana;
- Preventing drugged driving and the exacerbation of other adverse public health consequences associated with marijuana use;
- Preventing the growing of marijuana on public lands and the attendant public safety and environmental dangers posed by marijuana production on public lands; and
- Preventing marijuana possession or use on federal property.

Under the August 29 guidance, whether marijuana-related conduct implicates one or more of these enforcement priorities should be the primary question in considering prosecution

[Page 1 of 3 Obama's 'executive order' on "Guidance Regarding
Marijuana Related Financial Crimes", located at:
https://dfi.wa.gov/documents/banks/dept-of-justice-memo.pdf]

under the CSA. Although the August 29 guidance was issued in response to recent marijuana legalization initiatives in certain states, it applies to all Department marijuana enforcement nationwide. The guidance, however, did not specifically address what, if any, impact it would have on certain financial crimes for which marijuana-related conduct is a predicate.

The provisions of the money laundering statutes, the unlicensed money remitter statute, and the Bank Secrecy Act (BSA) remain in effect with respect to marijuana-related conduct. Financial transactions involving proceeds generated by marijuana-related conduct can form the basis for prosecution under the money laundering statutes (18 U.S.C. §§ 1956 and 1957), the unlicensed money transmitter statute (18 U.S.C. § 1960), and the BSA. Sections 1956 and 1957 of Title 18 make it a criminal offense to engage in certain financial and monetary transactions with the proceeds of a "specified unlawful activity," including proceeds from marijuana-related violations of the CSA. Transactions by or through a money transmitting business involving funds "derived from" marijuana-related conduct can also serve as a predicate for prosecution under 18 U.S.C. § 1960. Additionally, financial institutions that conduct transactions with money generated by marijuana-related conduct could face criminal liability under the BSA for, among other things, failing to identify or report financial transactions that involved the proceeds of marijuana-related violations of the CSA. *See, e.g.,* 31 U.S.C. § 5318(g). Notably for these purposes, prosecution under these offenses based on transactions involving marijuana proceeds does not require an underlying marijuana-related conviction under federal or state law.

As noted in the August 29 guidance, the Department is committed to using its limited investigative and prosecutorial resources to address the most significant marijuana-related cases in an effective and consistent way. Investigations and prosecutions of the offenses enumerated above based upon marijuana-related activity should be subject to the same consideration and prioritization. Therefore, in determining whether to charge individuals or institutions with any of these offenses based on marijuana-related violations of the CSA, prosecutors should apply the eight enforcement priorities described in the August 29 guidance and reiterated above.[1] For example, if a financial institution or individual provides banking services to a marijuana-related business knowing that the business is diverting marijuana from a state where marijuana sales are regulated to ones where such sales are illegal under state law, or is being used by a criminal organization to conduct financial transactions for its criminal goals, such as the concealment of funds derived from other illegal activity or the use of marijuana proceeds to support other illegal activity, prosecution for violations of 18 U.S.C. §§ 1956, 1957, 1960 or the BSA might be appropriate. Similarly, if the financial institution or individual is willfully blind to such activity by, for example, failing to conduct appropriate due diligence of the customers' activities, such prosecution might be appropriate. Conversely, if a financial institution or individual offers

---

[1] The Department of the Treasury's Financial Crimes Enforcement Network (FinCEN) is issuing concurrent guidance to clarify BSA expectations for financial institutions seeking to provide services to marijuana-related businesses. The FinCEN guidance addresses the filing of Suspicious Activity Reports (SAR) with respect to marijuana-related businesses, and in particular the importance of considering the eight federal enforcement priorities mentioned above, as well as state law. As discussed in FinCEN's guidance, a financial institution providing financial services to a marijuana-related business that it reasonably believes, based on its customer due diligence, does not implicate one of the federal enforcement priorities or violate state law, would file a "Marijuana Limited" SAR, which would include streamlined information. Conversely, a financial institution filing a SAR on a marijuana-related business it reasonably believes, based on its customer due diligence, implicates one of the federal priorities or violates state law, would be label the SAR "Marijuana Priority," and the content of the SAR would include comprehensive details in accordance with existing regulations and guidance.

[Page 2 of 3 Obama's 'executive order' on "Guidance Regarding Marijuana Related Financial Crimes", located at: https://dfi.wa.gov/documents/banks/dept-of-justice-memo.pdf]

Memorandum for All United States Attorneys   Page 3
Subject: Guidance Regarding Marijuana Related Financial Crimes

services to a marijuana-related business whose activities do not implicate any of the eight priority factors, prosecution for these offenses may not be appropriate.

The August 29 guidance rested on the expectation that states that have enacted laws authorizing marijuana-related conduct will implement clear, strong and effective regulatory and enforcement systems in order to minimize the threat posed to federal enforcement priorities. Consequently, financial institutions and individuals choosing to service marijuana-related businesses that are not compliant with such state regulatory and enforcement systems, or that operate in states lacking a clear and robust regulatory scheme, are more likely to risk entanglement with conduct that implicates the eight federal enforcement priorities.[2] In addition, because financial institutions are in a position to facilitate transactions by marijuana-related businesses that could implicate one or more of the priority factors, financial institutions must continue to apply appropriate risk-based anti-money laundering policies, procedures, and controls sufficient to address the risks posed by these customers, including by conducting customer due diligence designed to identify conduct that relates to any of the eight priority factors. Moreover, as the Department's and FinCEN's guidance are designed to complement each other, it is essential that financial institutions adhere to FinCEN's guidance.[3] Prosecutors should continue to review marijuana-related prosecutions on a case-by-case basis and weigh all available information and evidence in determining whether particular conduct falls within the identified priorities.

As with the Department's previous statements on this subject, this memorandum is intended solely as a guide to the exercise of investigative and prosecutorial discretion. This memorandum does not alter in any way the Department's authority to enforce federal law, including federal laws relating to marijuana, regardless of state law. Neither the guidance herein nor any state or local law provides a legal defense to a violation of federal law, including any civil or criminal violation of the CSA, the money laundering and unlicensed money transmitter statutes, or the BSA, including the obligation of financial institutions to conduct customer due diligence. Even in jurisdictions with strong and effective regulatory systems, evidence that particular conduct of a person or entity threatens federal priorities will subject that person or entity to federal enforcement action, based on the circumstances. This memorandum is not intended, does not, and may not be relied upon to create any rights, substantive or procedural, enforceable at law by any party in any matter civil or criminal. It applies prospectively to the exercise of prosecutorial discretion in future cases and does not provide defendants or subjects of enforcement action with a basis for reconsideration of any pending civil action or criminal prosecution. Finally, nothing herein precludes investigation or prosecution, even in the absence of any one of the factors listed above, in particular circumstances where investigation and prosecution otherwise serves an important federal interest.

---

[2] For example, financial institutions should recognize that a marijuana-related business operating in a state that has not legalized marijuana would likely result in the proceeds going to a criminal organization.
[3] Under FinCEN's guidance, for instance, a marijuana-related business that is not appropriately licensed or is operating in violation of state law presents red flags that would justify the filing of a Marijuana Priority SAR.

[Page 3 of 3 Obama's 'executive order' on "Guidance Regarding Marijuana Related Financial Crimes", located at: https://dfi.wa.gov/documents/banks/dept-of-justice-memo.pdf]

=== December 2014 ===

Sedentary jobs are very unhealthy as the heart gets little exercise while the body sits all day. But since the detective can't sing and can't dance, Hollywood wasn't calling. He kept working as his health took a hit. At the end of 2014 the detective was diagnosed with RA – Rheumatoid Arthritis, an autoimmune reaction, causing pain and swelling in some joints. Most of us will feel the effects of arthritis as we grow older, but for the young detective and his family, he couldn't afford the loss of his health and mobility while securing his family's future.

The doctors prescribed the detective a pharmaceutical immune-system suppressant drug; the same one given to pregnant mothers to abort fetuses. Now, forgive me if I explain the condition incorrectly, as I am not a doctor or medical practitioner (nor am I an attorney offering legal advice), but the way the detective explains it, the pain and swelling in joints is misidentified by the body as causing discomfort and putting the person ill at ease – or *'dis-ease'*. The body's immune system automatically reacts as it attacks the joints for causing the disease of pain. Of course, this only causes more swelling and further deformity of joints. The body's well-intentioned immune system becomes overactive in RA patients and is weakened by the pharmaceutical industry's immune-suppressant drug; or at least, that's the idea.

Beyond the drug's costs, there were problems. The doctor prescribed immune-suppressant carried a warning label as long as the detective's arm. The warnings included horrifying things for one's health including, but not limited to death – as if there is worse. One warning cautioned of liver and kidney damage. Another even warned not to operate heavy machinery. As the immune-suppressant pharmaceutical drug needs continual usage before it begins to work effectively, detective work, let alone driving for any job, would be tasking. Scary - that it was the same drug given to expecting mothers to terminate a pregnancy.

It was clear, in the detective's opinion, the pharmaceutical drug was not the best option for his health. The disease the drug claimed to treat had seemingly worse side-effects than the RA. If a safe way existed to reduce the swelling and damage caused to the joints, then the disease itself would be suppressed instead of suppressing the body's reactive immune system, which is still needed to immunize a body against infections.

The detective looked for healthier alternatives to treat his condition. Eventually, he found one. In 2013 Illinois had passed the *"Compassionate Use of Medical Cannabis Pilot Program [Law] Act"*. All the systems needed to be put into place before medical *'cannabis'* (a.k.a. marijuana) sales could begin to qualified-patients in his state. The detective's RA was one of the qualifying conditions.

The Illinois State Police would perform background checks for the patients via state licensed fingerprint vendors, who would never be given the reason why the patient was being *'fingerprinted'*. This would be done according to the Illinois Department of Public Health directives to qualify the patient as a compliant, non-felon to receive their cards from the same licensing agency that issues detectives their licenses, the Illinois Department of Financial and Professional Regulation (IDFPR).

The detective was skeptical when he heard the IDFPR and police were going to be involved. Marijuana was classified with the FDA (Food and Drug Administration) as a *"Schedule 1 controlled substance"*; that means it can be a felony to possess or prescribe. Marijuana's continued federal felony classification under Obama's DEA as a *'Schedule 1 controlled substance'* could cause problems for all Americans including detectives and law enforcement. Medical marijuana patients already have enough to battle; they don't need further mountains to climb.

The program identified dispensaries by state police districts as referenced in the *'Illinois State – Illinois Department of Public Health – Compassionate Use of Medical Cannabis Pilot Program Act – FAQ- 2014'*.

Where do I find a list of dispensaries?

There are currently no dispensaries in operation. Dispensaries are expected to be located in the districts made up of the following:

- District 1 – Carroll, Lee, Ogle and Whiteside counties
- District 6 – DeWitt, Livingston and McLean counties
- District 7 – Henry, Knox, Mercer and Rock Island counties
- District 8 – Marshall, Peoria, Stark, Tazewell and Woodford counties
- District 9 – Cass, Christian, Logan, Mason, Menard, Morgan and Sangamon counties
- District 10 – Champaign, Coles, Douglas, Edgar, Macon, Moultrie, Piatt, Shelby and Vermilion counties
- District 11 – Bond, Clinton, Madison, Monroe and St. Clair counties

Page 10

State of Illinois
Illinois Department of Public Health

Illinois Medical Cannabis Pilot Program
Frequently Asked Questions (FAQs)

- District 12 – Clark, Clay, Crawford, Cumberland, Effingham, Fayette, Jasper, Lawrence, Marion and Richland counties
- District 13 – Franklin, Jackson, Jefferson, Perry, Randolph, Washington and Williamson counties
- District 14 – Fulton, Hancock, Henderson, McDonough and Warren counties
- District 16 – Boone, Jo Daviess, Stephenson and Winnebago counties
- District 17 – Bureau, La Salle and Putnam counties
- District 18 – Calhoun, Greene, Jersey, Macoupin, Montgomery counties
- District 19 – Edwards, Gallatin, Hamilton, Saline, Wabash, Wayne and White counties
- District 20 – Adams, Brown, Pike, Schuyler and Scott counties
- District 21 – Ford, Iroquois and Kankakee counties
- District 22 – Alexander, Hardin, Johnson, Massac, Pope, Pulaski and Union counties
- DeKalb County
- DuPage County
- Grundy and Kendall counties
- Kane County
- Lake County
- McHenry County
- Will County
- Cook County, outside the city of Chicago
- City of Chicago

[portions of pages 10-11 'IDPH – Illinois Medical Cannabis Pilot Program - FAQs – July 2014']

Furthermore, private detectives are America's privatized public-option to government police; private eyes are the cop's competition on many levels and offer armed protective services to individuals, businesses and even schools, public and private. In fact, private detectives are capable of all the police do for a society and then some. Of course, private detectives would need to be contracted by the People before assuming law enforcement roles for our communities.

This isn't to say police aren't qualified; all American law enforcement officers are amply qualified to tackle the same duties licensed private detectives can perform. But it is the taxpayer-funded duty of the police to investigate crimes after they occur – not before. Never would a police officer investigate to validate an insurance claim when no suggestion of a crime was present. Nor would taxpayer-funded police investigate domestic issues involving separation of private assets. The taxpayers wouldn't stand for it. So private eyes exist for many valid causes. Though private detectives can protect our school children, sometimes us private detectives get the impression some cops don't appreciate the competition, for their armed services in particular.

In the past, other states had already legalized medical marijuana, and even its recreational usage. The detective learned marijuana was safe for human consumption. Though the state's Governor Quinn refused to sign the final authorization, Illinois grew anxious to treat their medical conditions with marijuana.

The detective saw the Illinois State Police website openly invite (and still does as I prepare this presentation) Illinois residents who are medical marijuana cardholders to exercise their 2nd Amendment with Firearm Owner's Identifications (FOID) and Concealed Carry Licenses (CCL) issued by the Illinois State Police.

Then, Illinois residents and the detective found their reassurance. America's private healthcare treatments and medical records would ultimately be protected by our 4th Amendment Right, as most Americans understand *'to be secure in their 'papers and effects'*; other state and federal laws protect the same. The State of Illinois could not single out a detective, his licenses or his family-business or else they would be doing the same to all Americans. The detective printed a copy of the State of Illinois' reassurance our private medical records would remain protected as residents applied for the medical marijuana program. The detective was relieved he would be able to continue in the business he had built to secure a future for his family.

State of Illinois
Illinois Department of Public Health

Illinois Medical Cannabis Pilot Program
Frequently Asked Questions (FAQs)

Are registry identification cards from other state medical cannabis programs valid in Illinois?

No. Only registry identification cards issued through the Illinois Department of Public Health Division of Medical Cannabis are valid in Illinois.

Am I protected under Illinois law if I'm visiting another state and using my medical cannabis?

No. The Compassionate Use of Medical Cannabis Pilot Program Act only applies in Illinois.

I live in another state and have one of the eligible debilitating medical conditions. May I apply?

No. You may only apply if the Compassionate Use of Medical Cannabis Program...

Is my confidentiality protected when I apply and if I am approved for the use of medical cannabis?

Yes. The following information received and records kept by the Illinois Department of Public Health Division of Medical Cannabis are subject to all applicable federal privacy laws, are confidential, are exempt from the Freedom of Information Act and are not subject to disclosure to any individual or public or private entity, except as necessary for authorized employees of the Department to perform official duties for the medical cannabis program.

1. applications, or renewals, their contents and supporting information submitted by qualifying patients and designated caregivers, including information regarding designated caregivers and physicians;

2. the individual name and other information identifying the person to whom the Illinois Department of Public Health Division of Medical Cannabis has issued registry identification cards; and

3. all medical records provided to the Department in connection with an application for a registry identification card.

Can I use medical cannabis anywhere I want?

No. Using medical cannabis is prohibited in a school bus, on the grounds of any preschool or primary or secondary school, in any correctional facility, in any motor vehicle, in a private residence used at any time to provide licensed child care or other similar social service care on the premises and in any public place where an individual could reasonably be expected to be observed by others. A public place includes all parts of buildings owned in a whole or in part, or leased, by the state or local unit of government. A public place does not include a private residence unless the private residence is used to provide licensed child care, foster care or other similar social service care on the premises. Using medical cannabis is also prohibited in a health care facility or any other place where smoking is prohibited by the Smoke-free Illinois Act and knowingly in close physical proximity to anyone under the age of 18.

[Page 13 'IL Department of Public Health – Illinois Medical Cannabis Pilot Program - FAQs – July 2014]

"State of Illinois – Illinois Department of Public Health – Compassionate Use of Medical Cannabis – Frequently Asked Questions (FAQs) – July 2014 [portion of page 13]"

"... Is my confidentiality protected when I apply and if I am approved for the use of medical cannabis?"

"Yes. The following information received and records kept by the Illinois Department of Public Health Division of Medical Cannabis are subject to all applicable federal privacy laws, are confidential, are exempt from the Freedom of Information Act and are not subject to disclosure to any individual or public or private entity, except as necessary for authorized employees of the Department to perform official duties for the medical cannabis program:

1. applications, or renewals, their contents and supporting information submitted by qualifying patients and designated caregivers, including information regarding designated caregivers and physicians;

2. the individual name and other information identifying the person to whom the Illinois Department of Public Health Division of Medical Cannabis has issued registry identification cards; and 3. all medical records provided to the Department in connection with an application for a registry identification card. ..."

[State of Illinois – IDPH – Compassionate Use of Medical Cannabis – Frequently Asked Questions (FAQs) – July 2014]

By the end of October 2015, the detective had received his medical cannabis card from the State of Illinois. The detective was relieved he would be able to continue in the business he labored for years to build as he Patriotically contribute to America's *'Free Market'* while securing a future for his family. The detective had witnessed corruption in the past at government levels, first hand, but he never expected what was in store for his family's future under Obama's continuing *'orders'*.

=== November 2015 ===

In November 2015, Illinois began the *'Compassionate Use of Medical Cannabis'* sales under Governor Bruce Rauner.

But relief would soon turn to puzzlement as Illinois patients were un-Constitutionally infringed despite state and federal laws protecting their medical records and *'Bill of Rights'*.

==== December 4, 2015 ===

"Illinois State Police erroneously seize medical marijuana cardholders' guns and gun cards."

A major Chicago newspaper had reported online on December 4, 2015, just weeks after Illinois's medical marijuana program began, Illinois State Police had seized guns and Firearm Owner's Identifications (FOID) cards from patients in the new medical program. The Illinois State Police admitted their erroneous un-Constitutional infringement and apologized by returning almost all the guns. A veteran from Rockford, Illinois had his gun-card seized along with his firearms. Family heirlooms went missing; no further word was reported. That vet likely moved out of Illinois.

The detective didn't learn of the mainstream media story published December 4, 2015 online until after the government seized the defined status of his family business's licensing. Yet still, it is important to mention this online MSM news report for the State of Illinois continues to deceive the American public about the detective's Firearm Control Card (FCC) defined license status.

But for the time, America went on, as did the detective and his family business. Clients were starting to become repeat customers and new business was calling on the phone. He even learned of unfortunate towns in Illinois that were so broke, devastated by government employee payrolls and police misconduct settlements, they no longer could afford a police department. Perhaps towns could use a team of affordable licensed detectives working directly for the People. Perhaps America would appreciate detective services for our counties or even their whole state. Maybe even the whole U.S.A.

=== Spring - 2016 ===

Toward the beginning half of 2016, during the warmer months in the *'Land of Lincoln',* the detective was driving through a town when he was stopped by a municipal police officer; the dark tinted windows of a detective's under-cover surveillance vehicle can often catch the eye of police as a vehicle performs a three-point turn on a blocked pathway.

The police officer was courteous as the detective politely handed him his driver's license and proof of insurance. The officer spoke into a two-way radio/speaker system attached near his shoulder, presumably to their police radio-dispatch as he called-in the detective's information. The officer understood why the detective had performed the unusual three-point-turn maneuver on the blocked roadway; it would be just a moment, the officer kindly explained.

The police radio dispatcher on the other end of the transmission promptly spoke back to the officer over the speaker at a level for neighborhood residents and patrons in the parking area of a nearby fast-food restaurant to hear as they took notice of the police squad-car's flashing lights. The dispatcher assured the police officer the detective had no outstanding warrants with a valid license. This publicly broadcast assurance over the officer's speaker-system prompted the officer to return the detective's credentials with well wishes.

As the officer began to walk away, the radio-dispatcher interrupted over the loud-speaker. The detective remembers the voice over the police officer's loud speaker say, *"Wait, he's got a medical marijuana card"*, as neighborhood residents continued to listen while the squad-car's lights flashed on their astounded faces. The police officer and nearby pedestrians appeared as shocked as the detective was to hear the voice on the officer's loud-speaker broadcast, over public airwaves, confidential, private medical records protected by state and federal laws.

Neighborhood residents scattered as the officer began to question the detective. The police officer asked if the detective had any marijuana with him; the detective uncomfortable at the discussion of his medical history and treatments, assured the officer he did not. Though the police officer did not ask if the detective had been using medical marijuana on that day, the detective assured he was not and would not use it on days when working or when driving was required, just as you wouldn't several over-the-counter drugs and certain prescription medications. The police officer again wished the detective well and departed in his squad-car. The detective hadn't broken any laws and was partially relieved at not being detained any longer. But…

The detective was astonished at the blatant disregard for our American Constitutional Rights by law enforcement; during the Obama administration, these changes became crystal clear. The detective immediately was puzzled to how his private medical information submitted to the Illinois Department of Public Health (IDPH) had become available to a random municipal police department not involved with the Illinois medical marijuana program. The IDPH assures, in the previously referenced *'Illinois Medical Cannabis FAQs'* document, only the IDPH will use and *"keep"* information submitted by patients, with all state and federal protections in place.

The violation against the detective's state, federal and even 4th Amendment protections *'to be secure'* in our medical records had set precedent for every individual citizen of the United States of America.

It seemed Obama and law enforcement agencies could now use any *'Schedule 1 controlled substance'* to hold Americans to a *'Bill of Attainder'*, punishing Americans for crimes they were not convicted of, even if all state and federal protections are guaranteed in writing to remain in place? To single-out a detective would be discriminatory. Obama's law enforcement directives are allowing police to diagnose medical marijuana patients as *'narcotic addicts'*, without their doctors. The detective never submitted his medical information for any other reason than for his healthcare. The FBI and Illinois State Police are not the keepers of such medical information and in doing so would be in violation of every American's 4th Amendment Rights and Illinois State Law.

The precedent was set. Now, would prescription drugs be targeted next for our *'Bill of Rights'*? It seemed all Americans could now have their 4th Amendment protections stripped if they are merely suspected of misuse by law enforcement — no trial necessary. To allow others to have any *'Schedule 1 controlled substance'* and not search their records for infringement purposes seems it would be unequal justice by discrimination. My hunch is, Obama grabbed all America's records.

Within months, the Illinois State Police would, *'jump-the-gun'* in their enforcement of Obama's *'new rules'* for our *'Bill of Rights'*, as they infringed the detective's 2nd Amendment firearm purchase from 2016, weeks prior to Obama's un-Constitutional *'rule'* change in 2017.

=== June 30, 2016 ===

The State of Illinois updated their medical marijuana law from 2013. In congruence with our 10th Amendment, further definitions were made, and qualifying conditions were added as the People of Illinois and their elected lawmakers reinforced the stipulations of compliant medical marijuana users as *"Lawful"* and never ever, *"unlawful"*.

"Public Act 099-0159' '(410 ILCS 130/5/7)' 'Compassionate Use of Medical Cannabis Pilot Program Act'

"...'(f) States are not required to enforce federal law or prosecute people for engaging in activities prohibited by federal law. Therefore, compliance with this Act does not put the State of Illinois in violation of federal law.

(g) State law should make a distinction between the medical and non-medical uses of cannabis. Hence, the purpose of this Act is to protect patients with debilitating medical conditions, as well as their physicians and providers, from

arrest and prosecution, criminal and other penalties, and property forfeiture if the patients engage in the medical use of cannabis. (Source: P.A. 98-122, eff. 1-1-14.)

(410 ILCS 130/7 new)

Sec. 7. Lawful user and lawful products. For the purposes of this Act and to clarify the legislative findings on the lawful use of cannabis:

(1) A cardholder under this Act shall not be considered an unlawful user or addicted to narcotics solely as a result of his or her qualifying patient or designated caregiver status.

(2) All medical cannabis products purchased by a [page break'] qualifying patient at a licensed dispensing organization shall be lawful products and a distinction shall be made between medical and non-medical uses of cannabis as a result of the qualifying patient's cardholder status under the authorized use granted under State law."

[http://www.ilga.gov/legislation/publicacts/fulltext.asp?Name= 099-0519]

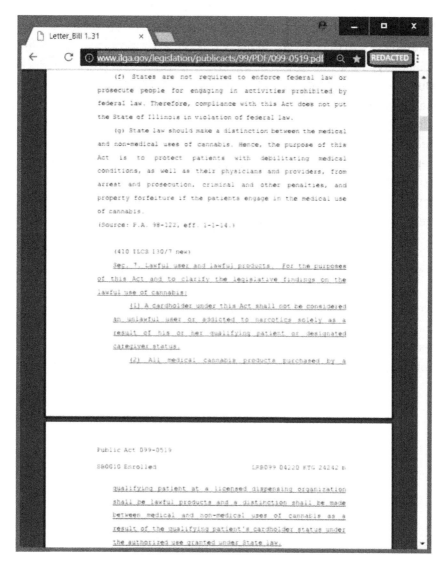

[IL 'Compassionate Use of Medical Cannabis Pilot Program Act' (Law)
(410 ILCS 130/5.f.-g. /7.1.2.) at:
http://www.ilga.gov/legislation/publicacts/99/PDF/099-0519.pdf]

Intelligence agencies, and corporations too, use a term called, *"compartmentalization";* a short definition could be to create several different departments to allow designed-confusion and plausible deniability to exist as a defense against any breaches of law or conduct. Multiple government departments were overseeing the medical marijuana for Illinois. But only two government departments legally held information about patient identity. The Illinois Department of Public Health was one government agency. The other was the Illinois Department of Financial and Professional Regulation; the IDFPR also issues detective licenses and the *'Firearm Control Cards' (FCC)* to detectives in order to use firearms in their profession. The commercial medical dispensary also had the detective's identifying information.

Had someone, or many, at one or several of these government regulated departments, allowed the detective's protected medical records to be violated? The detective considered if this was true, it meant likely he wasn't the only patient who suffered the same. Perhaps some may argue a legal *'pharmacy-reporting'* loophole exists? But loopholes really don't exist if they instantly change the *'Bill of Rights'* for millions of Americans, overnight without elected lawmakers or the patient's doctor.

=== August 31, 2016 ===

Mainstream media headlines reported a story online that seems to imply something far grander than what occurred. Many Americans suspected headlines like this under Obama, as did the detective. Barack Obama's *'fence-sitting'* on the medical marijuana issue had contradictions built into his own *'executive orders'.* Mainstream media, if more beholden to the truth, may have used this headline instead:

"US 9th Circuit Court of Appeals upholds dismissal of lower court ruling that Obama's DEA kept Medical Marijuana a Felony."

One federal appellate circuit court can't change the *'Bill of Rights'* for hundreds of millions of Americans; that takes our elected Congress. And our government is prohibited from creating an 'after-the-facts' *'ex post facto Law'* and *'Bill of Attainder'*. The report of the court decision was auspiciously timed for Obama's *'UN Small Arms Treaty'* he was desperately trying to get passed in the Senate before a new American President was elected and inaugurated. The federal appellate court's ruling was to uphold a dismissal of a lower court's filing which cited the *'Gun Control Act of 1968'*. The federal appellate court cited a 1974 federal case claiming Americans are now exempt from their 5th Amendment's *"due process"*. *'We the People'* already had our *'due process'* in 1974 – that's the story the US 9th Circuit is going with for our *'Bill of Rights'*.

Another conveniently-timed event would be Obama's upcoming revision of *'Form 4473 - Revised October 2016'*. Obama's September 29, 2009 *'order'*, already implies anyone in the state authorized medical marijuana program and in possession of a legal firearm is not in, *"...clear and unambiguous compliance with applicable state laws and may indicate illegal drug trafficking activity of potential federal interest...".*

=== November 16, 2016 ===

On November 16, 2017, Obama's Federal Bureau of Alcohol, Tobacco and Firearms (ATF) announced changes to become effective on January 16, 2017 for the federal firearm transfer *'Form 4473 Revised October 2016',* attempting to prevent firearm sales to medical marijuana cardholders. I still hear folks falsely claim Obama's not coming for our 2nd Amendment. But, Barrack Obama's lasting new *'rules'* under *'executive order'* would continue into the new President's administration as he was investigated for unsubstantiated allegations of *'Russian collusion'*. This left President Trump stifled to act with the full weight of our *'Executive Office'* in defense of our *'Bill of Rights'*.

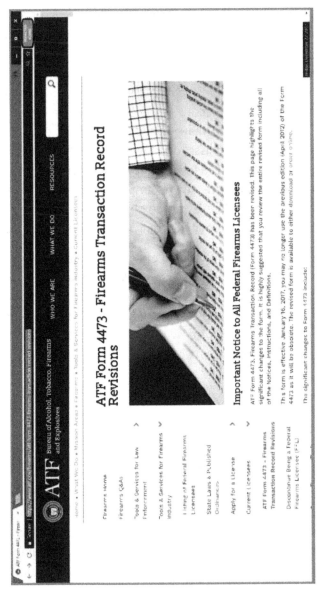

[ATF announcement – January 16, 2017 launch of 'Revised form 4473' - located at: https://www.atf.gov/firearms/atf-form-4473-firearms-transaction-record-revisions]

"ATF - Important Notice to All Federal Firearms Licensees

ATF Form 4473, Firearms Transaction Record (Form 4473) has been revised. This page highlights the significant changes to the form. It is highly suggested that you review the entire revised form including all of the Notices, Instructions, and Definitions.

This form is effective January 16, 2017, you may no longer use the previous edition (April 2012) of the Form 4473 as it will be obsolete. The revised form is available to either download or order online.'..."

[https://www.atf.gov/firearms/atf-form-4473-firearms-transaction-record-revisions]

The previous image and citation are of the *'public domain'* ATF webpage demonstrating the *"effective"* date of January 16, 2017, weeks after the detective would attempt to make 2nd Amendment firearm purchases for their detective agency. Illinois State Police would disobey this federal effective date, hastening infringement upon America's 2nd Amendment.

All the gun-shops in the greater Chicagoland area the detective visited still used the *'Form 4473 – Revised April 2012'.* Why would anyone do otherwise in a *'Free Market'*? It wasn't until Christmas 2016 that the detective learned of the upcoming changes Obama was overseeing at the federal level set to take effect in all 50 states on January 16, 2017, days before America's new President Trump would assume our Oval Office.

Again, for at least the second time, Obama found the need to revise America's access to our 2nd Amendment. Licensed gun-shops would use the federal *"Form 4473 Revised April 2012"* for the entire year of 2016 and into the third week of 2017. It is unclear if all gun-shops would even have access to this newly revised form until it became effective. As one can clearly see, Obama's new un-Constitutional *'Form 4473 Revised October 2016'*, would not be in effect as the detective attempted to purchase firearms on December 27, 2016.

=== December 2016 ===

The Illinois Department of Financial and Professional Regulation (IDFPR) renewed the detective's Firearm Control Card (FCC or *'tan card'* as it was once tan-colored). The FCC and FOID cards are required in tandem for detectives to use firearms in their line of work.

No infringements were presented by the State of Illinois in December of 2016 as the detective's Firearm Control Card was renewed via their IDFPR typical *'congratulations'* email. The email link was sent by the IDFPR to the detective, so he may print out his new license; it is a private link the public cannot access. The detective, uninfringed, printed his FCC card, signed and put it in his wallet as law required.

The detective learned at Christmas time in 2016, of Obama's ATF announcement of an upcoming, newly revised, *'Form 4473'* for firearm transfers. The detective thought he should purchase firearms to expand his family business before Obama's un-Constitutional changes could affect their *'Obligation of Contracts"*, future operations, the safety of their family, while ultimately affecting the safety of our United States.

Article I. Section 9.

" ' No Bill of Attainder or ex post facto Law shall be passed.'..."

Article. I. Section. 10.

"No State shall... ' pass any Bill of Attainder, ex post facto Law, or Law impairing the Obligation of Contracts..."

It is elected lawmakers of *'We the People',* who determine what changes will be made to our US Constitution and America's access to our *'Bill of Rights'.* Linking healthcare to access of America's Constitutional Rights sets a perverted and dangerous precedent for every American, including law enforcement, as age diminishes everyone's health.

The impossible standards of nothing less than *'time-travel'*, to avoid the inevitable *'Bill of Attainder'* under the Obama-era *'ex post facto Law'* will place more Americans at risk each day. King George III's *'ex post facto Laws'* and *'Bill of Attainder'* prompted our *'Declaration of Independence'* and Revolutionary War.

=== December 13, 2016 ===

Getting treated by a medical specialist proved impossible even prior to the detective's insurance expiration. By November 2016 the detective was without health insurance. So, he went to the Illinois exchange website for health insurance; it was the only place to apply. Self-employed health insurance applications are a bit complicated. Invoices are received at random intervals at the detective's family business; several weeks can pass without receiving a payment. The *'exchange'* website identified the detective's income over the past 30 days as below the poverty-line, though when averaged with the rest of the year he was not below the poverty-line. Yet, the cut-off date to apply for healthcare was approaching. Regardless of having the money available, the *'exchange'* wouldn't let the detective, a resident of Illinois, purchase healthcare since he qualified for 100% subsidy with income (on paper) below the poverty line for the last 30 days. No one at the helplines was answering, even after hours on hold. Insurance brokers ran into the same *'30-day-income-window scenario'* for the self-employed detective.

On December 13, 2016 the detective sent the application in electronically over the internet and waited. If his income reflected what it averaged for the whole year, he would have been able to purchase a regular insurance policy. Prevented from reporting his average income on the *'exchange'*, he was allowed, by law, only a 30-day window. Seven months would pass before the detective would receive any notification about being able to access any kind of healthcare under Obama's ACA.

=== December 15, 2016 ===

By December 15, 2016 the Illinois Administrative Code was updated to enact rules for enforcement, confidentiality, redactions of patient identifying information and criminal penalty. Citations follow:

"TITLE 77: PUBLIC HEALTH

CHAPTER I: DEPARTMENT OF PUBLIC HEALTH

SUBCHAPTER u: MISCELLANEOUS PROGRAMS AND SERVICES

PART 946 COMPASSIONATE USE OF MEDICAL CANNABIS PATIENT REGISTRY"

"Section 946.60 Confidentiality"

" a) The following information received and records kept by the Department for purposes of administering this Part are subject to all applicable federal privacy laws, are confidential, are exempt from the Illinois Freedom of Information Act, and are not subject to disclosure to any individual or public or private entity, except as necessary for authorized employees of the Department to perform official duties of the Department pursuant to this Part:

1)   Applications or renewals, their contents and supporting information submitted by qualifying patients and designated caregivers, including information regarding designated caregivers and physicians;

2)   The individual names and other information identifying persons to whom the Department has issued registry identification cards; and

3) All medical records provided to the Department in connection with an application for a registry identification card.'..."

"...' e)   The Department of Agriculture, the Department of Financial and Professional Regulation and the Illinois State Police may verify registry identification cards. Law enforcement personnel shall have access to the Department's on-line verification system to verify application date and application status of qualifying patients who have submitted an application for a registry identification card.'..."

"...' h)   Nothing in the Act shall prevent a private business from restricting or prohibiting the medical use of cannabis on its property.'..."

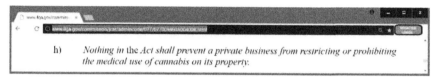

[http://www.ilga.gov/commission/jcar/admincode/077/077009460A00 400R.html]

"...' k)   Any person, including an employee or official of the Department of Public Health, Department of Financial and Professional Regulation, or Department of Agriculture or another State agency or local government, is guilty of a Class B misdemeanor with a $1,000 fine for breaching the confidentiality of information obtained under the Act (Section 145(c) of the Act) and Sections 946.270 and 946.275 of this Part.'..."

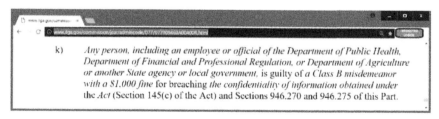

[http://www.ilga.gov/commission/jcar/admincode/077/077009460A00 400R.html]

=== December 27, 2016 ===

U.S. Department of Justice Bureau of Alcohol, Tobacco, Firearms and Explosives	OMB No. 1140-0020

Firearms Transaction Record Part I -
Over-the-Counter

Transferor's Transaction Serial Number *(if any)*

WARNING: You may not receive a firearm if prohibited by Federal or State law. The information you provide will be used to determine whether you are prohibited under law from receiving a firearm. Certain violations of the Gun Control Act, 18 U.S.C. §§ 921 *et. seq.*, are punishable by up to 10 years imprisonment and/or up to a $250,000 fine.

Prepare in original only. All entries must be handwritten in ink. Read the Notices, Instructions, and Definitions on this form. "PLEASE PRINT."

Section A - Must Be Completed Personally By Transferee (Buyer)

1. Transferee's Full Name

Last Name	First Name	Middle Name *(if no middle name, state "NMN")*

2. Current Residence Address (U.S. Postal abbreviations are acceptable. Cannot be a post office box.)

Number and Street Address	City	County	State	ZIP Code

3. Place of Birth U.S. City and State -OR- Foreign Country	4. Height Ft. ___ In. ___	5. Weight (Lbs.)	6. Gender ☐ Male ☐ Female	7. Birth Date Month Day Year

8. Social Security Number *(Optional, but will help prevent misidentification)*	9. Unique Personal Identification Number *(UPIN)* if applicable *(See Instructions for Question 9.)*

10.a Ethnicity	10.b. Race *(Check one or more boxes.)*
☐ Hispanic or Latino ☐ Not Hispanic or Latino	☐ American Indian or Alaska Native ☐ Black or African American ☐ White ☐ Asian ☐ Native Hawaiian or Other Pacific Islander

11. Answer questions 11.a. *(see exceptions)* through 11.l. and 12 *(if applicable)* by checking or marking "yes" or "no" in the boxes to the right of the questions.

	Yes	No
a. Are you the actual transferee/buyer of the firearm(s) listed on this form? **Warning: You are not the actual buyer if you are acquiring the firearm(s) on behalf of another person.** If you are not the actual buyer, the dealer cannot transfer the firearm(s) to you. *(See Instructions for Question 11.a.)* Exception. **If you are picking up a repaired firearm(s)** for another person, you are **not** required to answer 11.a. and may proceed to question 11.b.	☐	☐
b. Are you under indictment or information in any court for a **felony**, or any other crime, for which the judge could imprison you for more than one year? *(See Instructions for Question 11.b.)*	☐	☐
c. Have you ever been convicted in any court of a **felony**, or any other crime, for which the judge could have imprisoned you for more than one year, even if you received a shorter sentence including probation? *(See Instructions for Question 11.c.)*	☐	☐
d. Are you a fugitive from justice?	☐	☐
e. Are you an unlawful user of, or addicted to, marijuana or any depressant, stimulant, narcotic drug, or any other controlled substance?	☐	☐
f. Have you ever been adjudicated mentally defective *(which includes a determination by a court, board, commission, or other lawful authority that you are a danger to yourself or to others or are incompetent to manage your own affairs)* **OR** have you ever been committed to a mental institution? *(See Instructions for Question 11.f.)*	☐	☐
g. Have you been discharged from the Armed Forces under **dishonorable** conditions?	☐	☐
h. Are you subject to a court order restraining you from harassing, stalking, or threatening your child or an intimate partner or child of such partner? *(See Instructions for Question 11.h.)*	☐	☐
i. Have you ever been convicted in any court of a misdemeanor crime of domestic violence? *(See Instructions for Question 11.i.)*	☐	☐
j. Have you ever renounced your United States citizenship?	☐	☐
k. Are you an alien **illegally** in the United States?	☐	☐
l. Are you an alien admitted to the United States under a nonimmigrant visa? *(See Instructions for Question 11.l.)* If you answered "no" to this question, do **NOT** respond to question 12 and proceed to question 13.	☐	☐
12. If you are an alien admitted to the United States under a nonimmigrant visa, do you fall within any of the exceptions set forth in the instructions? (If "yes," the licensee must complete question 20c.) *(See Instructions for Question 12.)* If question 11.l. is answered with a "no" response, then do **NOT** respond to question 12 and proceed to question 13.	☐	☐

13. What is your State of residence *(if any)?* *(See Instructions for Question 13.)*	14. What is your country of citizenship? *(List/check more than one, if applicable. If you are a citizen of the United States, proceed to question 16.)* ☐ United States of America ☐ Other *(Specify)*	15. If you are not a citizen of the United States, what is your U.S.-issued alien number or admission number?

Note: Previous Editions Are Obsolete Page 1 of 6	**Transferee (Buyer) Continue to Next Page** **STAPLE IF PAGES BECOME SEPARATED**	ATF Form 4473 (5300.9) Part I Revised April 2012

[page 1 of 6 - Form 4473 - Revised April 2012 – firearms transaction record, via Wikimedia Commons attributed US Federal Government]

e. Are you an unlawful user of, or addicted to, marijuana or any depressant, stimulant, narcotic drug, or any other controlled substance?   Yes   No

['Form 4473 -Revised April 2012' effective thru January 15, 2017]

"Are you an unlawful user of, or addicted to any depressant, stimulant, narcotic drug or any other controlled substance?"

" Yes   No "

" [ ]   [X] "

[Question 11.e., 'Form 4473 -Revised April 2012' effective thru January 15, 2017 – located at:
https://upload.wikimedia.org/wikipedia/commons/d/d5/Atf-f-4473-1.pdf]

The detective visited a local family-owned gun-shop to exercise his 2nd Amendment Right and make firearm purchases for his family business expansion. First, he would need to put a down-payment on one firearm and fill out the firearms transfer *'Form 4473 - Revised April 2012'*.

Licensed gun-shops owners would use the federal *"Form 4473 Revised April 2012"* for the entire year of 2016 and into the third week of 2017. It wouldn't any make sense whatsoever for gun-shops to utilize non-effective forms.

Of course, the detective checked the box for, *"NO"*, on question *'11.e.'* according to the Illinois State Police website, and most importantly Illinois' medical marijuana Law. Illinois democratically elected lawmakers had added additional protections to patients and their specific distinction as *"Lawful"*, to the Illinois medical marijuana law earlier in 2016.

Perhaps law enforcement could have chosen to consider it just as much a crime to answer in the affirmative to the question being *"unlawful"* under Barack Obama's un-Constitutional methods. The Obama logic has law-abiding Americans, lawmakers and law enforcement at odds with other elements within law enforcement. A portion of the Illinois medical marijuana Law is cited as follows:

"Public Act 099-0159' '(410 ILCS 130/5, /7)'

'Compassionate Use of Medical Cannabis Pilot Program Act'

'... [Section 5.] (g) State law should make a distinction between the medical and non-medical uses of cannabis. Hence, the purpose of this Act is to protect patients with debilitating medical conditions, as well as their physicians and providers, from arrest and prosecution, criminal and other penalties, and property forfeiture if the patients engage in the medical use of cannabis.

(Source: P.A. 98-122, eff. 1-1-14.)

(410 ILCS 130/7 new)

Sec. 7. Lawful user and lawful products. For the purposes of this Act and to clarify the legislative findings on the lawful use of cannabis: ..."

"(1) A cardholder under this Act shall not be considered an unlawful user or addicted to narcotics solely as a result of his or her qualifying patient or designated caregiver status.

(2) All medical cannabis products purchased by a ['page break'] qualifying patient at a licensed dispensing organization shall be lawful products and a distinction shall be made between medical and non-medical uses of cannabis as a result of the qualifying patient's cardholder status under the authorized use granted under State law.'..."

[http://www.ilga.gov/legislation/publicacts/99/PDF/099-0519.pdf]

The following document is the detective's firearm down-payment receipt for his attempted firearm purchases on *"12-27-16"*

(December 27, 2016) weeks before Obama's revised *'order'* took effect infringing millions of Americans from our 2nd Amendment Rights. The date of the detective's denied firearm purchase predates, by weeks, the effective un-Constitutional *'rule'* changes by Obama's ATF.

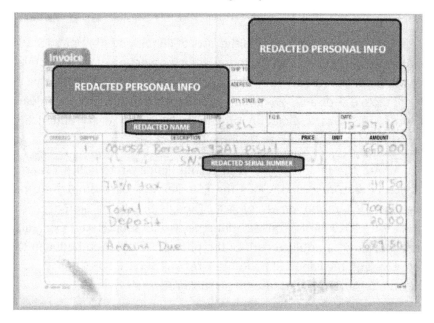

[The detective's 12/27/2016 receipt – dated before Obama's changes.]

=== January 4, 2017 ===

The detective received a voicemail from the gun-shop owner where he had made a down-payment on his firearm purchases. The gun-shop owner's message stated the Illinois State Police had denied his firearm purchase but had not left a reason why. After calling the gun-shop back, the detective was provided with a telephone number for the Illinois State Police Firearms Service Bureau (FSB).

The detective immediately called the Illinois State Police Firearms Service Bureau (FSB) on the afternoon of January 4, 2017. The police officer stated the Illinois State Police didn't care about state laws, our Constitution or what America's Founders believed as the detective explained he had filled out the correct *'Form 4473 - Revised April 2012'*.

The Police officer stated the laws of Illinois and the United States of America don't matter as the feds were in possession of the detective's private medical records. They did not have permission to obtain or keep the detective's, or any law-abiding Illinois resident's medical marijuana records; this was a violation of Illinois laws and every American's Constitutional protections to their medical records.

Are the phone calls placed to the Illinois State Police Firearms Service Bureau recorded? Does the FSB claim to be exempt from our *'Freedom of Information [Law] Act'*. Though the police stated on the January 4th, 2017 phone conversation, they would send a letter explaining their *'new law'*, a public record of the phone conversation between the detective and the Illinois State Police Firearms Service Bureau may prove valuable to America's defense of our *'Bill of Rights'*.

=== January 10, 2017 ===

The Illinois State Police dated their infringement letter, *"1/10/2017"*, six days after the detective's telephone conversation with them, and several days prior to Obama's un-Constitutional changes to our US Constitution, set to take effect January 16, 2017.

The Illinois State Police webpage answers the American public's concerns about medical marijuana. The Illinois State Police statement can be read as follows in its citation as it invites Americans to partake in what they refer to as a legal program:

> *"Medical marijuana cardholders will not have their FOID or CCL cards revoked, or be denied issuance of a FOID or CCL card, due to their status as a medical marijuana cardholder. Such cards are governed by the State law, and State law requires that a person's status as a medical marijuana cardholder not result in the denial of any right or privilege."*
>
> *[https://www.ispfsb.com/Public/Faq.aspx]*
>
> *Illinois State Police 2017-2018*

And at the same exact time the State of Illinois also, simultaneously informed the detective:

> *"You are federally prohibited from purchasing firearms for the reason(s) listed below:*
> *18 USC (g) (3) – People who are unlawful users of addicted to any controlled substance.*
> *MEDICAL CANNABIS LICENSE VALID PATIENT...."*
>
> *Illinois State Police – January 10, 2017*
> *Illinois Governor Bruce Rauner – January 10, 2017*
> *Barack Obama – "federally prohibited" – January 10, 2017*
> *[IL State Police infringement letter 1/10/2017]*

The Illinois State Police infringement letter, though dated January 10, 2017 during the Obama administration, would eventually be sent in an envelope postdated February 14, 2017, Valentine's Day, by the United States Postal Service (USPS). The letter was dated six days before Obama's un-Constitutional *'rule'* change and 10 days before America saw Donald J. Trump inaugurated as our 45th President of the United States.

Obama's *"form is effective January 16, 2017"*, according to the ATF webpage published November 16, 2016, just days after Obama's Democratic Party lost the election to Donald J. Trump. Did Obama think he had more time to advance his UN agenda if Clinton won? It's uncertain who Obama was catering to, but it didn't seem to be Americans.

ILLINOIS STATE POLICE
Division of Administration

Bruce Rauner
Governor

Leo P. Schmitz
Director

1/10/2017

REDACTED

Dear **REDACTED**

Your Firearm Transaction # **REDACTED** has been DENIED. You are federally prohibited from purchasing firearms for the reason(s) listed below:

- 18 USC 922 (g) (3) - Persons who are unlawful users of or addicted to any controlled substance.
  MEDICAL CANNABIS LICENSE - VALID PATIENT   EXP DATE   COUNTY

REDACTED

You are prohibited from purchasing firearms for one year from the date of the expiration of your Medical Cannabis License. 18 USC 922 (g)(3). You may submit an appeal to challenge the accuracy of the record that was used as the basis of your denial. 28 CFR 25.10(c). To file an appeal or challenge the accuracy of the record used to deny your firearm transaction, please complete the attached form and return it to the Illinois State Police Firearms Services Bureau.

As an alternative, you may elect to direct your challenge to the accuracy of the record, in writing, to the FBI, NICS Operations Center, Criminal Justice Information Services Division, 1000 Custer Hollow Road, Module C-3, Clarksburg, West Virginia 26306-0147.   28 CFR 25.10(d).

You may also contest the accuracy or validity of a disqualifying record by bringing an action against the state or political subdivision responsible for providing the contested information, or responsible for denying the transfer, or against the United States, as the case may be, for an order directing that the contested information be corrected or that the firearm transfer be approved. 28 CFR 25.10(f).

For additional information, please call the Customer Service Call Center at 217.782.7980 to speak to a representative of the Firearms Services Bureau.

Illinois State Police
Firearms Services Bureau

Firearms Services Bureau
801 South Seventh Street • Suite 400-M
Springfield, IL 62703
(217) 782-7980 (voice) • 1 (800) 255-3323 (TDD)
www.illinois.gov • www.isp.state.il.us

[IL State Police Infringement letter holding the detective to Obama's 'Bill of Attainder' from the 'ex-post-fact-Law' –1/10/2017]

=== January 16, 2017 ===

"Are you an unlawful user of, or addicted to, marijuana, or any depressant, stimulant, narcotic drug, or any other controlled substance? Yes [or] No

[attributed to the US Federal Government at https://commons.wikimedia.org/wiki/File:Atf-f-4473-1.pdf]

Obama's new un-Constitutional *'order'* replaced the previous question *'11.e'* on the federal firearm transfer *'Form 4473'* with the revised question (to follow), thereby enabling his *'Ex-Post-Facto Government Gun Grab'*, to begin targeting our American 2nd Amendment:

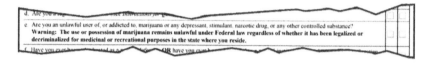

[US Government: https://www.atf.gov/file/61446/download]

"Are you and unlawful user of, or addicted to, marijuana or any depressant, stimulant, narcotic drug, or any other controlled substance? ***Warning: The use or possession of marijuana remains unlawful under Federal law regardless of whether it has been legalized or decriminalized for medicinal or recreational purposes in the state where you reside.***

[Yes] (or) [No]"

[US Government: https://www.atf.gov/file/61446/download]

Obama's new infringement *'rule'* took effect just days before President Trump assumed our Oval Office. The following is page one of six, of Obama's new *'Form 4473 Revised October 2016'*:

U.S. Department of Justice
Bureau of Alcohol, Tobacco, Firearms and Explosives

OMB No. 1140-0020

Firearms Transaction Record

Transferor's/Seller's Transaction Serial Number *(If any)*

WARNING: You may not receive a firearm if prohibited by Federal or State law. The information you provide will be used to determine whether you are prohibited from receiving a firearm. Certain violations of the Gun Control Act, 18 U.S.C. 921 et. seq., are punishable by up to 10 years imprisonment and/or up to a $250,000 fine.

Read the Notices, Instructions, and Definitions on this form. Prepare in original only at the licensed premises *("licensed premises" includes business temporarily conducted from a qualifying gun show or event in the same State in which the licensed premises is located)* unless the transaction qualifies under 18 U.S.C. 922(c). All entries must be handwritten in ink. "**PLEASE PRINT.**"

Section A - Must Be Completed Personally By Transferee/Buyer

1. Transferee's/Buyer's Full Name *(If legal name contains an initial only, record "IO" after the initial. If no middle initial or name, record "NMN".)*
Last Name *(Including suffix (e.g., Jr, Sr, II, III))* | First Name | Middle Name

2. Current State of Residence and Address *(U.S. Postal abbreviations are acceptable. Cannot be a post office box.)*
Number and Street Address | City | County | State | ZIP Code

3. Place of Birth
U.S. City and State -OR- Foreign Country | 4. Height Ft. In. | 5. Weight (Lbs.) | 6. Sex ☐ Male ☐ Female | 7. Birth Date Month Day Year

8. Social Security Number *(Optional, but will help prevent misidentification)* | 9. Unique Personal Identification Number *(UPIN) if applicable (See Instructions for Question 9.)*

10.a. Ethnicity
☐ Hispanic or Latino
☐ Not Hispanic or Latino

10.b. Race *(In addition to ethnicity, select one or more race in 10.b. Both 10.a. and 10.b. must be answered.)*
☐ American Indian or Alaska Native   ☐ Black or African American   ☐ White
☐ Asian   ☐ Native Hawaiian or Other Pacific Islander

11. Answer the following questions by checking or marking "yes" or "no" in the boxes to the right of the questions. | Yes | No

a. Are you the actual transferee/buyer of the firearm(s) listed on this form? **Warning: You are not the actual transferee/buyer if you are acquiring the firearm(s) on behalf of another person. If you are not the actual transferee/buyer, the licensee cannot transfer the firearm(s) to you.** *Exception. If you are picking up a repaired firearm(s)* for another person, you are **not** required to answer 11.a. and may proceed to question 11.b. *(See Instructions for Question 11.a.)* | ☐ | ☐

b. Are you under indictment or information in any court for a **felony**, or any other crime for which the judge could imprison you for more than one year? *(See Instructions for Question 11.b.)* | ☐ | ☐

c. Have you ever been convicted in any court of a **felony**, or any other crime for which the judge could have imprisoned you for more than one year, even if you received a shorter sentence including probation? *(See Instructions for Question 11.c.)* | ☐ | ☐

d. Are you a fugitive from justice? *(See Instructions for Question 11.d.)* | ☐ | ☐

e. Are you an unlawful user of, or addicted to, marijuana or any depressant, stimulant, narcotic drug, or any other controlled substance? **Warning: The use or possession of marijuana remains unlawful under Federal law regardless of whether it has been legalized or decriminalized for medicinal or recreational purposes in the state where you reside.** | ☐ | ☐

f. Have you ever been adjudicated as a mental defective **OR** have you ever been committed to a mental institution? *(See Instructions for Question 11.f.)* | ☐ | ☐

g. Have you been discharged from the Armed Forces under **dishonorable** conditions? | ☐ | ☐

h. Are you subject to a court order restraining you from harassing, stalking, or threatening your child or an intimate partner or child of such partner? *(See Instructions for Question 11.h.)* | ☐ | ☐

i. Have you ever been convicted in any court of a misdemeanor crime of domestic violence? *(See Instructions for Question 11.i.)* | ☐ | ☐

12.a. Country of Citizenship: *(Check/List more than one, if applicable. Nationals of the United States may check U.S.A.)*
☐ United States of America *(U.S.A.)*   ☐ Other Country/Countries *(Specify)* | Yes | No

12.b. Have you ever renounced your United States citizenship? | ☐ | ☐

12.c. Are you an alien **illegally** or **unlawfully** in the United States? | ☐ | ☐

12.d.1. Are you an alien who has been admitted to the United States under a nonimmigrant visa? *(See Instructions for Question 12.d.)* | ☐ | ☐

12.d.2. If "yes", do you fall within any of the exceptions stated in the instructions? | ☐ N/A | ☐ | ☐

13. If you are an alien, record your U.S.-Issued Alien or Admission number *(AR#, USCIS#, or I94#)*:

Previous Editions Are Obsolete
Page 1 of 6

Transferee/Buyer Continue to Next Page
STAPLE IF PAGES BECOME SEPARATED

ATF E-Form 4473 (5300.9)
Revised October 2016

[Page 1 of 6 - Obama's NEW 'Form 4473 Revised October 2016' located at: https://www.atf.gov/firearms/atf-form-4473-firearms-transaction-record-revisions]

The detective still waited for the infringement letter promised to him by the Illinois State Police FSB. Whence the letter arrived the detective would have evidence of the *'Bill of Attainder'* being enforced on law-abiding Americans, one of which would be medical marijuana recipient and former President of the United States, Jimmy Carter.

The detective wasn't sure where to turn. It was intimidating to have his 2nd Amendment denied after such a deception from his law enforcement competitors. Obama's un-Constitutional *'rule'* changes were destroying the detective's family business and placing Americans, including his family, in harm's way. The Illinois State Police were carrying out Obama's commands as if they were laws passed by our elected representatives – they were not. Nor would Obama be around much longer. Unless in the shadows?

=== January 20, 2017 ===

America saw a new President sworn into our White House as the detective searched for answers. His family's safety and that of all America's had been put in danger by the actions of the Illinois State Police Department, preemptively following Obama's un-Constitutional *'rules'* to invade Americans' protected medical records.

The detective was puzzled at the infringements and the vulnerability this would inflict unto the National Security of our United States. The detective knew it was wrong and un-Constitutional which makes the infringement illegal. But what had happened?

The Illinois State Police website continued to invite (and currently still do at their website) Americans to exercise their 2nd Amendment even if they are medical marijuana cardholders. Former President of the United States Jimmy Carter is a medical marijuana user treating a cancer diagnosis; Jimmy Carter claims he is cancer free now.

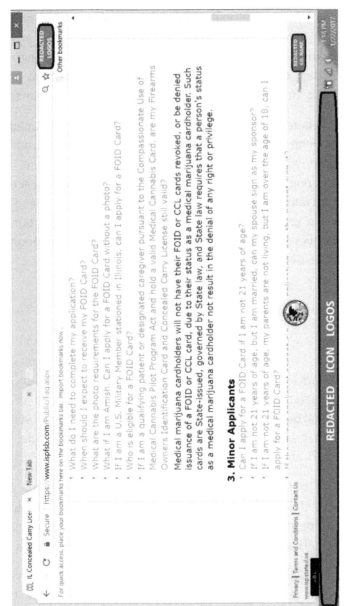

*[IL State Police invite marijuana cardholders to exercise 2nd Amendment
-screenshot 01/22/2017 found at:*
https://www.ispfsb.com/Public/Faq.aspx]

So, what had happened to America and our *'Equal Access to Justice Law'*? Are working-class Americans not entitled to the same fair and equal treatment as medical pot user, President Jimmy Carter? Political activists and media personalities in support of Obama's DNC (Democratic National Committee) instantly started to attack America's new President Donald J. Trump with claims of *"Russian collusion"* which couldn't be supported with any kind of solid evidence to present to Congress or the American People. The detective could see things were taking a turn for the worse for other Americans too. Though America saw a new President, Obama's war against our *'Bill of Rights'* had just begun.

=== February 14, 2017 ===

Valentine's Day 2017

The US Postal Service received the Illinois State Police infringement letter being sent to the detective, and postdated the envelope on February 14, 2017, Valentine's Day, well past President Trump's inauguration. The letter was received by the detective much after the letter's January 10th, 2017 date or the January 4th, 2017 over-the-phone infringement. The letter came more than 1100 hours after the 72-hour legal obligation the police have, to uphold our 2nd Amendment.

The Illinois State Police included in their mailing a *'Request for Appeal'* document which calls for a person to testify against themselves in violation of America's 5th Amendment. The following link is for an already existing *"Illinois State Police' FOID Appeal 'non-Mental Health"*. Why wouldn't they send the *'non-Mental Health FOID Appeal'* to medical marijuana cardholders instead of inventing a *'new'* form? The existing *'non-Mental Health Appeal'* the police did *NOT* send can be viewed at:

[Form NOT sent to medical marijuana cardholders in Illinois at:
https://ispfsb.com/Public/Firearms/FOID/NonMentalHealth.pdf]

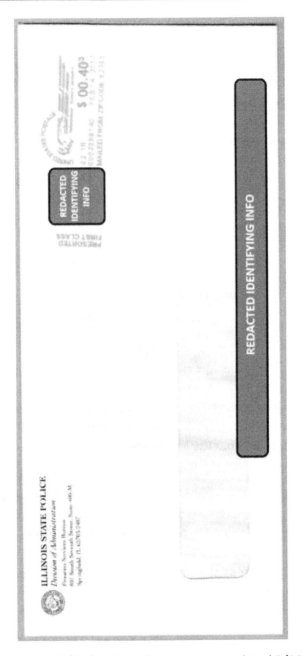

[gun purchase 12/27/2016 – infringement postdated 2/14/2017]

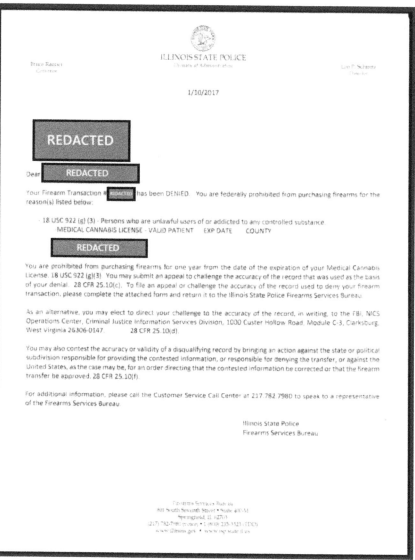

[IL State Police 2nd & 4th Amendment Infringement with a 'Bill of Attainder' from a new, 'ex-post-fact-Law' – dated 1/10/2017, six days before the new 'Form 4473 Revised October 2016' takes effect 1/16/2017]

Illinois State Police – Firearms Services Bureau
Request for Appeal
DENIAL OF A FIREARM TRANSFER

I, _____, am requesting an appeal of the denial of my firearm transfer.

By completing and signing this form, I am appealing to the Director of the Illinois State Police the denial of my firearm transfer. I understand my review will not occur until all requested documentation is received by the Illinois State Police, Firearms Services Bureau, Appeals Section.

☐ The decision to deny my firearm transfer was made in error. I am challenging the record used to determine my eligibility to purchase a firearm. I do not currently possess or have never possessed a medical marijuana license.

☐ I am appealing the decision to deny my firearm transfer. I no longer possess a medical marijuana license. I have enclosed supporting documents.

Printed Name: _____ Date of Birth: _____

Signature _____ Date: _____

ADDITIONAL COMMENTS:

This form must be completed, signed, dated, and returned to:
Illinois State Police
Firearms Services Bureau -- ATTN: APPEALS
801 South 7th Street, Suite 400-M
Springfield, IL 62703

Page 1 of 1

[The detective's scanned copy of IL State Police 'invented' "Appeal" citing no legal reference in lieu of their FOID "Non-Mental Health Appeal" which does cite legal references.]

Perhaps the Illinois State Police feel they can deactivate a medical patient's FOID card from the source instead of physically seizing it by sending their newly conjured *'Denial Appeal'* form without any legal references or citations to laws included on the form? All of their other forms have legal reference citations to our laws – this one didn't.

The existing *'non-Mental Health Appeal'* form is technically for a FOID revocation appeal. The detective still had his FOID card but was told by state police he would not be able to renew it unless he surrendered his medical marijuana card on or before August 31, 2018, one year prior to his FOID card's expiration on September 1, 2019 - regardless of assurances of powerless lawmakers, elected by *'We the People'*.

The *'Request for Appeal'* newly invented document the Illinois State Police sent to the detective doesn't cite any laws like the official document I was able to locate online for *"non-Mental Health Appeals"* which cites in its lower left-hand corner *'430 ICLS 65/10'* and *'IL Admin Code, Title 20, ['] 1230.70'*.

Obama's *'rules'*, seemingly catering to an agenda outside of our American *'Bill of Rights'*, had placed every American in jeopardy including the detective and his family. Now things got stranger as the Illinois State Police were inventing a new form, free of legal reference, specifically to deny marijuana cardholders their Rights.

The Illinois State Police newly invented *'Request for Appeal'* form is in violation of our 5th Amendment protections from testifying against one's self. The form was designed to contest the medical marijuana cardholder's medical records the Illinois State Police and Obama's Federal Bureau of Investigation (FBI NCIS) had already obtained in violation of our state laws, federal laws and our Constitutional Rights.

Any which way the detective rolled the dice, the *'Countdown-Clock'* was ticking. It had been started by the FBI and Illinois State Police infringement of the detective's FOID status and threatened renewal as this un-Constitutional precedent draws ever nearer for all Americans.

=== March 30, 2017 ===

Shortly after opening a new family business checking account at a more convenient location nearer the detective's home office, the detective discovered the 24-hour ATM card did not access cash. The bank repeatedly assured the detective the card worked – yet, it still never withdrew cash. When he again inquired, the bank president first offered to correct the bank's error; then, all of a sudden, stated, over the phone, the detective's bank account would be closed and they no longer wished to do business with him as they felt they could not satisfy his banking needs with their advertised 24-hour ATM banking (which never worked).

Did the banks also have access to America's private and legally protected medical records as did the police departments and Obama's FBI-NCIS? Obama's fourth *'executive order'* on marijuana directs banking enforcement directives from the federal government upon those suspected of being involved with *"Suspicious Activity, money laundering, criminal enterprises"* and *"cartels"*. But medical marijuana is not a crime.

At first, the detective assumed the bank's president became just as frustrated with the detective's ATM card complaints as the detective was by being misled about their 24-hour ATM card many times. But, after looking further into Obama's *'executive orders'* and seeing the *'guidance'* Obama used to go after marijuana prosecutions within his DOJ's memos on marijuana, the detective knew his options for help were running thin. America remained in the dark for the most part on Obama's *'rules'* as they are misled by mainstream media. And the detective needed answers too.

Not long after the detective's family business checking account was closed at one bank, the detective's personal bank accounts began having issues. Checks were returned *'NSF'* (Non-Sufficient Funds) when funds were available, generating more returned check fees; mysterious fees for replacement ATM cards appeared – yet none were ordered. Glitches can occur, but glitches don't explain away our *'Bill of Rights'*.

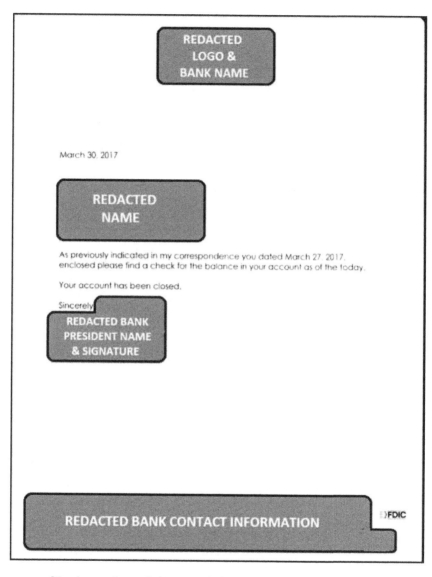

[Bank terminated detective's business account 3/30/2017]

=== April 28, 2017 ===

The detective continued to cautiously search for answers in a delicate environment of marijuana laws, infringements and chaos created by Obama's *'Bill of Attainder'* and *'ex post facto Law'*. Fearful of losing what he worked for his whole life, the detective was about to learn of a new seizure, in violation of state and federal laws, by the Illinois Department of Financial and Professional Regulation (IDFPR). It was time to renew his detective license; and the detective did just that. The State of Illinois again emailed a link to the non-public licensee page where the detective could print his new license. But something was wrong.

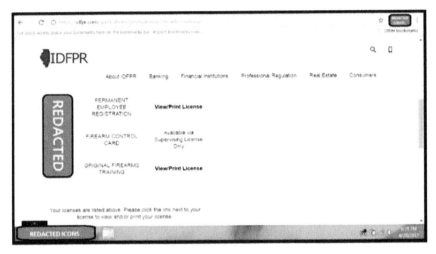

[non-public detective license print-license webpage –"FIREARM CONTROL CARD – Available via Supervising License Only" – 4/28/2017]

This law-abiding, family-business owner of a detective agency, who already had his 2nd Amendment firearm purchase un-Constitutionally and unlawfully infringed by his competition, the Illinois State Police and FBI, in violation of federal and state laws according to the Illinois State Police and ATF's own websites, was now faced with a government *'seizure'* of his family business property.

The State of Illinois's IDFPR, without notice, had un-Constitutionally seized the defined legal status of the detective's Firearm Control Card (FCC) license, destroying their family business with Obama's *'Bill of Attainder'* and *"ex post facto Law"*. Obama's un-Constitutional 'after-the-fact' *'Bill of Attainder'* remains in violation of Article I - Sections 9 through 10 of our United States Constitution. These Constitutional protections were provided by America's Founders to answer the corruption saw under a king's rule. Illinois residents find similar protections in their State Constitution's *'Illinois Bill of Rights'*.

The Illinois Department of Financial and Professional Regulation (IDFPR) seized the defined status of the detective's Illinois State issued Firearm Control Card (FCC), claiming it was now for *"Supervising License Only"*. It became apparent the IDFPR was also likely using their knowledge of patients' private medical records without patient consent or their doctor's approval, in violation of state and federal laws.

This infringement has prevented the detective from being able to offer his armed protective services to schools to secure our children when they're away from home. The news of school-shootings has many concerned for our children and our Rights. With the Illinois State Police and IDFPR misleading folks, can *'We the People'* continue to trust those who are appointed instead of elected or hired directly by Americans? As law enforcement becomes more focused on *"fake news"*, more of our children remain vulnerable. Even commenters on social media criticize the national rifle lobbies as they call their members are *"cowards"*. I can assure you, this is not the case as many are cops, vets and active military.

This change in the detective's licensing for his family-business came months after the IDFPR renewed the detective's FCC card in December of 2016. The detective was able to print-out the FCC without any notifications or infringements from the state or federal government. This mysterious *'FCC redefinition'* discovery became evident to the detective when renewing his detective license in April of 2017. What else did Obama have in store for Americans upon his departure from office?

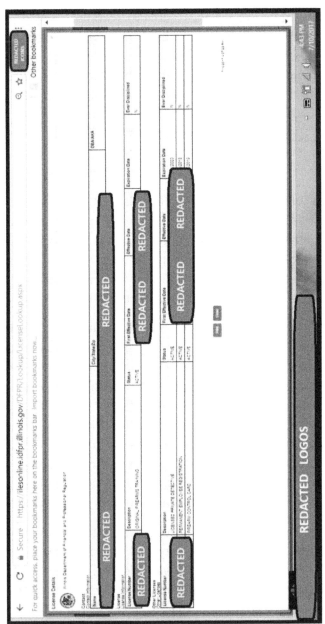

[public view FCC – still 'ACTIVE' & 'N' discipline – 7/10/2017 at:
https://ilesonline.idfpr.illinois.gov/DFPR/Lookup/LicenseLookup.aspx]

The previous documented Illinois *'License LookUp'* public-search webpage demonstrates the ongoing cover-up conducted by the State of Illinois and their IDFPR. The State of Illinois continues to inform the American People the detective's licenses are *"ACTIVE"* and without discipline, assuring them they can hire this fully licensed and armed detective who is compliant with all laws.

So much for the State of Illinois' concept of a *"well regulated Militia"?* The Illinois private detectives are solely governed by the IDFPR under the laws of the *'Illinois Private Detective Act (224 ILCS 447/)'.* As professional detectives, we work vehemently to keep up to date on such law changes. There is no provision for this in the *'Illinois Private Detective Act of 2004'*; there is no provision for this in the recent updates to laws.

Remember, private detective agencies like the detective's business offer competition for the monopoly the Illinois State Police and FBI hold over the allocation of tax-dollars spent on state and federal law enforcement and investigative services for duties which also include providing armed protective services, like the detective and his 2nd Amendment American Right. The IDFPR and Illinois State Police had, *"deprived"* the detective of, *"property without due process of law,"* as they took their competition's (the detective's) ability to compete for law enforcement services. The State of Illinois allowed the detective's, *"private property to be taken for public use, without just compensation."*

The government seized the detective's ability to remain in competition with taxpayer-funded police departments and federal agencies. If allowed to continue, Obama's *'Ex-Post-Facto Government Gun Grab'* will leave the United States also vulnerable to tyrannical threats with his policy's mass disarming of the citizenry at state levels, continuing under the radar of the new Trump Administration.

This ever growing and imminent threat could serve the interest of America's enemies and the *'UN disarmament treaties'* Obama had worked so hard to pass in our United States Congress.

As all of America and the rest of the World can see, the Illinois Department of Financial and Professional Regulation (IDFPR) offers their assurance to the public that they can hire this fully licensed and legally compliant private detective with a valid, current, *"ACTIVE"* and never disciplined FCC-Firearm Control Card with confidence.

This cover-up is an extremely dangerous and irresponsible, precedent-setting infringement upon every American's Constitutional Rights. If the Illinois State Police and IDFPR can do this to a fully compliant, licensed detective, how long before they come for every American's Rights? Should *'We the People'* believe Barack Obama supporters when they say he didn't make *'rules'* to infringe our American 2nd Amendment? Should Americans not concern themselves because Obama is no longer influencing our laws? His *'executive orders'* are.

=== July 17, 2017 ===

At the end of June 2017, the Illinois Department of Health and Human Services (IHHS) finally sent a letter to the detective asking for supporting documentation for his self-employment. He gathered his documentation and sent it back to them. For over 200 days from December 13, 2016, the detective had finally received health coverage.

Illinois sent more correspondence including a notification dated August 28, 2017. The letter informed the detective he could receive compensation for medical expenses from January 28, 2017 to July 13, 2017; unless of course it was for medical marijuana, but the detective used minimal amounts. It should be noted: the Illinois medical marijuana laws are for those who have qualifying conditions with an *"ongoing"* doctor-patient relationship. Denying a law-abiding patient healthcare is not American; yet, they did it to the detective in violation of *'(410 ILCS 130/40.2.) Compassionate Use of Medical Cannabis Pilot Program [Law]'*.

State of Illinois
Department of Healthcare and Family Services
Illinois Department of Human Services

100 South Grand Avenue, East
Springfield, IL 62762

NOTICE OF POSSIBLE ELIGIBILITY FOR PAYMENT
COHEN COURT ORDER

REDACTED
IDENTIFYING
INFORMATION

Date: August 28, 2017

Case Number: REDACTED

You have already been notified that your application for medical assistance was approved by the Illinois Department of Human Services. Your application was approved after the legal time limit. If you (or someone on your behalf) paid for your medical care after you applied for assistance, you may be entitled to repayment from the Department. You will only be eligible for this payment if:

1) You received the medical services after the date you applied for assistance December 13, 2016 and

2) You (or someone on your behalf) paid for the medical services between January 28, 2017 and July 13, 2017.

To receive this payment from the department, you must get proof from the medical provider that you (or someone on your behalf) paid for the services. This proof must show the date of the service, the date of the payment and a description of the type of services. You may show this letter to the medical provider to explain why you need proof of payment. Present the proof to the DHS local office or the KidCare Unit indicated below:

Lake FCRC
2000 N Lewis Avenue Suite#100
Waukegan, IL 60087-

cc: Local Office Administrator

HFS 2379 (R-4-11)   106

['Cohen Court Order' allows for reimbursement for the uninsured time from January, 28, 2017 to July 13, 2017 – the detective and his dehabilitating medical condition went without healthcare for 7 months.]

Though he had the money for health insurance, late invoices caused the state's exchange to identify the detective's income as below the poverty-line for the last 30 days; he was forced to accept *'Medicaid'* under *'Obamacare'*. More than 200 days would pass before the detective received health insurance again. His rheumatologist had retired in 2016; he found receiving any kind of treatment from a specialist proved impossible for any of the detective's ailments in 2016. 2017 was an insurmountable battle as he suffered without healthcare for more than seven months. Acquiring healthcare under the ACA was like trying to run through molasses in January as Obamacare targeted the self-employed.

=== July 25, 2017 ===

[non-public private-licensee-webpage - IDFPR issued new 'invented license' without license #, to detective who never applied for license.]

Not long after the detective discovered the defined *"ACTIVE"* status of his Firearm Control Card (FCC) had been *'seized'* and covertly redefined by the IDFPR, the detective searched for his original email he received after his FCC renewal from the state in December 2016. The email had contained a private link that redirected to a new, private licensee-webpage.

There was a new license the detective had never applied for. Not ever. The *"Supervisory"* FCC card doesn't exist in the *'Illinois Private Detective Act of 2004'* nor in the supplements or addendums as far as any of my colleagues or myself can see. Did the IDFPR invented a new license discriminating against *"Lawful"* medical marijuana cardholders?

Why would they issue a *'make-believe license'* to someone who never applied for such licensing? It's very irresponsible and endangering to America. Was this so the State of Illinois could attempt to escape accountability to our 5th Amendment's *'just compensation'* and *'due process'?* All while distracting from the government's 4th Amendment exploitation of *"Lawful"* residents' seized medical *'papers and effects'?*

The IDFPR doesn't even issue a license number for their newly invented *"Supervisory"* FCC license for public searches. All are encouraged to see for themselves, so they too can feel comfortable questioning the legitimacy of this newly invented, congressionally bypassed *"Supervisory FCC license"*. See if any of these *"Supervisory"* licenses are listed for any detectives? Before you search, know that the IDFPR updated their website search page. One can no longer generically search for a detective or a detective agency; the *"detective"* selections have been removed from the drop-down menu list at the website since mid-2017.

The Illinois Department of Financial and Professional Regulation (IDFPR) never sent the detective notification for the *"Supervisory"* FCC license. I wonder why? Was it because the license doesn't actually exist? Were they trying to sneak it in under America's radar? I'd be certainly interested to know what the IDFPR was thinking as it seems they are discriminating against *"Lawful"* patients. Did the IDFPR think ignoring patient laws and *'The Constitution of the United States'* was a good thing?

The famous quote, some attribute to Samuel Clemens, comes to mind as we see an invented license, not searchable by the public...

"It ain't what you don't know that gets you into trouble.

It's what you know for sure that just ain't so."

The detective never applied for such a license *"Supervised Firearm Control Cards and/or Canine Authorization Cards"*. There are no provisions in *the 'Illinois Private Detective Act of 2004'* as far as I, or any of my private detective colleagues can determine. Addendums to laws exist but the detective wasn't notified of any changes. I searched those addendums and law-additions. I can't find any changes in the Illinois laws governing the private detective's FCC cards. In fact, all laws speak to the contrary of the actions of the IDFPR and the Illinois State Police.

Whence the detective clicked the link on the *'Supervisory FCC'* the webpage redirected him to his original FCC printable card he had renewed in December of 2016 without infringements or notifications. No changes were present on the card. No words referring to *"Supervisory"* are found on it. It was the exact same card they had issued before.

You are invited to see for yourself. The following are links to the Illinois Laws governing private detectives. As one can determine, there is no such law that provides for *"Supervisory"* Firearm Control Cards:

(225 ILCS 447/) Private Detective, Private Alarm, Private Security, Fingerprint Vendor, and Locksmith Act of 2004'.

[http://www.ilga.gov/legislation/ilcs/ilcs5.asp?ActID=2474&Cha pterID=24]

The police in Illinois aren't exempt from protecting our American *'Bill of Rights'*, as indicated by the following links to the laws governing Illinois police officers:

'State Police Act - (20 ILCS 2610/0.01) (from Ch. 121, par. 307.01) - Sec. 0.01. Short title. This Act may be cited as the State Police Act. - (Source: P.A. 86-1324.)' webpage defining their laws follows:

[http://www.ilga.gov/legislation/ilcs/ilcs3.asp?ActID=346&ChapterID=5]

The local police also are not exempt from violating our American *'Bill of Rights'* with Obama's *'Bill of Attainder'* and *'ex post facto Law'*. The *'Illinois Police Training Act'* doesn't provide for such criminal infractions; the law can be read at the following link:

'(50 ILCS 705/) Illinois Police Training Act.'

[http://www.ilga.gov/legislation/ilcs/ilcs3.asp?ActID=731&ChapterID=11]

The detective had contacted his legal insurance providers as this infringement was now destroying all he had worked for, not to mention the physical endangerment. He was a legal-insurance customer for over 14 years and never missed a payment. He knew his legal insurance providers could refer a Civil Rights attorney to address these governmental attacks against his compliant family business and his Constitutional Rights. His own lawyers didn't believe him and hung-up on him thinking he was prank-calling them. He called the corporate office to explain it was not a prank and legitimately needed legal counsel.

The next day after the detective's lawyers hung up on him, they called back. The detective was able to have the lawyer look up his licenses. The lawyer agreed that the state was informing the public he had a valid detective's FCC license. The detective relayed to his attorneys, Illinois was informing him differently in non-public email links. How could the government get away with such deceptions? The State of Illinois had inflicted upon him an *'ex post facto Law'* and *'Bill of Attainder'*, prohibited by Illinois laws and *'The Constitution of the United States'*.

The detective informed his attorneys of the mysteriously closed business checking account and state license seizure. The detective became concerned at the way multiple government agencies, and perhaps now banks, were treating patients in the state's medical program. This was *"Lawful"* medication President Jimmy Carter and the detective were taking. The detective's attorneys had provided him with a referral attorney's telephone number who specialized in Civil Rights. The *'Civil Rights'* attorney never returned the detective's message he left.

This was wrong. The detective is a law-abiding, Patriotic American. Law enforcement had violated our laws and now the detective's 5th Amendment as they asked for the detective to testify against himself with the *'Firearm Transfer Denial Appeal Request'* specifically aimed at medical marijuana. Again, the government had set another precedent for changing the law without elected representatives of *'We the People'* involved. His attorneys wouldn't help. Justice wasn't answering phones for America under Obama's *'rules'*.

=== September 6, 2017 ===

Once the clock hits 365 days prior to the detective's FOID card's expiration, he would need to surrender his medical marijuana card or face non-renewal of his Firearm Owner's Identification. On September 1, 2019, the detective's FOID gun-card would expire. August 31, 2018 became the deadline Obama's law enforcement had sentenced unto the law-abiding medical patient, their competition, without *'due process'*.

It was evident, once law-abiding Americans found themselves classified as felonious narcotic users by Obama's FBI-NICS, held to his *'Bill of Attainder'* under his un-Constitutional *'ex post facto Law'*, yet without any criminal conviction in courtrooms. Our American Forefathers warned us of these same measures Obama was employing, retroactively.

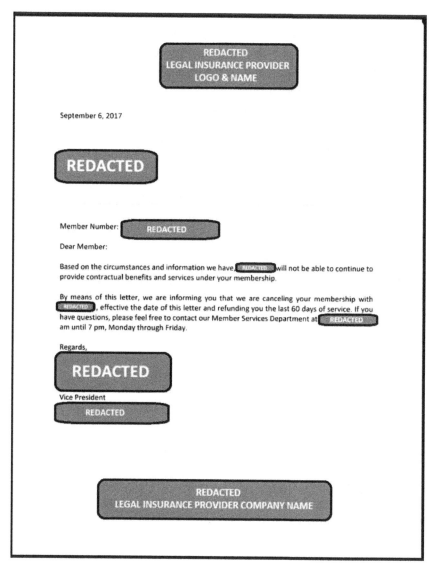

[Legal Insurance Company cancels detective's contract 9/06/2017]

After informing his attorneys at his pre-paid legal insurance providers that the un-Constitutional infringements were not by President Donald Trump, but instead committed under Obama and his Attorney General Loretta Lynch with cooperation from their FBI-NCIS, the Illinois State Police and perhaps the Illinois Department of Financial and Professional Regulation, the detective's attorneys mysteriously terminated his contract when he needed them most – and without any explanation. It looked like the detective and his family business would need a more appropriate shield for *'legal'* protection?

Without explanation of their cancelation from the detective's attorneys at his pre-paid legal insurance providers, the detective's family lost complete faith in our FBI, the Illinois State Police and their accomplices within the Illinois Department of Professional Regulation. Some, or all, had willfully chosen to violate Illinois State Law and the Constitutional Rights of Americans with the Obama-era *'Ex-Post-Facto Government Gun Grab'*, spilling its un-Constitutionality into President Trump's tenure as the democratically elected leader of the *'Free World'*.

=== February 14, 2018 ===

Valentine's Day - 2018

The detective's assigned medical marijuana dispensary has grown more peculiar; they currently have *'tip-jars'* atop the counter at the *"medical"* dispensary. Once friendly toward customers, he explained the dispensary's demeanor changed toward select customers after some patients shared information on the medical program while in their waiting room in the autumn of 2016. Since then, the detective discovered he was labeled a *"difficult patient"* by the dispensary after declining to share his phone number to join their *"customer rewards program"*. *'Reward'* programs evolve, yet hopefully not only around patient-income.

The detective's a working man and of course would appreciate partaking in all discounts to save on healthcare expenses; but his family business had already been victimized by the government's actions. He didn't need any more troubles from conflicting law enforcement orders or text messages to his phone he uses for business from those selling what Obama said was a felonious *'Schedule 1 controlled substance'.* The dispensary asked why he wouldn't share his phone number and the detective told them again on December 9, 2017, he wouldn't share his number. The detective's number started getting their marketing texts after that visit. The dispensary may have taken his number, against his wishes, from their admission documents and entered it in their *"customer rewards program"* after that visit. The dispensary's seizing of the detective's phone number for their marketing purposes seems *"unlawful"*, but there's no one to tell without violating our 5th Amendment Right. The police overseeing medical cannabis have already told him, they didn't care about ours laws. Who are you going to call?

Regardless of their attitude toward select customers, the detective's assigned medical cannabis dispensary offered *'Remedies'* to patients they forcefully entered into their *'customer rewards program'*. The dispensary text-marketed their *'Schedule 1 controlled substance'*, with invitations to pick-up *'Valentine'* gifts and products to enjoy the *[REDACTED 'PRO-FOOTBALL BOWL-NAME']*. As a reminder, marijuana is currently only legal to state-issued medical marijuana cardholders in Illinois. Yet, the dispensary suggested cardholders distribute what to other folks? Unless they assume every medical marijuana cardholder has a *'Valentine"* who is also a medical marijuana cardholder? Maybe some do, but certainly not all.

The Illinois State Police, who earn a living overseeing the state's *'Lawful medical marijuana cartel',* didn't seize the dispensary's licenses. The same investors may own two dispensaries and perhaps interest in a grow facility too? Others in GOP-voting counties got declined for even one medical dispensary license after investing vast fortunes.

counts and liver and kidney function, may be performed to monitor progress or to check for side effects. KEEP ALL DOCTOR AND LABORA APPOINTMENTS while you are using this medicine. BEFORE YOU HAVE MEDICAL OR DENTAL TREATMENTS, EMERGENCY CARE, OR SURGEF doctor or dentist that you are using this medicine. THIS MEDICINE MAY DIZZINESS, DROWSINESS, OR BLURRED VISION. DO NOT DRIVE, OPE MACHINERY, OR DO ANYTHING ELSE THAT COULD BE DANGEROUS know how you react to this medicine. Using this medicine alone, with ot medicines, or with alcohol may lessen your ability to drive or to perform potentially dangerous tasks. Check with your doctor before you drink alc you are taking this medicine. THIS MEDICINE MAY CAUSE you to becon more easily. Avoid exposure to the sun, sunlamps, or tanning booths unt how you react to this medicine. Use a sunscreen or protective clothing if be outside for a prolonged period. THIS MEDICINE MAY REDUCE THE N BLOOD CELLS WHICH ARE NEEDED FOR CLOTTING. Avoid activities tf cause bruising or injury. Tell your doctor if you have unusual bruising or or if you notice dark, tarry, or bloody stools. THIS MEDICINE MAY LOW

KEEP OUT OF REACH OF CHI

DETECTIVE'S NAME REDACTED

DATE: 12/18/14

METHOTREXATE 2.5MG TABLETS - YELLOW
QTY: 25   5 REFILLS BEFORE 12/17/15

REDACTED DOCTOR'S NAME
REACTED PRESCRIPTION-CODING
& REDACTED PHARMACY COMPANY

[The Detective's Rheumatoid Arthritis prescription.]

I suppose medical marijuana is more inviting to others than an *'abortion-pharmaceutical'*. What would you make of a *"Medical"* dispensary's invitation to pick-up something for your *'significant other'* on *'Saint Valentine's Day'* or for your *'pro-football championship'* party?

=======

The detective checked all the Illinois and federal laws he could. None of what Obama, the IDFPR, the IDPH or the Illinois State Police were allowing to happen was provided for in our laws as far as he could determine. I checked and made links to many of the laws and legal information available herein this presentation. The following are links to Illinois laws and regulations governing the Illinois Firearm Owner's Identification cards (FOID cards) allowing Illinois residents to legally possess, purchase and transport firearms and ammunition in the state. The following is what Illinois Law states about FOID revocations, though the detective's FOID was never revoked. The citations are as follows:

"(430 ILCS 65/10) (from Ch. 38, par. 83-10)"

"Sec. 10. Appeal to director; hearing; relief from firearm prohibitions. "

"(a) Whenever an application for a Firearm Owner's Identification Card is denied, whenever the Department fails to act on an application within 30 days of its receipt, or whenever such a Card is revoked or seized as provided for in Section 8 of this Act, the aggrieved party may appeal to the Director of State Police for a hearing upon such denial, revocation or seizure, unless the denial, revocation, or seizure was based upon a forcible felony, stalking, aggravated stalking, domestic battery, any violation of the Illinois Controlled Substances Act,..."

[http://www.ilga.gov/legislation/ilcs/fulltext.asp?DocName=04 3000650K10]

===

Another Illinois Law speaks to the FOID card's revocation; though nothing in the law indicates medical marijuana cardholders are *"unlawful"*. The law reference and link is provided as follows:

"(430 ILCS 65/9.5)

Sec. 9.5. Revocation of Firearm Owner's Identification Card."

[http://ilga.gov/legislation/ilcs/documents/043000650K9.5.htm]

===

The next law I located perhaps explains how the Illinois State Police thought they could perform what they did to the detective while committing a *"Class B misdemeanor"* in violation of a medical marijuana cardholder's confidentiality as defined by *'Illinois Administrative Code, Title 77, Part 946, Section 946.40, subsection k'* and, *'Section 946.60, subsections a., a.1, a.2., a.3.'* and, *'subsection e'* (noted in Chapter 1); partially cited as follows:

"(430 ILCS 65/8) (from Ch. 38, par. 83-8)"

"Sec. 8. Grounds for denial and revocation. The Department of State Police has authority to deny an application for or to revoke and seize a Firearm Owner's Identification Card previously issued under this Act only if the Department finds that the applicant or the person to whom such card was issued is or was at the time of issuance: ...',"

"... (d) A person addicted to narcotics;.."

"... (n) A person who is prohibited from acquiring or possessing firearms or firearm ammunition by any Illinois State statute or by federal law;..."

"... (f) A person whose mental condition is of such a nature that it poses a clear and present danger to the applicant, any other person or persons or the community;

(g) A person who has an intellectual disability;
[http://www.ilga.gov/legislation/ilcs/fulltext.asp?DocName=04
3000650K8]
===

For good measure I checked and provided the *"Illinois Controlled Substances Act"*. The law only speaks to non-medical marijuana; references are cited as follows:

"CRIMINAL OFFENSES

(720 ILCS 570/) Illinois Controlled Substances Act.

Sec. 100

It is not the intent of the General Assembly to treat the unlawful user or occasional petty distributor of controlled substances with the same severity as the large-scale, unlawful purveyors and traffickers of controlled substances.

(720 ILCS 570/101) (from Ch. 56 1/2, par. 1101)"

Sec. 101. This Act shall be known as and may be cited as the "Illinois Controlled Substances Act.

(Source: P.A. 77-757.)"

[http://www.ilga.gov/legislation/ilcs/ilcs5.asp?ActID=1941&Cha pterID=53]
===

Illinois has a *'Cannabis Control Act',* which doesn't contain any wording to deny the *'Bill of Rights',* to *"Lawful"* medical marijuana cardholders. The references are cited as follows:

"(720 ILCS 550/1) (from Ch. 56 1/2, par. 701)

(720 ILCS 550/2) (from Ch. 56 1/2, par. 702)

Sec. 2. This Act shall be known and may be cited as the "Cannabis Control Act".

(Source: P.A. 77-758.)"

[http://www.ilga.gov/legislation/ilcs/ilcs3.asp?ActID=1937&]
===

The detective knew what was happening was not right. He understood he was probably not the only one who was facing these quietly carried out infringements upon our *'Bill of Rights'*. Our Constitutional Rights and Liberty were being threatened by Obama's *'new rules'*. Without anywhere else to turn, the detective knew an Illinois licensed private detective could provide assistance. That's when my skills were called upon.

As I am a private detective, the detective knew I would not be able to divulge his unredacted medical records or breach confidentiality afforded to clients. The detective knew I had a cursory understanding of our US Constitution and state laws. And the detective knew he had to make this information available to the American People who are kept dangerously in the dark under Obama's *'new'* law enforcement directive.

The detective, along with other patients have already faced enormous retaliation from law enforcement. But with Obama's federal *'orders'* still unlawfully being enforced by state police departments according to interpretations invented during Obama's time at the White House, all Americans are now sharing in the loss of our *'Bill of Rights'*.

To assist the detective and his family, I began looking for remedies to the problems caused by Obama's *'Ex-Post-Facto Government Gun Grab'*. I contacted another Illinois private detective who also had a state issued FCC card, in an attempt to see if he could assist in providing services to the detective's family until a remedy could be found.

The other detective's FCC card, though listed as *"ACTIVE"* by the IDFPR, was also *'in question'* as the Illinois Department of Financial and Professional Regulation (IDFPR) claimed to have lost his original *"Firearms Training Certificate"*, which he had submitted about 20 years ago to obtain his first Firearm Control Card. The IDFPR wanted this other private detective I spoke with, to resubmit the original, not a copy, that they had lost. The IDFPR had the original – how could anyone resubmit what they lost? The other detective couldn't find legal counsel either.

=======

Did Obama smoke marijuana as a youngster? Many Americans claim he smokes marijuana today. But why would he wage war on our Constitutional Rights? Had he not done his homework on American Civics? That didn't make sense, as he boasted of studying at Harvard. Surrendering our *'Bill of Rights'* was not going to solve more problems than it created. So why did Obama act in such ways?

Could it be that Obama had obligations to those outside the United States? He ran to Wall Street to collect huge cantor fees after leaving our White House. He now leads the *'Obama Foundation'*, assisting the United Nations in educating youths all around the world.

=======

No juries were present. No elected lawmakers were involved with the Obama-era *'rule'* changes affecting millions of Americans. No laws were broken by medical marijuana cardholders as proven by background checks performed by the Illinois State Police. All cardholders were compliant according to our State laws and our US Constitution. Something was not right.

In the next section, we will take a step back from the detective's viewpoint and examine the historical attacks on our American Freedom with a broader, worldwide perspective of the chronology of events leading to *'The Ex-Post-Facto Government Gun Grab'*. You are invited to discover *'The Modus Operandi'*, slithering its way into America's future and Donald J. Trump's Presidency.

Chapter 3

The Modus Operandi.

The Method of Operation.

During the detective's January 04, 2017 afternoon telephone conversation with the Illinois State Police Firearms Service Bureau, the Illinois State Police officer informed the detective he would need to surrender his Illinois State issued medical marijuana card no less than 365 days prior to the expiration date displayed on his current and valid (yet no longer honored) Illinois State Police issued Firearm Owner's Identification (FOID) card, or else the Illinois State Police would not renew the detective's FOID card upon its September 1, 2019 expiration.

Law-abiding Americans, like an Iraq-War veteran in Rockford, Illinois, have already had their family's firearms seized and gone missing once in police hands. Without an Illinois Firearm Owners Identification card, the firearm-owner has an opportunity to transfer to someone else they know with a FOID card or surrender the firearms to police. An Illinois detective's Firearm Control Card is valid only with an Illinois FOID card.

Obama-era directives prompted the Illinois State Police and FBI to start their *'Countdown-Clock'* during Barack Obama's tenure with an *'after-the-fact'* sunset-date of August 31, 2018 for the detective's 2nd Amendment and ultimately, their family owned business. The numbers of disarmed, law-abiding Americans will grow increasingly as time edges forward, unveiling Obama's ongoing, *'Ex Post Fact Government Gun Grab'*. These un-Constitutional disarmament measures destroy our last line of defense *'being necessary to the security of a free State.'* Meanwhile, America sinks into the blinding abyss of *"fake news"*. Will President Trump act in time to stop this ongoing siege and subsequent government cover-up to disrupt the tyranny of *'The Modus Operandi'?*

This endangering *'deadline'* Obama has installed into the Trump Presidency sets dangerous precedents for *'The Constitution of the United States'*, with its *'Bill of Attainder'*, punishing Americans for crimes they were never charged with, nor a jury to hear their defense. America's enemies, work tirelessly for the disarmament of the People of the United States. Obama's commands are still being carried out at municipal, state, federal and even international agencies.

For the rest of Americans who have access to the same medication President Jimmy Carter used to treat his cancer, beginning on January 16, 2017, they would also need to build a *'Time Machine'* in order to travel back one year, and surrender their access to their healthcare before Obama's *'after-the-fact'* *'ex post facto Law'* held them to his ongoing *'Bill of Attainder'* denying Americans our Constitutional Rights without ever being charged or convicted of a crime.

Retroactive laws are impossible to comply with; anyone who thinks otherwise is not in alignment with America's Founders or the current understanding of quantum physics required for *'time-travel'*. Author H.G. Wells wrote fiction. *'The Constitution of the United States'* is non-fiction.

For the detective, well, let's just say the Illinois State Police *'jumped-the-gun'* when they unlawfully, and un-Constitutionally enforced the Obama-era retroactive *'ex post facto Law'*, prior to its effective date classifying him and all compliant medical marijuana patients as felonious *'Schedule 1'* narcotic users with the FBI's NCIS. Under a *'Bill of Attainder'* these patients are denied their *'due process'* lest they can build a *'Time-Machine'* to remain in compliance.

Jimmy Carter, the detective, and the growing number of millions of extensively background-checked legal medical marijuana patients are not spies and are not exempted from our American 5th Amendment as these are definitely not *"...cases arising in the land or naval forces, or in the Militia, when in actual service in time of War or public danger...".*

True-Blooded Americans would be able to make this distinction. But with extremely powerful lobbies behind the UN disarmament treaties, no American's 2nd Amendment is safe from tyranny waiting in the shadows.

To infringe upon an Americans' 2nd Amendment with information obtained by a 4th Amendment violation seizing our medical *'papers and effects',* is a crime beyond imagining. The government went further with the detective as they violated his 5th Amendment when the state *'deprived'* his commercial business license as it was *'taken for public use, without just compensation'.* The only remedy offered was for the detective *'to be a witness against himself',* with their *'newly invented' 'Appeal Request'* discriminating against medical marijuana patients.

On January 4, 2017 the Illinois State Police told the detective on the phone, and a dated letter from January 10, 2017, sent in a postdated envelope from February 14, 2017, that his firearm purchase from December 27, 2016 had been *"federally prohibited"* by Barack Obama's *'new rules',* which bypassed elected lawmakers becoming effective, weeks later, on January 16, 2017. Will it happen to you too?

===

On January 15, 2017, Americans with a qualifying condition could have sought a medical marijuana card like Jimmy Carter's and purchased a firearm. But in the blink of an eye…….

On January 16, 2017, Obama's *'ex post facto Law'* kicked-in and those law-abiding Americans would no longer have a 2nd Amendment guaranteed by our Founding Fathers unless a *'Time Machine'* was nearby.

===

Obviously *'Time-Machines'* are outrageous. Yet, Obama's *'Countdown-Clock'* for our *'Bill of Rights'* continues to tick into America's future and Donald Trump's Presidency. For the detective, his time is running short before he is forced to surrender his medical card and set a precedent for our American *'Bill of Rights',* unless President Trump acts to stop the ongoing Obama-era attack on our American Constitution. *'Tick-Tock'* says America's Clock.

Government contradictions are plentiful, which surprises few. But it is the ongoing concealment and misleading nature of messaging from Obama and law enforcement agencies, which is what troubles Americans as they become aware of the Obama-era cover-ups within state and federal governments followed by media-blackouts.

The Obama-era changes in our *'Bill of Rights'* access were made by non-elected law-enforcement, non-elected regulators and non-elected judges. Department heads can hold their jobs for several years and justices can be appointed for life. Nevertheless, medical marijuana patients, including the detective, were assured by the government their Rights would never be infringed.

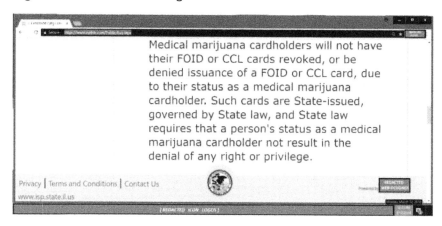

Medical marijuana cardholders will not have their FOID or CCL cards revoked, or be denied issuance of a FOID or CCL card, due to their status as a medical marijuana cardholder. Such cards are State-issued, governed by State law, and State law requires that a person's status as a medical marijuana cardholder not result in the denial of any right or privilege.

Privacy | Terms and Conditions | Contact Us
www.isp.state.il.us

[March 12, 2018 – Illinois State continues its cover-up at:
https://www.ispfsb.com/Public/Faq.aspx]

For an explanation of the siege on American's Freedoms one may possibly examine the *'Hegelian Dialectic'* from 19th century philosopher, Georg Wilhelm Friedrich Hegel. Hegel's logical assimilation presented a three-stage concept of *'thesis - antithesis - synthesis',* or as some refer to it, *'Problem-Reaction-Solution'.* The thesis presents a perceived problem like *'gun-violence'*. The antithesis is the public's reaction of *'shock and dismay'*. The synthesis is the solution to the perceived problems with *'The Ex Post Facto Government Gun Grab'*. It is a plan for tyrants.

A chronological recap of events, laws, court interpretations, enforcement measures, admissions of law enforcement errors, Barack Obama's interpretations, the United Nations agendas and mainstream media perceptions are examined to introduce a broader scope over the timeline of world events in the spectrum of *'The Modus Operandi'* for Obama's ongoing *'Ex-Post-Facto Government Gun Grab'*.

=== 1750 ===

The American Colonists recited the words, some historians accredit to Reverend Johnathan Mayhew, preached during a sermon in 1750, *"No taxation without representation."* Soon the tyrannical King George III of Great Britain would hear the American Colonists.

"Taxation without representation is tyranny."

Declared by 'We the People' since the 1750's.

=== July 4, 1776 ===

With Benjamin Franklin's concept of the *'Free Press'* running strong, word soon infiltrated the British Isles and the ear of King George III. The King threatened to have the head of any American Colonist who would make such a *"Declaration of Independence"*.

Declaration of Independence

Signed - July 4, 1776

When hearing of the tyrannical King's threats against those who would sign our *'Declaration of Independence'*, American Patriot John Hancock signed his name large and centered making certain to send King George III a clear message of defiance. The *'public domain'* transcription of our *'Declaration of Independence"* can be found at the following link:

https://www.archives.gov/founding-docs/declaration-transcript

=== September 17, 1787 to December 15, 1791 ===

"The Constitution of the United States"

Our American Forefathers fought and won our Independence. On October 19, 1781 British General Cornwallis surrendered at Yorktown. Liberty had arrived, but our New Nation feverishly debated between the States. Compromises were made granting *'States Rights'* with considerations to include a state's equal representation in the legislature and also, representation based upon a state's population. Our Forefathers established securities, preserving our American way of life.

Our country would have a two-house elected legislative body, the Senate equally representing the States regardless of their geographic size or populations. The other, a House of Representatives weighted solely by its population. A judiciary branch would exist to interpret the laws as legal conflicts arose. And a Chief Executive would be a civilian, born in the United States of America, no younger than 35 years of age and held to Preside over the administration of our laws and military as they preserve, protect and defend *'The Constitution of the United States'*.

Final conditions needed to be met to provide further securities to *'We the People'*, before all the States would agree to ratify our federal Constitution. *'We the People'* needed protections *'being necessary to the security of a free State,'*.

The King of Great Britain had been holding American Colonists accountable for actions in the past that he currently deemed illegal with an *'ex post facto Law'*; for instance, American Colonists were punished for not paying a tax when none existed at the time they didn't pay. Colonist were held to punishments in the King's *'Bill of Attainder'* without conviction of crimes that weren't illegal when the Colonists took such actions. Our American Founders made our *'Declaration of Independence'* on July 4, 1776. By December 15, 1791 America's Founding Fathers ratified our First Ten Amendments known as our *'Bill of Rights'*.

'The Constitution of the United States', Article I., Section 9., prevents our federal government from performing this ongoing Obama-era *'Government Gun Grab'*, while Section 10. Prohibits the states from enacting the same *'Bill of Attainder'* and *'ex post facto Law'*.

<u>*'The Constitution of the United States'*</u>

<u>*Article 1. Section 9. "…' No Bill of Attainder or ex post facto Law shall be passed.'…"*</u>

<u>*Article. 1. Section. 10. "No State shall… ' pass any Bill of Attainder, ex post facto Law, or Law impairing the Obligation of Contracts…"*</u>

What is the *'Bill of Attainder'* and an *'ex post facto Law'*?

A *'Bill of Attainder'* is a legislative action holding a person or a group of people to punishments of a crime without a trial or a conviction.

An *'ex post facto Law' (Latin for 'after the facts')* is a law which retroactively changes the consequences of actions, relationships or rules of evidence that were legal before the law was enacted.

'The Constitution of the United States'
https://www.archives.gov/founding-docs/constitution-transcript

America's *'Bill of Rights'*
https://www.archives.gov/founding-docs/bill-of-rights-transcript

'*Amendments XI through XXVII*'
https://www.archives.gov/founding-docs/amendments-11-27

=== 1850 ===

"World's first Detective Agency opens in Chicago, Illinois, USA."

Alan Pinkerton, born in Glasgow, Scotland on August 25, 1819, immigrated to America and became a Chicago police officer. By 1849, Pinkerton was named Chicago's first police detective. In the following year, 1850, he opened the *"Pinkerton Detective Agency"*, in Chicago, Illinois. He soon built an agency with a team of private detectives serving the United States of America protecting public and private interests.

Before long, Private Detective Alan Pinkerton would go on to successfully guard President Abraham Lincoln from spies and assassins throughout the entirety of America's Civil War.

=== April 15, 1865 ===

America's Civil War raged between the Northern Union Army and the Southern Confederate Army, pitting Brother against Brother from its official onset on April 12, 1861. After President Abraham Lincoln preserved our Union, he cordially dismissed his personal security detail, Private Detective Alan Pinkerton, against Pinkerton's pleas.

Shortly thereafter John Wilkes Booth, *'Knights of the Golden Circle' 'secret-society'* member, assassinated President Lincoln at Ford's Theater on April 15, 1865. Not only America, but every person on Earth lost a great leader. The world certainly could have used Abraham Lincoln's *'Private Eye'* on that fateful night.

[Chicago Private Detective Alan Pinkerton guarding President Lincoln in the company of Union General John A. McClernand (on the right); this 'public domain' photo was made available by the Library of Congress at: *http://www.loc.gov/pictures/resource/cwpb.04326/]*

=== June 18, 1878 ===

'Posse Comitatus Act'

From 1867 to 1877 the United States Army occupied the Southern States during the period of *'Reconstruction'* following the Civil War. Reports of abuses and crimes were alleged by the former Confederate citizens living in the occupied territory. Presidential candidate Samuel J. Tilden of New York won the popular vote in the 1876 election and took home more electoral votes. But the 20 disputed, undecided electoral votes prompted Congress to act, and strike a deal granting Hayes the Presidency. America was in great controversy.

On June 18, 1878 President Rutherford B. Hayes signed the *'Posse Comitatus Act',* prohibiting the US Army from occupying American, civilian soil outside of military bases. In 1956 the law was amended to include the US Air Force. The Navy and Marines are not mentioned in the law but were added later under Department of Defense regulations.

=== January 16, 1920 to December 5, 1933 ===

Prohibition

Not long after the end of World War I, the 18th Amendment to our US Constitution became effective on January 16, 1920 creating the prohibition of alcoholic beverages in the USA.

Crime syndicates instantly arose to meet the *'Free Market's'* desire for alcohol. US Treasury Agent Eliot Ness and his team of *'Untouchables'* fought government corruption and gangsters on the streets of my hometown of Chicago, Illinois. Today, Chicago remains the murder capital of the world with gang violence endangering our families.

IN THE DISTRICT COURT OF THE UNITED STATES
FOR THE NORTHERN DISTRICT OF ILLINOIS
EASTERN DIVISION.

UNITED STATES
    VS   NOS. 22852
ALPHONSE CAPONE   23232 } Consolidated.

We, the Jury find the Defendant NOT
GUILTY as charged in Indictment No. 22852 and we find the
Defendant GUILTY on Counts *one- five- nine- thirteen- eighteen*
and NOT GUILTY on Counts *2-3-4-6-7-8-10-11-12-14-15-16-17- 19 20-21-22*
Indictment No. 23232.

[Verdict in United States v. Alphonse Capone, 10/ 17/1931, located at:
https://www.archives.gov/exhibits/american_originals/capverd.jpg]

"When I sell liquor, it's called bootlegging; when my patrons serve it on Lake Shore Drive, it's called hospitality."

Al Capone – former Chicago crime boss

The 19th Amendment was added to our US Constitution allowing women the Right to vote. In the coming years, America saw a different approach to the prohibition of alcohol consumption. By December 5th, 1933 America had added the 20th Amendment to the US Constitution ending the prohibition of alcohol. The crime syndicates which had evolved around the stifling infringements had withered in strength as the *'Free Market'* became available to law-abiding Americans. Transcripts of Amendments *'XI'* through *'XXVII'*, are at the following:

https://www.archives.gov/founding-docs/amendments-11-27

=== 1934 ===

The United States Congress passed the first *'Gun Control Act'*, in response to previous alcohol-prohibition related violence. America's law would be modified and replaced by others in years to come as the income-gap began to widen even further in our United States. Crime rose accordingly making robber-barons nervous of a well-Armed populace. The law would see amendments and outright revisions in America's tempestuous future.

=== December 7, 1941 ===

"... A date which will live in infamy.'..."

President Franklin Delano Roosevelt

Our Island of Hawaii and our US Naval Base at its Pearl Harbor were hit by Japanese bombers from the air, killing American service members and civilians. Foreign tyranny arrived to the shores of our country. The next day, President Franklin Delano Roosevelt would ask Congress to declare War on Japan.

The US government held Japanese Americans in internment camps, stripping them of their Constitutional protections as *'We the People'* engaged in World War II. Victory over Japan was achieved soon after dropping atomic weapons on Hiroshima and Nagasaki, Japan.

=== Jun 6, 1944 ===

D-Day

The United States joined Allied Forces as a coordinated attack was launched against the Nazi occupation along France's Normandy Beach. Allied Forces eventually pushed the German dictator, Adolph Hitler back from the Western Front as Russia stopped the Nazis from the East. Reports of Hitler committing suicide circulated, yet his death was never visually confirmed by the Western *'Free Press'*. Russians claimed to have taken the body of the genocidal dictator.

Soon Europe was divided between Free Western States and a communist Eastern Block ruled over by Russia's United Soviet Socialist Republic (USSR). The *'Iron Curtain'* kept Western influence away from the Eastern Block population with armed guards on either side of the border.

The Cold War between West and East began as the ensuing *'Arms Race'* led to increased funding for a new industry, the *'Military Industrial Complex'* (MIC). The power to develop nuclear weapons is kept in the *'private sector'*, preventing any one branch of the military from hungering for power under the temptation of advanced weapon technologies.

=== July 8, 1947 ===

"The intelligence office of the 509th Bombardment Group at Roswell Army Air Field announced at noon today, that the field has come into the possession of a Flying Saucer."

Major Jesse Marcel – US Army Intelligence – press statement.

Before eyes begin to roll, the significance of this event is vastly important outside of *'Little Green Men'.* Roswell, New Mexico was the only base in the world that housed nuclear atomic weapons. Shortly thereafter the reported *'Flying Saucer'*, the US Army Air Force OSS (Office of Strategic Services) had new competition in its monopoly over foreign intelligence gathering. The Central Intelligence Agency (CIA) was launched on July 26, 1947. By September 18, 1947 the Air Force had split from the Army and would no longer be known as the US Army Air Force.

As the Cold War intensified with Russia, the Military Industrial Complex (MIC) had evolved into an industry of darkness, shadows and secrecy. On January 17, 1961, President Dwight D. Eisenhower in his farewell address would warn of the MIC's growing strength and influence; the dangers that develop from its unchecked secrecy are what concerned President Eisenhower. It was President Eisenhower, a former General, who forced the MIC's disclosure of secret bases in Nevada to the White House. The world was kept in the dark as new programs evolved in the *'Technological Revolution'* that America saw following the 1940's.

USAPS or *'Unacknowledged Special Access Projects'* soon developed. They are funded through mostly covert, un-Constitutional and thereby illegal means as they are kept secret from the American public. USAPS are so exclusive, even American Presidents are denied access on a *"Need-to-Know"* basis. Suppression of alternative energy solutions and weaponized technologies, arguably, are what fuels the USAPS and MIC quest for continued secrecy to the detriment of America.

=== January 17, 1961 ===

"...In the councils of government, we must guard against the acquisition of unwarranted influence, whether sought or unsought, by the military-industrial complex. The potential for the disastrous rise of misplaced power exists and will persist.'..."

President Dwight D. Eisenhower

Excerpt from his 'Farewell Address'.

President Dwight D. Eisenhower, a former General, oversaw the emergence of a dangerous new industry in our United States. After the 'Atomic-Age' had begun, a need for research and advanced weapon technologies became necessary to guard America against this new kind of warfare. Though a necessary industry, Eisenhower immediately saw the potential for a grave threat against the United States and our People. It was President Eisenhower, as rumor has it, who stood up to the Military Industrial Complex when he demanded access to the notorious *'Area 51'*.

=== April 27, 1961 ===

"... The very word 'secrecy' is repugnant in a free and open society... We decided long ago that the dangers of excessive and unwarranted concealment of pertinent facts far outweighed the dangers which are cited to justify it."

JFK addresses the 'Free Press'.

President John F. Kennedy spoke to the mainstream media at a famous hotel, in New York City on April 27, 1961. He addressed concerns for government-insider intelligence leaks to the press that caused dangerous disruptions in the peaceful endeavors of our United States.

=== November 22, 1963 ===

President John F. Kennedy was assassinated in his first term after bravely speaking out against *"secrecy"* within our government. The government investigated many, including themselves, resulting in the later debunked *'Warren Report'*, which claimed a lone-gunman assassinated JFK with multiple rapid-shots fired from six stories up, at a moving target with a bolt-action rifle, obtained from a mail-order catalog.

Despite the accused's claims of innocence, Lee Harvey Oswald was summarily assassinated, execution-style, in a room full of armed law enforcement officers by night club owner, Jack Ruby. Jack Ruby was found guilty of Oswald's murder but died in prison pending an appeal. The later debunked *'Warren Report'* found Jack Ruby acted alone.

America would soon answer the demands of transparency, but it would not last long. The dark, sinister forces of a *'Shadow Government'* were present in the annals of our United States. Few have the courage to take them on. President John Fitzgerald Kennedy was one of the few.

=== July 4, 1966 to July 4, 1967 ===

America enacted FOIA, the *'Freedom of Information [Law] Act - 5 U.S.C. SECT. 552, AS AMENDED BY PUBLIC LAW NO. 104-231, 110 STAT. 3048'* on America's Independence Day in 1966. It would be one full year before it would become effective on July 4, 1967. This delay most likely allowed time for those who thrive on concealment within our government to secure what they needed, keeping their *"secret society"* and the People's documents hidden from the eyes of American Justice. In 1996 the law was amended to become the *'Electronic Freedom of Information [Law] Act'* under America's 42nd President, Bill Clinton.

The *'FOIA/FOIL'* Law can be viewed at the following archived webpage link:

https://www.justice.gov/oip/blog/foia-update-freedom-information-act-5-usc-sect-552-amended-public-law-no-104-231-110-stat

=== October 22, 1968 ===

'Gun Control Act of 1968'

Many events in history attributed to where we are as a planet today. In 1934, the United States of America passed the first *'Gun Control Act'*. However, things changed in 1963 with the assassination of President John F. Kennedy. Some are still believing the *'lone-gunman theory'* as they place faith in our government's debunked *'Warren Report'*.

The *'Warren Report'* alleged a lone gunman purchased a rifle through a mail-order catalog and committed the assassination of JFK by himself. It seems obvious there is likely much more to JFK's assassination than *'We the People'* were led to believe by the mainstream media and our government. Lawmakers reacted nonetheless.

On October 22, 1968, President Lyndon B. Johnson signed into law the new, *'Gun Control Act of 1968'*. Some claim it is this law that allowed Illinois State Police and other states to seize guns from law-abiding medical patients and infringe upon America's 2nd Amendment when placed in conjunction with Obama's *'executive orders'* on medical marijuana.

The following is a link to the *'Gun Control Act of 1968'*:

https://www.gpo.gov/fdsys/pkg/STATUTE-82/pdf/STATUTE-82-Pg1213-2.pdf

=== October 26, 1970 ===

The US government enacted the *'The Financial Recordkeeping and Reporting of Currency and Foreign Transactions Act of 1970 (31 U.S.C. 5311 et seq.)'* or as it's known by its shorter title, the *'Bank Secrecy Act of 1970'* (BSA). The federal government's *'Financial Crimes Enforcement Network'* (FinCEN) has made available a collection of the links to the citations which mostly compose the BSA. The link is provided as follows:

https://www.fincen.gov/resources/fincens-mandate-congress

=== October 27, 1970 ===

On October 27, 1970 the federal government enacted the *'Controlled Substance Act of 1970',* (CSA) or as it is longer titled, the *'Comprehensive Drug Abuse Prevention and Control Act of 1970'.*

The 1968 Gun Control Act did not directly specify marijuana as an element which would prevent Americans from accessing their 2nd Amendment Rights. It was congress who repealed the *'Stamp Act'* as it included a marijuana stamp tax that was self-incriminating any American who purchased it under varying state laws. The changes needed in the *'Stamp Act'* stemmed from the federal case, *'Leary Vs. The United States of America'* and a 5th Amendment claim of Americans being forced to act as witnesses against themselves. Now, the Illinois State Police send *'Denial Appeals Request Forms'* requiring Americans to violate their own 5th Amendment protection against being a witness against themselves.

Congress passed the *'Controlled Substance Act'* in 1970 but had left marijuana off until a review could be conducted by the government. President Richard M. Nixon appointed the *'Shafer Commission',* formally known as the *'National Commission on Marihuana (Marijuana) and Drug*

Abuse" to conduct the study. The Shafer Commission released their report which seemed to favor marijuana to be treated as alcohol consumption. The commission suggested marijuana users were calm, unlike those under the influence of alcohol. The *'National Criminal Justice Reference Service'* (NCJRS) provides an abstract from the findings and, also details about the 1200+ page report.

The NCJRS link to the CSA abstract follows:

https://www.ncjrs.gov/App/publications/Abstract.aspx?id=45382

The following link is provided by the US Food and Drug Administration (FDA) found online referencing the *'1970 Controlled Substance Act'*:

https://www.fda.gov/ohrms/dockets/ac/03/briefing/3978B1_07_A-FDA-Tab%206.pdf

The US Government Publishing Office has also made information available relating to the *"Scheduling classifications"* of the referenced law; the following link is provided for your convenience:

https://www.gpo.gov/fdsys/granule/USCODE-2011-title21/USCODE-2011-title21-chap13-subchapI-partB-sec812/content-detail.html

The complete text for the CSA can be viewed on a PDF document at the following link:

https://www.gpo.gov/fdsys/pkg/STATUTE-84/pdf/STATUTE-84-Pg1236.pdf

=== October 25, 1978 ===

FISA

The 95th Congress passed *'Public Law 95-511'*, also known as the *'Foreign Intelligence Surveillance Act of 1978'* (FISA). Future medical marijuana cancer patient President Jimmy Carter signed the bill into law under advisement of his National Security Advisor, Zbigniew Brzezinski. Brzezinski is father to a mainstream media personality, and son to a former Eastern Soviet Block communist diplomat. Zbigniew Brzezinski passed away on May, 26, 2017 during the research for this presentation.

Just months before America saw a new President Reagan, President Carter, under Brzezinski's advisement, got the idea to open the borders to Cuban refugees from April 15 to October 31, 1980. Americans soon saw a flood of cocaine gangsters spill into Miami with violence not witnessed since the days of Capone. Brzezinski also armed and trained the *'mujahideen'* freedom-fighters, made-up partly of the Taliban, to oust occupying Russian forces from their home country of Afghanistan.

Zbigniew Brzezinski previously authored works from the 1960's prognosticating America's future surveillance state, and the 1990's predicting tragic global events and a future need for legislation to strip American Freedoms for our own safety. Was America drawn into the Hegelian *'Problem-Reaction-Solution'* of the *'USA PATRIOT Act of 2001'*?

In addition, Brzezinski was on the *'Council on Foreign Relations'* by the 1990's, advising UN member states. He was also a founding member of the *'Tri-Lateral Commission'*, a private consulting think-tank advising the United Nations among others. Brzezinski openly admitted to attending a meeting at the Bilderberg Group, which is a private consortium of wealthy individuals including bankers, industrialists and politicians; they meet secretly, once a year, away from public eyes and ears, while they plot a future of globalization.

To add to Brzezinski's resume, he began his career in higher politics as a counselor for President Lyndon B. Johnson from 1966 to 1968. After being NSA director for Carter from 1977 to 1981, *'Zbig'*, as his friends liked to call him, went on to advise Bill Clinton and Barack Obama on foreign and domestic policies. Barack Obama went on to push total forfeiture of our Rights including the 2nd Amendment in line with UN disarmament treaties, which Constitutionally require a *"Super Majority"* vote in the US Senate to become adopted by *'We the People'.*

Barack Obama also seemed to have embedded a sunset-date for his extension on the protections afforded his own actions on DACA (Deferred Action for Childhood Arrivals). The children were brought to the United States, trafficked across an international border to bypass immigration laws. Since Senator Orin Hatch (now retired) in 2000 introduced the, *'Development, Relief, and Education for Alien Minors Act'*, or the *DREAM Act'* as it became known, the undocumented immigrants, or *'illegal aliens"* (as Bill Clinton would refer to them), liked to call themselves, *"DREAMers"* incorporating the Act's name to their desires to bypass existing immigration laws. Did Brzezinski advise Obama on allowing more undocumented immigration to spill onto our streets as Miami saw Cuban prisons dumped onto our American streets and into our neighborhoods in 1980 under President Carter?

In years to come, FISA warrants would find ample usage after the horrid events of September 11, 2001. The law was designed to prevent covert investigations of foreign operatives being exposed through public records of warrants and FOIA requests. Accusations of FISA court abuse would surround Obama's post White House life. A link to FISA follows:

https://www.gpo.gov/fdsys/pkg/STATUTE-92/pdf/STATUTE-92-Pg1783.pdf

=== 1985 to 1986 ===

Congress debated, then passed the *'Money Laundering Control Act of 1986'.* It was signed into law by President Ronald Reagan. The congressional archives offer two H.R. (House Resolution) numbers for the MLCA. The first link is H.R. 5077; the second link is to 5217 from the same 99th US Congress.

Some Americans may argue it is this law, working in conjunction with others which made law enforcement to feel justified when allowing America's private medical records to be used as a means to deny firearm purchases to law-abiding Americans who treat their ailments with a *"Lawful" 'Controlled Substance'*.

A link to H.R. 5077 is at the following:

https://www.congress.gov/bill/99th-congress/house-bill/5077

The link to H.R. 5217 follows:

https://www.congress.gov/bill/99th-congress/house-bill/5217

A PDF reference of the law follows:

https://www.ffiec.gov/bsa_aml_infobase/documents/regulations/ml_control_1986.pdf

=== March 23, 1994 ===

Congress enacted the *'Money Laundering Suppression Act of 1994 '* (MLSA), designed to go after criminal enterprises as it encroached upon Constitutional privacy protections for law-abiding American with a 4th Amendment violation in the absence of a *'Writ of Habeas Corpus'*.

It is likely this law would be one of many used in conjunction with one another including the *'USA PATRIOT Act of 2001'*, the *'Controlled Substance Act of 1970'*, and the *'Gun Control Act of 1968'* as Barack Obama committed his ongoing, un-Constitutional *'Ex Post Facto Government Gun Grab'*. A link to the government archive of the MLSA follows:

https://www.congress.gov/bill/103rd-congress/house-bill/3235/text

=== August 21, 1996 ===

'HIPAA'

Congress passed the *'Health Insurance Portability and Accountability Act of 1996' (HIPAA)*; it was signed into law by Bill Clinton. This law does allow for the government to seize medical records under very specific circumstances relating to prescribed drugs; medical marijuana is not a prescribed drug. Yet treatments in Illinois do require a doctor to acknowledge the patient has a qualifying condition.

However, since the medical records regarding medical cannabis in Illinois are required, by law, to be redacted of all patient identifying information, the federal government would not have access to such information without Illinois State laws being broken by the patients, dispensaries or by the federal and/or state governments.

This seems to indicate either someone in the State of Illinois committed a *"Class B misdemeanor"* and leaked medical records of the state's medical marijuana patients to Obama's FBI, or a FISA (Foreign Intelligence Surveillance Act) warrant was issued under Barack Obama's 2009 *'executive order'* classifying *"firearms"* as not being in *"clear and unambiguous compliance"* with state law when a 2nd Amendment Right is exercised by a law-abiding medical marijuana cardholder.

Law enforcement is absolutely necessary to prevent crime and bring criminals to Justice. Yet, weakening America's Constitutional protections only feeds into Obama's continuing siege against American Freedoms with his *'Ex Post Facto Government Gun Grab'* on unsuspecting and law-abiding medical patients. A link to HIPAA follows:

https://www.congress.gov/bill/104th-congress/house-bill/3103/text

A PDF version is available at the following link:

https://www.congress.gov/104/plaws/publ191/PLAW-104publ191.pdf

=== October 30, 1998 ===

The US government enacted the *'Money Laundering and Financial Crimes Strategy Act of 1998',* to further strengthen its security state watching over the American public and our finances, excusing themselves in the public's best interest. This law would be one of many used in conjunction with the others including the *'USA PATRIOT Act',* the *'Controlled Substance Act of 1970',* and the *'Gun Control Act of 1968'* as Barack Obama encroached into America's *'Bill of Rights'* with his *'orders'.* A link to the government archives for the law follows:

https://www.congress.gov/bill/105th-congress/house-bill/1756

=== September 11, 2001 ===

America watched in horror as the events of 9/11 unfolded. Thousands of American lives were lost in the senseless violence. Not long afterwards, America would react with military might against the accused countries and enact legislation to weaken our American Rights to privacy, surrendering our Freedoms for temporary safety.

Could the *'Hegelian Dialectic'* of *'Problem-Reaction-Solution'* be applied to the tragic events of 9/11? The nicknamed *'USA PATRIOT Act'* was introduced almost immediately to Congress. Despite its complexity, the *'USA PATRIOT Act'* was together within weeks of the tragic events of September 11, 2001 as America was distracted by our new war.

The Military Industrial Complex (MIC) never before saw such booming business. *"Fake News"* based upon faulty and misleading intelligence was used as an excuse to search for WMDs *(Weapons of Mass Destruction)* in the sovereign country of Iraq while terrorists were hunted in Afghanistan. Though most accused were citizens of Saudi Arabia.

=== October 26, 2001 ===

Congress responded to the events of 9/11 by swiftly passing the *'USA PATRIOT Act'* (Uniting and Strengthening America by Providing Appropriate Tools Required to Intercept and Obstruct Terrorism Act). The law is partly designed to protect America from threats, including the financing of terrorism. George W. Bush's Presidential administration was quick to remind Americans that terrorism can be financed through illegal drugs. This suggested anyone using marijuana could be a potential threat to the United States and may be subject to investigation by federal authorities under a FISA warrant issued secretly for foreign operatives working against the interests of the United States.

The *'USA PATRIOT Act'* suspended *'Habeas Corpus'* for law-abiding Americans. The federal government would no longer need *'Habeas Corpus'* (Latin for *'body of the crime'*), as outlined in Article I., Section 9., clause 2 of *'The Constitution of the United States'*, before they decided to investigate Americans. Suspicion alone was sufficient cause for President George W. Bush's administration and Barack Obama's.

'The Constitution of the United States'

Article I., Section 9., "... The Privilege of the Writ of Habeas Corpus shall not be suspended unless when in Cases of Rebellion or Invasion the public Safety may require it.'..."

The privileged *'Writ of Habeas Corpus'* guarantees Americans their Right to *'due process'* in a courtroom with evidence of a crime presented. Without *'the body'* of a crime, the accused is Free and without punishments held unto them. Without the evidence of a crime, our government cannot legally investigate Americans under normal circumstances; but *'Habeas Corpus'* is a *'Privilege'*, not a *'Right'*. That being said, medical marijuana patients are not a *'Rebellion or Invasion'* endangering *'public Safety',* and therefore require individual protections, each, provided by our US Constitution's *'Bill of Rights'.*

Did the federal government, under Barack Obama, believe they had a right to seize medical records of all medical marijuana users if they dare try to exercise their 2nd Amendment Rights? The *'USA PATRIOT Act'* Section 215., speaks specifically to medical records.

However, the medical marijuana patient's status alone could not be used to grant a FISA (Foreign Surveillance Intelligence Act) warrant unless the states ignore the US Constitution's 10th Amendment and cooperate with Obama's 2009 un-Constitutional *'executive order'* designating, without trial, any American who has a 2nd Amendment and a medical marijuana card as *"not in clear and unambiguous compliance with state law"* for suspicion of *"money laundering"* for *"drug cartels".* The following text is from the *'USA PATRIOT Act of 2001':*

"... Public Law 107-56

107th Congress

An Act

To deter and punish terrorist acts in the United States and around the world, to enhance law enforcement investigatory tools, and for other purposes. <<NOTE: Oct. 26, 2001 - [H.R. 3162]>>

Be it enacted by the Senate and House of Representatives of the United States of America <<NOTE: Uniting and Strengthening America by Providing Appropriate Tools Required to Intercept and Obstruct Terrorism (USA PATRIOT ACT) Act of 2001.>> in Congress assembled,

SECTION 1. SHORT TITLE AND TABLE OF CONTENTS.

(a) Short <<NOTE: 18 USC 1 note.>> Title.--This Act may be cited as the ``Uniting and Strengthening America by Providing

Appropriate Tools Required to Intercept and Obstruct Terrorism (USA PATRIOT ACT) Act of 2001''. ''

''...''

"SEC. 215. ACCESS TO RECORDS AND OTHER ITEMS UNDER THE FOREIGN INTELLIGENCE SURVEILLANCE ACT.

Title V of the Foreign Intelligence Surveillance Act of 1978 (50 U.S.C. 1861 et seq.) is amended by striking sections 501 through 503 and inserting the following:

``SEC. 501. <<NOTE: 50 USC 1861.>> ACCESS TO CERTAIN BUSINESS RECORDS FOR FOREIGN INTELLIGENCE AND INTERNATIONAL TERRORISM INVESTIGATIONS.

``(a)(1) The Director of the Federal Bureau of Investigation or a designee of the Director (whose rank shall be no lower than Assistant Special Agent in Charge) may make an application for an order requiring the production of any tangible things (including books, records, papers, documents, and other items) for an investigation to protect against international terrorism or clandestine intelligence activities, provided that such investigation of a United States person is not conducted solely upon the basis of activities protected by the first amendment to the Constitution.

``(2) An investigation conducted under this section shall--

``(A) be conducted under guidelines approved by the Attorney General under Executive Order 12333 (or a successor order); and

``(B) not be conducted of a United States person solely upon the basis of activities protected by the first amendment to the Constitution of the United States.

``(b) Each application under this section--

``(1) shall be made to--

``(A) a judge of the court established by section 103(a); or

``(B) a United States Magistrate Judge under chapter 43 of title 28, United States Code, who is publicly designated by the Chief Justice of the United States to have the power to hear applications and grant orders for the production of tangible things under this section on behalf of a judge of that court; and

[[Page 115 STAT. 288]]

``(2) shall specify that the records concerned are sought for an authorized investigation conducted in accordance with subsection (a)(2) to obtain foreign intelligence information not concerning a United States person or to protect against international terrorism or clandestine intelligence activities.

``(c)(1) Upon an application made pursuant to this section, the judge shall enter an ex parte order as requested, or as modified, approving the release of records if the judge finds that the application meets the requirements of this section.

``(2) An order under this subsection shall not disclose that it is issued for purposes of an investigation described in subsection (a).

``(d) No person shall disclose to any other person (other than those persons necessary to produce the tangible things under this section) that the Federal Bureau of Investigation has sought or obtained tangible things under this section.

``(e) A person who, in good faith, produces tangible things under an order pursuant to this section shall not be liable to any other person for such production. Such production shall not be *deemed to constitute a waiver of any privilege in any other proceeding or context.*

``SEC. 502. <<NOTE: 50 USC 1862.>> CONGRESSIONAL OVERSIGHT.

``(a) On a semiannual basis, the Attorney General shall fully inform the Permanent Select Committee on Intelligence of the House of Representatives and the Select Committee on Intelligence of the Senate concerning all requests for the production of tangible things under section 402.

``(b) On a semiannual basis, the Attorney General shall provide to the Committees on the Judiciary of the House of Representatives and the Senate a report setting forth with respect to the preceding 6-month period--

``(1) the total number of applications made for orders approving requests for the production of tangible things under section 402; and

``(2) the total number of such orders either granted, modified, or denied.''.

``...''

The *'USA PATRIOT Act'* can be viewed at the following links:

https://www.congress.gov/bill/107th-congress/house-bill/03162

A text link follows:

https://www.congress.gov/bill/107th-congress/house-bill/3162/text

A link to a PDF version of the *'USA PATRIOT Act'* follows:

https://www.gpo.gov/fdsys/pkg/BILLS-107hr3162enr/pdf/BILLS-107hr3162enr.pdf

In congruence with the *'Bank Secrecy Act of 1970' (BSA)*, the *'Money Laundering Control Act of 1986'*, the *'Money Laundering Suppression Act of 1994'*, and the *'Money Laundering and Financial Crimes Strategy Act of 1998'*, and the *'USA PATRIOT Act of 2001'*, the *'Foreign Intelligence Surveillance Act of 1978'* (FISA) court warrants could be issued under Barrack Obama, secretly on any American with a 2nd Amendment who was suspected of using medical or recreational marijuana according to his medical marijuana *'executive orders'* beginning in 2009 for the purpose of *'Anti-Money Laundering'* (ALM) defenses for America against terrorism and foreign threats.

Again, medical marijuana patient President Jimmy Carter doesn't put the fear into me the way it does Barrack Obama and his foreign policy advisors. Perhaps they have ulterior motives?

=== October 29, 2002 ===

An Appellate Court from the Northern District of California decided on the case, *'Walters vs. Conant'*. By 2003 the US Supreme Court upheld the decision to allow for doctors, who have no financial interest in marijuana, to recommend the *'Schedule 1 Controlled Substance'* marijuana to patients.

This decision paved the way for states to begin medical marijuana programs as a legitimate medical treatment for American patients to benefit from the same healthcare our allies, including Israel, already provide to their citizens through their national healthcare systems.

The Northern District court decision is at the following link:

https://www.justice.gov/osg/brief/walters-v-conant-petition

=== October 7, 2003 ===

"United States Patent 6,630,507"

"Cannabinoids as antioxidants and neuroprotectants"

"Cannabinoids have been found to have antioxidant properties, unrelated to NMDA receptor antagonism. This new found property makes cannabinoids useful in the treatment and prophylaxis of wide variety of oxidation associated diseases, such as ischemic, age-related, inflammatory and autoimmune diseases. The cannabinoids are found to have particular application as neuroprotectants, for example in limiting neurological damage following ischemic insults, such as stroke and trauma, or in the treatment of neurodegenerative diseases, such as Alzheimer's disease, Parkinson's disease and HIV dementia. Nonpsychoactive cannabinoids, such as cannabidoil, are particularly advantageous to use because they avoid toxicity that is encountered with psychoactive cannabinoids at high doses useful in the method of the present invention. A particular disclosed class of cannabinoids useful as neuroprotective antioxidants is formula (I) wherein the R group is independently selected from the group consisting of H, CH.sub.3, and COCH.sub.3. ##STR1##"

[http://patft.uspto.gov/netacgi/nph-Parser?Sect1=PTO1&Sect2=HITOFF&d=PALL&p=1&u=/netahtml/PTO/srchnum.htm&r=1&f=G&l=50&s1=6630507.PN.&OS=PN/6630507&RS=PN/6630507]

As one can determine, the US government owned patent is for the medical use and applications of marijuana's ingredient, *'Cannabinoids'* as *'anti-oxidants and neuroprotectants".* Yet Obama's DEA re-reclassified medical marijuana as a felony *'Schedule 1 controlled substance'* by August 10, 2016, claiming it does not have any medical applications or uses. Why did the US Government register the Patent?

US006630507B1

(12) **United States Patent**
Hampson et al.

(10) Patent No.: **US 6,630,507 B1**
(45) Date of Patent: **Oct. 7, 2003**

(54) **CANNABINOIDS AS ANTIOXIDANTS AND NEUROPROTECTANTS**

(75) Inventors: **Aidan J. Hampson**, Irvine, CA (US); **Julius Axelrod**, Rockville, MD (US); **Maurizio Grimaldi**, Bethesda, MD (US)

(73) Assignee: **The United States of America as represented by the Department of Health and Human Services**, Washington, DC (US)

(*) Notice: Subject to any disclaimer, the term of this patent is extended or adjusted under 35 U.S.C. 154(b) by 0 days.

(21) Appl. No.: **09/674,028**

(22) PCT Filed: **Apr. 21, 1999**

(86) PCT No.: **PCT/US99/08769**
§ 371 (c)(1),
(2), (4) Date: **Feb. 2, 2001**

(87) PCT Pub. No.: **WO99/53917**
PCT Pub. Date: **Oct. 28, 1999**

Related U.S. Application Data

(60) Provisional application No. 60/082,589 filed on Apr. 21, 1998, and provisional application No. 60/095,993, filed on Aug. 10, 1998.

(51) Int. Cl. **A61K 31/35**
(52) U.S. Cl. **514/454**
(58) Field of Search 514/454

(56) **References Cited**

U.S. PATENT DOCUMENTS

2,304,669 A	12/1942	Adams
4,876,276 A	6/1989	Mechoulam et al.
5,227,537 A	7/1993	Mess et al.
5,284,867 A	2/1994	Kloog et al.
5,434,295 A	5/1995	Mechoulam et al.
5,462,946 A	10/1995	Mitchell et al.
5,512,270 A	4/1996	Ghio et al.
5,521,215 A	5/1996	Mechoulam et al.
5,538,993 A	7/1996	Mechoulam et al.
5,635,530 A	6/1997	Mechoulam et al.
5,696,109 A	12/1997	Malfroy-Camine et al.
6,410,588 B1	6/2002	Feldmann et al.

FOREIGN PATENT DOCUMENTS

EP	477918 A1	5/1991
EP	576357 A1	12/1993
EP	650354 A1	6/1995
EP	658546 A1	6/1995
WO	WO93/05031 A1	3/1993
WO	WO94/12667 A1	6/1994
WO	WO96/12485 A1	5/1996
WO	WO96/28050 A1	6/1996
WO	WO97/09063 A1	5/1997
WO	94/53917	* 10/1999

OTHER PUBLICATIONS

Windholz et al., The Merck Index, Tenth Edition (1983) p. 241, abstract No. 1723.*
Mechoulam et al., "A Total Synthesis of dl-Δ'-Tetra-hydrocannabinol, the Active Constituent of Hashish," *Journal of the American Chemical Society,* 87:14 3273–3275 (1965)
Mechoulam et al., "Chemical Basis of Hashish Activity," *Science,* 18:611–612 (1970)
Ottersen et al., "The Crystal and Molecular Structure of Cannabidiol," *Acta Chem Scand B.31,* 9:807–812 (1977)
Cunha et al., "Chronic Administration of Cannabidiol to Healthy Volunteers and Epileptic Patients'," *Pharmacology* 21:175–185 (1980)
Consroe et al., "Acute and Chronic Antiepileptic Drug Effects in Audiogenic Seizure-Susceptible Rats," *Experimental Neurology,* Academic Press Inc., 70:626–637 (1980)
Turkanis et al., "Electrophysiologic Properties of the Cannabinoids," *J. Clin. Pharmacol.,* 21:449S–463S (1981)
Carlini et al., "Hypnotic and Antiepileptic Effects of Cannabidiol," *J. Clin. Pharmacol.,* 21:417S–427S (1981)
Karler et al., "The Cannabinoids as Potential Antiepileptics," *J. Clin. Pharmacol.,* 21:437S–448S (1981)
Consroe et al., "Antiepileptic Potential of Cannabidiol Analogs," *J. Clin. Pharmacol.,* 21:428S–436S (1981)

(List continued on next page.)

Primary Examiner—Kevin E. Weddington
(74) *Attorney, Agent, or Firm*—Klarquist Sparkman, LLP

(57) **ABSTRACT**

Cannabinoids have been found to have antioxidant properties, unrelated to NMDA receptor antagonism. This new found property makes cannabinoids useful in the treatment and prophylaxis of wide variety of oxidation associated diseases, such as ischemic, age-related, inflammatory and autoimmune diseases. The cannabinoids are found to have particular application as neuroprotectants, for example in limiting neurological damage following ischemic insults, such as stroke and trauma, or in the treatment of neurodegenerative diseases, such as Alzheimer's disease, Parkinson's disease and HIV dementia. Nonpsychoactive cannabinoids, such as cannabidiol, are particularly advantageous to use because they avoid toxicity that is encountered with psychoactive cannabinoids at high doses useful in the method of the present invention. A particular disclosed class of cannabinoids useful as neuroprotective antioxidants is formula (I) wherein the R group is independently selected from the group consisting of H, CH₃, and COCH₃.

26 Claims, 7 Drawing Sheets

[http://pdfpiw.uspto.gov/.piw?Docid=06630507&homeurl=http://patft. uspto.gov/netacgi/nph-Parser?Sect1%3DPTO1%2526Sect2%3DHITOFF%2526d%3DPALL%2526p %3D1%2526u%3D/netahtml/PTO/srchnum.htm%2526r%3D1%2526f%3 DG%2526l%3D50%2526s1%3D6630507.PN.%2526OS%3DPN/6630507% 2526RS%3DPN/6630507&PageNum=&Rtype=&SectionNum=&idkey=NO NE&Input=View+first+page]

Since the US Government isn't recognizing the Patent to provide those valuable healthcare treatments for *'We the People'*, would the US government mind so much if they put it up for grabs to the highest bidder? I offer *'two-bits'* to start the bidding. Is that how that works? Probably not.

=== 2004 ===

The State of Illinois updated its private detective laws. Illinois private detectives are solely governed by the *'(225 ILCS 447/) Private Detective, Private Alarm, Private Security, Fingerprint Vendor, and Locksmith Act of 2004'*. A link to the Illinois State law follows:

http://www.ilga.gov/legislation/ilcs/ilcs3.asp?ChapterID=24&ActID=247 4

Private Detectives have been around for many years. The first private detective on record was Alan Pinkerton of the Pinkerton Detective Agency located right in my hometown of Chicago, Illinois. Established prior to the Civil War, Alan Pinkerton's detective agency was eventually tasked with keeping President Abraham Lincoln alive with the detective's armed protective services against armies and assassins bent on the destruction of the Union and our cherished President.

After the Civil War ended, Lincoln dispatched Pinkerton's detective services against the detective's concerns. Shortly thereafter, the tragic assassination of America's great leader occurred as the American President remained vulnerable without his armed, private detective security detail at his side at Ford's Theater on that fateful night of April 14th, 1965.

In my youth, I remembered researching what it took to become a private detective in the State of Illinois after being inspired by detectives of literature, film and even our American Heritage. Detectives weren't always required to be licensed in Illinois. By the end of the 1980s the laws had changed; several detectives were receiving official Illinois State licensing. Illinois passed a new act replacing the old in 2004. The *'(225 ILCS 447/) Private Detective, Private Alarm, Private Security, Fingerprint Vendor, and Locksmith Act of 2004'* is the sole law governing private detectives in Illinois. It would not make sense for other regulatory agencies or state police to enforce regulations as Illinois private detectives work as special investigators investigating state employees and even police at times.

Private Detectives can be contracted to do many different things and by different entities. I have personally worked on behalf of the government bodies, businesses, and individual American citizens in my line as a special investigator; for this reason, the People of Illinois thought it best for private detectives to be governed by someone other than their competition, the government pensioned police force.

=== October 14, 2009 ===

"UNODA - United Nations Office for Disarmament Affairs"

"UN Register of Conventional Arms"

"Transparency in armaments is a key confidence-building measure. It may encourage restraint in the transfer or production of arms, and can contribute to preventive diplomacy."

[https://www.un.org/disarmament/convarms/register/]

On October 14, of 2009 Obama and his Secretary of State Clinton were negotiating an *"Arms Treaty"* with the United Nations introduced by the President of Costa Rica, Oscar Arias. Supporters of our *'Bill of Rights'* felt this would threaten American Freedoms and ultimately, our

United States and the People leaving us vulnerable to threats, foreign and domestic. The United Nations has a specific office, *'UNODA' (United Nations Office for Disarmament Affairs).* Their website boasts of gun registration to be sent from countries to their collective database in what the UN calls the UNROCA (UN Registry of Conventional Arms).

The UN goes further on linked pages to make more statements of the infringements to be imposed onto our American *'Bill of Rights'.* Was Obama trying to use medical marijuana to seize millions of American civilian guns for a United Nations Agenda for the 21st Century?

The UNODA citation reads as follows:

"United Nations Office for Disarmament Affairs"

"Transparency in Armaments"

"Governments can report to the United Nations their arms imports and exports. Reporting voluntarily on weapons transfers shows domestic confidence: a mature readiness by the authorities to have some key national defence policies scrutinized by media, academia and others. Also, sharing such information can create trust between countries, and can contribute to early warning and preventive diplomacy. Being open about armaments may even encourage restraint in the transfer or production of weaponry."

"Transparency is as important for those countries that are large-scale arms traders, as it is for those importing or exporting few or no weapons."

"The United Nations Register of Conventional Arms is an annual reporting mechanism through which governments can share information on weapons they transferred the previous year. Member States reporting to it provide information on the build-up and volume of the conventional arsenals which it deems

essential to maintain a credible defence and perform effective peacekeeping tasks."

"The UN Register of Conventional Arms (UNROCA) has received reports from more than 170 States. The vast majority of official arms transfers are captured by it."

[https://www.un.org/disarmament/convarms/transparency-in-armaments/]

As one can determine, the United Nations gives no consideration for America's 2nd Amendment, or any of our *'Bill of Rights'* for that.

=== October 19, 2009 ===

"MEMORANDUM FOR SELECTED UNITED STATES ATTORNEYS"

Obama's DOJ

Every President's administration, since 1970, kept marijuana classified as *"Schedule 1",* a felonious *"controlled substance"*, that if possessed could result in one losing their American Right to exercise their 2nd Amendment, among other possible penalties.

On October 19, 2009 Obama's *'executive order'* issued by his DOJ, denied the federal government from allocating any resources to investigate, prosecute or infringe upon the Rights and privileges of valid state-issued medical marijuana cardholders. Yet his promises didn't last.

Barack Obama really went after medical marijuana programs and the American patients alleviating their de-habilitating conditions. Obama's efforts were celebrated in the press as being *'pro-medical marijuana'*. Yet, after reading his first *'executive order'* on medical marijuana, Americans saw mainstream media misreport his intentions. The following screenshot references Obama's *'order'*.

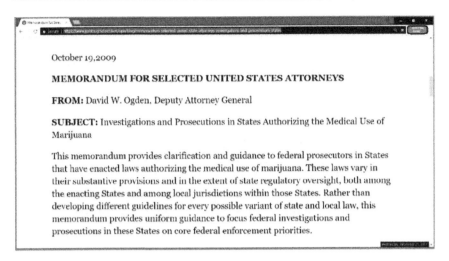

[portion of the Obama 'executive order' October 19, 2009 located at: https://www.justice.gov/archives/opa/blog/memorandum-selected-united-state-attorneys-investigations-and-prosecutions-states]

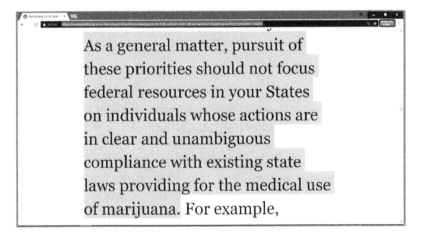

[portion of the Obama 'executive order' October 19, 2009 located at: https://www.justice.gov/archives/opa/blog/memorandum-selected-united-state-attorneys-investigations-and-prosecutions-states]

Obama's *'executive order'*, then created a paradox for law enforcement's misinterpretations, bypassing our courts and lawmakers.

Typically, when any of the following characteristics is present, the conduct will not be in clear and unambiguous compliance with applicable state law and may indicate illegal drug trafficking activity of potential federal interest:

- unlawful possession or unlawful use of firearms;
- violence;
- sales to minors;
- financial and marketing activities inconsistent with the terms, conditions, or purposes of state law, including evidence of money laundering activity and/or financial gains or excessive amounts of cash inconsistent with purported compliance with state or local law;
- amounts of marijuana inconsistent with purported compliance with state or local law;
- illegal possession or sale of other controlled substances; or
- ties to other criminal enterprises.

Of course, no State can authorize violations of federal law, and the list of factors above is not intended to describe exhaustively when a federal prosecution may be warranted. Accordingly, in prosecutions under the Controlled Substances Act, federal prosecutors are not expected to charge, prove, or otherwise establish any state law violations. Indeed, this memorandum does not alter in any way the Department's authority to enforce federal law, including laws prohibiting the manufacture, production, distribution, possession, or use of marijuana on federal property. This guidance regarding resource allocation does not "legalize" marijuana or provide a legal defense to a violation of federal law, nor is it intended to create any privileges, benefits, or rights, substantive or procedural, enforceable by any individual, party or witness in any administrative, civil, or criminal matter. Nor does clear and unambiguous compliance with state law or the absence of one or all of the above factors create a legal defense to a violation of the Controlled Substances Act. Rather, this memorandum is intended solely as a guide to the exercise of investigative and prosecutorial discretion.

[https://www.justice.gov/archives/opa/blog/memorandum-selected-united-state-attorneys-investigations-and-prosecutions-states]

I have made underscores of particular interest in the following citation. Obama's October 19, 2009 *"MEMORANDUM FOR SELECTED UNITED STATES ATTORNEYS"* is cited as follows:

> " '... As a general matter, pursuit of these priorities should not focus federal resources in your States on individuals whose actions are in clear and unambiguous compliance with existing state laws providing for the medical use of marijuana. For example, prosecution of individuals with cancer or other serious illnesses who use marijuana as part of a recommended treatment regimen consistent with applicable state law, or those caregivers in clear and unambiguous compliance with existing state law who provide such individuals with marijuana, is unlikely to be an efficient use of limited federal resources. On the other hand, prosecution of commercial enterprises that unlawfully market and sell marijuana for profit continues to be an enforcement

priority of the Department. To be sure, claims of compliance with state or local law may mask operations inconsistent with the terms, conditions, or purposes of those laws, and federal law enforcement should not be deterred by such assertions when otherwise pursuing the Department's core enforcement priorities.

Typically, when any of the following characteristics is present, <u>the conduct will not be in clear and unambiguous compliance with applicable state law and may indicate illegal drug trafficking activity of potential federal interest</u>:

- *<u>unlawful possession or unlawful use of firearms;</u>*
- *violence;*
- *sales to minors;*
- *financial and marketing activities inconsistent with the terms, conditions, or purposes of state law, including evidence of money laundering activity and/or financial gains or excessive amounts of cash inconsistent with purported compliance with state or local law;*
- *amounts of marijuana inconsistent with purported compliance with state or local law;*
- *illegal possession or sale of other controlled substances; or*
- *ties to other criminal enterprises.*

Of course, no State can authorize violations of federal law, and the list of factors above is not intended to describe exhaustively when a federal prosecution may be warranted.'..."

[https://www.justice.gov/archives/opa/blog/memorandum-selected-united-state-attorneys-investigations-and-prosecutions-states]

Draw your attention to the first button-point in the previously cited quote from Barack Obama's DOJ that I have personally underlined along with their qualifying statement. Obama's attempt to change *'The*

Constitution of the United States' while bypassing our elected representatives is evident in this *'executive order'* of his.

Furthermore, the underlined phrases indicate a clear call to usurp *'due process'* guaranteed by our 5th Amendment as law enforcement is infringing on the 2nd Amendment without convicting anyone of crimes under Obama's *'Bill of Attainder'*. The US 9th Circuit Court of Appeals has their own *'opinions'* on why Americans are now exempt from our guaranteed *'due process'*; we will examine the court's opinions later.

Draw your attention to the Obama-era illogical and un-Constitutional infringement on our Rights from Obama's 2009 DOJ statement:

> *"... 'when any of the following characteristics is present, the conduct will not be in clear and unambiguous compliance with applicable state law and may indicate illegal drug trafficking activity of potential federal interest: - unlawful possession or unlawful use of firearms; ......' – illegal possession or sale of other controlled substances...."*

What Barack Obama attempted to do is leave the door open for legal firearms to disqualify law-abiding Americans from legal medical marijuana. While at the exact same time Obama made what his own DOJ has described as *'legal medical cards'* to disqualify Americans from our Right, *"to keep and bear Arms"*. Obama's got Americans coming and going. Americans can't have Jimmy Carter's cure for cancer if they expect to have a *'Bill of Rights'*; at least according to Barack Obama and those who continue to carry out Obama's un-Constitutional *'executive orders'*.

Now that *"Lawful"* medical marijuana cards can disqualify Americans from their 2nd Amendment because they are *'unlawful'*, will legal medical marijuana cardholders be disqualified from legal medical marijuana card renewals because they are also, simultaneously, unlawful under the *'Controlled Substance Act of 1970'*?

The detective was puzzled when his competitors, the Illinois State Police denied his December 27, 2016 firearm purchases on January 4th, 2017 and in a letter received after Valentine's Day dated January 10th, 2017. It would seem residents of Illinois cannot possess an Illinois State issued medical marijuana card if they are guilty of being *"an unlawful user"* of anything, especially a felonious *'controlled substance'*.

The Illinois State Police see to the background checks for medical marijuana patients; but they weren't supposed to keep the patient's medical records. That was against our 4th Amendment *'right of the people to be secure in their persons, houses, papers, and effects, against unreasonable searches and seizures, shall not be violated, and no Warrants shall issue, but upon probable cause, supported by Oath or affirmation, and particularly describing the place to be searched, and the persons or things to be seized.'*

Breaching patient confidentiality is also considered to be a *'Class B misdemeanor'* by Illinois Law. And remember, Obama didn't implement his firearm transfer background check changes on *'Form 4473'* to include medical marijuana until *"January 16, 2017"* according to Obama's ATF.

=== October 31, 2009 ===

A 'Fast and Furious' Halloween.

The *'Fast and Furious'* scandal began to haunt the Obama administration from its beginnings on Halloween 2009. Supporters of Barack Obama claimed the previous administration's measures known as *'Operation Wide Receiver'* from 2006 under George W. Bush set a precedent for Obama's program to run guns into Mexico in an attempt to track illegal arms traders. Obama's *'Fast and Furious'* guns were later found in Arizona near the dead body of gunned-down Federal Border Patrol Agent Brian Terry.

=== March 23, 2010 ===

Obamacare, also known to some as the *"Affordable"* Care Act (ACA), was signed into law. The law mandated healthcare to be purchased by anyone with taxable income. The ACA claimed to provide healthcare for anyone without the means to afford it through *'Medicare/Medicaid'*.

The law certainly did get government involved with private medical records belonging to Americans. From the Internal Revenue Service to law enforcement, Obama's rules had touched every American life whether it was welcomed or not. Now, state governments would jump on the Obama *'bandwagon'* of un-Constitutionality and government seizures.

Another troubling aspect of the *'Obamacare'* law for all Americans is a section included for a physician's *"coding-system"* based on the United Nations' World Health Organization's (WHO) *"International Classification of Diseases"* (ICD) quoted as follows:

> *"... Legal execution: All executions performed at the behest of the judiciary or ruling authority (whether permanent or temporary) as: asphyxiation by gas, <u>beheading, decapitation (by guillotine)</u>, capital punishment, electrocution, hanging, poisoning, shooting, other specified means.'..."*

> *['UN WHO International Disease Classifications']*

Some bloggers lobbying for Obama's *'rules'* claimed the reference to *"...beheading, decapitation (by guillotine)..."* is used only for the coding system, ICD-9 which was updated to ICD-10 in 2014. I didn't believe in such things as *"conspiracy-theories"*, *"FEMA Camps"*, and *"Government Gun Grabs"*; yet, now that I have held in my hands very real evidence of Obama's *'Ex-Post-Facto Government Gun Grab'*, I am much less dismissive of any claims, as outlandish as they may sound.

=== September 21, 2011 ===

Barack Obama's DOJ released his second *'executive order'* on medical marijuana in our United States addressed to federal firearms licensees – also known as licensed gun-sellers in the USA. The order called for the licensees not to sell firearms to medical marijuana users.

But how would gun-shop owners know what is included in an American's private medical records unless their private medical records were made public? Why did Obama want to breach the 10th Amendment to deny Constitutional Rights to Americans seeking alternative treatments to those produced by his *'Big Pharma'* campaign contributors and *'speaking-fee'* employers as he cantered down Wall Street upon his departure from our Oval Office? Did Obama try to appease the United Nations Office for Disarmament Affairs (UNODA) with his *'Gun Grab'*? The following is a link to Obama's *'executive order'*:

https://www.atf.gov/press/releases/2011/09/092611-atf-open-letter-to-all-ffls-marijuana-for-medicinal-purposes.pdf

=== September 11, 2012 ===

Benghazi, Libya

Barack Obama had backed a rebellion of Muammar Gaddafi, the leader the African country of Libya. Gaddafi was noted to support the highest standard of living for citizens in all of North Africa. He employed an all-woman security staff and was reported to offer free college education to all his citizens. Many countries, including the United States had mixed feelings on the dictator. Gaddafi was associated with terrorists, yet often met with American politicians, including Obama.

Gaddafi did not recognize the US Dollar or world banking. He wanted to issue gold as currency to all his citizens. This would disrupt the world markets and affect changes outside of his country. Some speculate that is the true reason he was killed.

Chaos erupted in the months following Gaddafi's slaying in the streets. US Ambassador Chris Stevens made a visit outside of the capital city of Tripoli to the war-tattered city of Benghazi, Libya following the end of Gaddafi's rule. Not long after the Ambassador's arrival, on the anniversary of the September 11, 2001 attack on the United States, the US Embassy Outpost fell under siege from an organized enemy attack. Ambassador Stevens was among those who died in the *'13-Hour'* attack.

According to those who were in Benghazi, help was never sent by Barack Obama or his Secretary of State, Hillary Rodham Clinton, though the Pentagon was forwarding the live feed from the reconnaissance drone flying above the ongoing attack. The only help they received was from the brave American men and women with a few Libyan contractors working for the secret CIA base in Benghazi and its American security contractors in country. Security personnel in the main US Embassy in Tripoli were forced to obtain a privately rented plane to fly from Tripoli to Benghazi. The rented plane was too small. So, several trips had to be made back and forth from the Benghazi airport to the secret CIA base a mile away from the burning US Embassy Outpost for extraction of the remaining survivors, abandoned by Obama's White House. The men and women who worked together, fought together and bled together are heroes all. America will not forget Sean Smith, Tyrone Woods, Glen Doherty and Chris Stevens.

=== March 27, 2013 ===

"Obama signed the 'Farmers Provisions' protecting 'GMO' producers."

Obama signed the provision which was loosely titled as a protection act for one of the industry's major patent holders for GMOs (Genetically Modified Organisms). GMOs are used to alter the genetics of food so as to withstand stronger and more pervasive use of pesticides. The bill, against the popular will of the American People, prevents GMO-labeling of food so Americans are prevented from knowing what they're feeding their families. The law was later expanded upon by the, *'DARK Act';* that's a coined-name by representatives on both sides of the aisle.

Some critics argue a greater conspiracy is at play, as genetically modified food is unnecessary, and unhealthy according to several governments around the world who have outlawed such products. Obama felt it is none of America's business what we feed our children as his later signing of the *'DARK Act'* indicates. The outlawing of genetically modified food in individual States across America has met with great political opposition since Obama's tenure. The provisions signed by Obama are refenced at the following link:

https://www.congress.gov/bill/113th-congress/house-bill/933/text

=== April 02, 2013 ===

"United Nations ' 67/234. The Arms Trade Treaty…"

"…4. Calls upon all States to consider signing and, thereafter, according to their respective constitutional processes, becoming parties to the Treaty at the earliest possible date;…"

[http://undocs.org/A/RES/67/234%20B]

The UN worked with the Obama administration on more disarmament of law-abiding US citizens. Though Obama's administration denied it, some Americans called this a *'gun-control backdoor loophole'* for Obama's *'Gun Grab'* desires. By mid-April of 2013, mainstream media reported on it, quietly online, without much fanfare.

Several UN *'Arms Treaties'* were negotiated during Barrack Obama's occupation of the White House. But two, in particular, are noteworthy for their timing. This 2013 UN Arms Treaty fell just prior to the passing of Illinois' medical marijuana law.

The other UN Arms Treaty we will examine further on in this chapter, after Donald J. Trump won the Presidential election, in what some *"Fake News"* followers call, a surprise victory for Donald Trump, over one of the least popular candidates in Democratic Party history, Hillary Rodham Clinton (according to mainstream media's portrayal of Clinton). The recent United Nations Disarmament Arms Trade Treaties can be viewed via their webpage for the *'United Nations Office for Disarmament Affairs' (UNODA)* at the following URL:

https://www.un.org/disarmament/att/

=== May 14, 2013 ===

Obama's IRS scandal became exposed as his administration was caught using the Internal Revenue Service (IRS) to target financial supporters of his party's political adversaries by denying or delaying their legally permittable tax-exempt status as Obama and DNC (Democratic National Committee) financial supporters were allowed to use the same status in a timely manner. Did Obama weaponize the IRS to financially attack his party's political competition? From the leaking of the America's private medical records, it became evident something was askew inside our legal system. King George III was holding law-abiding American Colonists criminally accountable for actions that were legal when performed under his *'Bill of Attainder'* and *'ex post facto Laws'*. It is alarming to understand, Obama knows how the King's actions resulted.

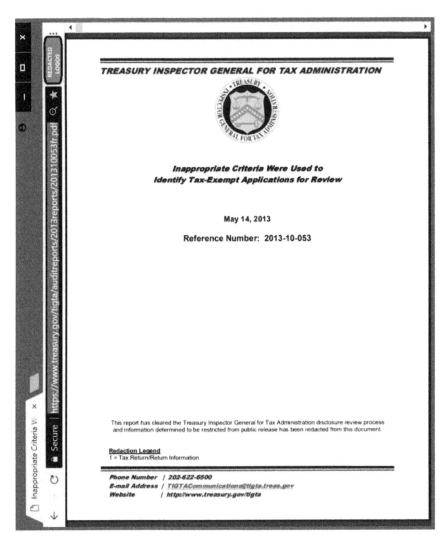

[Page 1 of 48 — Treasury Inspector General for Tax Administration report located at:

https://www.treasury.gov/tigta/auditreports/2013reports/201310053fr.pdf]

=== August 01, 2013 ===

"On August 1, 2013, the Compassionate Use of Medical Cannabis Act ('Act'), Public Act 98-0122, became effective.'..."

"Illinois Department of Public Health"

[*http://www.dph.illinois.gov/topics-services/prevention-wellness/medical-cannabis*]

This Illinois law was later updated with *"Public Act 099-0519"* on June 30, 2016. The original law includes sections *'5. f.-g.'*

"Public Act 099-0159' '(410 ILCS 130/5) '

'Compassionate Use of Medical Cannabis Pilot Program Act'

"...'(f) States are not required to enforce federal law or prosecute people for engaging in activities prohibited by federal law. Therefore, compliance with this Act does not put the State of Illinois in violation of federal law.

(g) State law should make a distinction between the medical and non-medical uses of cannabis. Hence, the purpose of this Act is to protect patients with debilitating medical conditions, as well as their physicians and providers, from arrest and prosecution, criminal and other penalties, and property forfeiture if the patients engage in the medical use of cannabis. (Source: P.A. 98-122, eff. 1-1-14.)

[*http://www.ilga.gov/legislation/publicacts/fulltext.asp?Name=099-0519*]

The new *'Section 7.'* Of Illinois' medical marijuana law, was later added with *"Public Act 099-0519"* on June 30, 2016. Citations follow:

(410 ILCS 130/7 new)

Sec. 7. Lawful user and lawful products. For the purposes of this Act and to clarify the legislative findings on the lawful use of cannabis:

(1) A cardholder under this Act shall not be considered an unlawful user or addicted to narcotics solely as a result of his or her qualifying patient or designated caregiver status.

(2) All medical cannabis products purchased by a [page break'] qualifying patient at a licensed dispensing organization shall be lawful products and a distinction shall be made between medical and non-medical uses of cannabis as a result of the qualifying patient's cardholder status under the authorized use granted under State law.'..."

[http://www.ilga.gov/legislation/publicacts/fulltext.asp?Name=099-0519]

Since Illinois indicates a cardholder under the state law, *"...shall not be considered an unlawful user or addicted to narcotics solely as a result of his or her qualifying patient or designated caregiver status...,"* was Obama suggesting American medical marijuana patients like the detective and President Jimmy Carter become *"addicted"* whence they exercise their 2nd Amendment Constitutional Right? Science has yet to show any conclusive evidence that marijuana is *'addictive'* in any traditional sense of the scientific definition.

Illinois Governor Pat Quinn signed the *"Compassionate Use of Medical Cannabis Act"* into law. Though Governor Quinn never authorized the production or sales (the next Governor Rauner would), the law designated the Illinois Department of Public Health to regulate the medical qualifications and eligibility while the Illinois State Police perform the background checks on the applicants to make certain they are law-abiding residents, in order for the Illinois Department of Financial and Professional Regulation to issue patients their medical cannabis identification cards.

The Illinois medical marijuana law provides for several government agencies to oversee the program. Even Obama's Department of Agriculture gets in on the action to see the crops are being grown in federal compliance. I'm not really certain how anything Obama continued to call a felony could be brought into compliance in his narrow thinking; but our 10th Amendment protects the States and Americans.

Amendment X

The powers not delegated to the United States by the Constitution, nor prohibited by it to the States, are reserved to the States respectively, or to the people.

Any leaks of medical records to law enforcement agencies are ultimately a violation of our 4th Amendment Rights as Americans, including residents of Illinois when the Illinois law specifically states medical marijuana is *"Lawful"*. Only the State of Illinois holds those private *"medical"* records according to the IDPH. The actions of Obama's ongoing law enforcement measures, following his un-Constitutional agenda, is discouraging Americans from seeking healthcare when citizens understand they could have their Constitutional Rights denied by an illegal *'ex post facto Law'* under his ongoing *'Bill of Attainder'*.

Amendment IV

The right of the people to be secure in their persons, houses, papers, and effects, against unreasonable searches and seizures, shall not be violated, and no Warrants shall issue, but upon probable cause, supported by Oath or affirmation, and particularly describing the place to be searched, and the persons or things to be seized.

Though the detective cannot speak for other medical marijuana cardholders, he never gave his medical information to the State of Illinois for any other reason than for his medical treatment under *'430-ILCS 130/ The Compassionate Use of Medical Cannabis Pilot Program [Law] Act'*. Compliant cardholders weren't served a warrant or criminally charged.

==== August 29, 2013 ===

Barack Obama released his third *'executive order'* on medical marijuana programs within our United States, as he attempted, yet again to bypass democratically elected lawmakers and our US Constitution. Obama's *'order'*, like his others before, continued to suggest medical marijuana cards can trigger an investigation into anyone who has a 2nd Amendment, which can be a tool of *"gangs, and cartels"*; adversely, those who legally exercise their 2nd Amendment may be denied a medical marijuana card. But again, these un-Constitutional *'orders'* are being carried out at state levels and spilled their blame unto President Donald J. Trump's administration. *'We the People'* face discriminatory lawsuits with Trump's Attorney General named as the defendant – not Obama and AG Lynch where this all began.

Barack Obama's *'Bill of Attainder'*, couldn't use the suspended *'Habeas Corpus'* from the *'USA PATRIOT Act of 2001'*, to use our *'Foreign Intelligence Surveillance Act'* *(FISA)* to bypass Constitutionally required *'Warrants'* and *'due process'* to spy on Americans who haven't done anything to break the law; could he? He did set up his 2015 *'FAST Act'* highway authority with some allocated federal funding he previously said he would not use for medical marijuana. Obama's 2013 *'order'* is cited:

"MEMORANDUM FOR ALL UNITED STATES ATTORNEYS…"

"… SUBJECT: Guidance Regarding Marijuana Enforcement"

"… As the Department [of Justice] noted during its previous guidance, Congress has determined that marijuana is a dangerous drug and that the illegal distribution and sale of marijuana is a serious crime that provides a significant source of revenue to large scale- criminal enterprises, gangs, and cartels. The Department of Justice is committed to enforcement of the CSA [Controlled Substances Act of 1970] consistent with those determinations. The Department of

Justice is also committed to using its limited investigative and prosecutorial resources to address the most significant threats in the most effective, consistent, and rational way. In furtherance of those objectives, as several states enacted laws …"

"…relating to the use of marijuana for medical purposes, the Department in recent years has focused its efforts on the certain enforcement priorities that are particularly important to the federal government:

- *Preventing the distribution of marijuana to minors;…*
- *Preventing revenue from the sale of marijuana from going to criminal enterprises, gangs, and cartels;*
- *Preventing the diversion of marijuana from states where it is legal under state law in some form to other states;*
- *Preventing state-authorized marijuana activity from being used as a cover or pretext for the trafficking of other illegal drugs or other illegal activity;*
- *Preventing violence and the use of firearms in the cultivation and distribution of marijuana;*
- *Preventing drugged driving and the exacerbation of other adverse public health consequences associated with marijuana use;*
- *Preventing the growing on public lands and the attendant public safety and environment dangers posed by marijuana production on public lands; and*
- *Preventing marijuana possession or use on federal property.*

These priorities will continue to guide the Department's enforcement of the CSA against marijuana-related conduct. Thus, this memorandum serves as guidance to the Department attorneys and law enforcement to focus their enforcement resources and efforts, including prosecution on persons or organizations whose conduct interferes with any one of more of these priorities, regardless of state law. (1)

Outside of the enforcement priorities, the federal government has traditionally relied on states and local law enforcement agencies to address activity through enforcement of their own narcotic laws. For example, the Department of Justice has not historically, devoted resources to prosecuting individuals whose conduct is limited to small amounts of marijuana for personal use on private property. Instead, the Department has left such lower-level or localized activity to state and local authorities and has stepped in to enforce CSA only when the use, possession, cultivation, or distribution of marijuana had threatened to cause one of the harms identified above.'..."

'... (1) These enforcement priorities are listed in general terms; each encompasses a variety of conduct that may merit civil or criminal enforcement of the CSA. By way of example only, the Department's interest in preventing the distribution of marijuana to minors would call for enforcement not just when and individual or entity sells or transfers marijuana to a minor, but also when marijuana trafficking takes place near an area associated to appeal to' minors; or when marijuana is being diverted, directly or indirectly, and purposefully or otherwise, to minors.... ' " [note MPK underscores above.]

[Obama's entire 2013 'executive order' can be viewed at:
https://www.justice.gov/iso/opa/resources/3052013829132756857
467.pdf]

Setting aside its un-Constitutionality, many key points are indicated in Obama's 2013 *'executive order'* on medical marijuana. One point is the discrimination present in many states, including Illinois. Beyond the detective's safety and business being put in jeopardy by the un-Constitutional and premature actions of the Illinois State Police declining a law-abiding American's 2nd Amendment, the actions also placed in danger our Founders' requirements, *'being necessary to the security of a free State'.* Another point is, the all-cash medical marijuana industry is overseen and ultimately regulated or, *"policed"* by the heavily armed Illinois State Police and heavily armed US Department of Agriculture.

The detective and his family-business were discriminated against by Obama's *"Guidance"*, as the medical marijuana industry utilizes law enforcement's firearms for their commercial business provided by taxpayers. Are cops in violation of Obama's *'ex post facto Law'* and *'Bill of Attainder'* too? Should the Illinois State Police surrender their arms used to protect Americans? I don't think that's a good idea at all. Is the design of the ongoing *'Ex-Post-Facto Government Gun Grab'* chaos and confusion for cops to be set at odds with *"Lawful"* Americans and police?

=== September 25, 2013 ===

Barack Obama's Secretary of State John Kerry, signed a United Nations Arms Treaty he claimed, to mainstream media, would not harm our American Rights. What do you think of Secretary Kerry's claims now? The United Nations published information on their disarmament treaty but doesn't readily share the body of the text. The UN link follows:

https://treaties.un.org/Pages/ViewDetails.aspx?src=IND&mtdsg_no=XX VI-8&chapter=26&lang=en

=== January 01, 2014 ===

Though Illinois hadn't authorized medical marijuana sales under Governor Quinn, the state added the law, *'(625 ILCS 5/Section 11-502.1) 'Possession of medical cannabis in a motor vehicle.'* The link follows:

http://www.ilga.gov/legislation/ilcs/fulltext.asp?DocName=062500050 K11-502.1

The Illinois *'Compassionate Use of Medical Cannabis Pilot Program [Law] Act',* also became effective, yet sales weren't authorized.

But searches and seizures under *'probable cause'* at medical marijuana dispensaries were authorized with a *'hold harmless'* for cops.

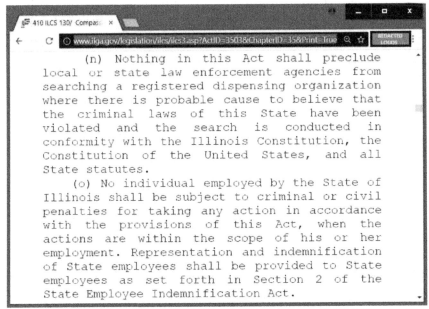

[http://www.ilga.gov/legislation/ilcs/ilcs3.asp?ActID=3503&ChapterID=35&Print=True]

The State of Illinois again exempted themselves from breaking our laws, if they feel there is *'probable cause'* But as the detective's credentials are all without discipline, why would they continue with Obama's *'orders'* outside of our laws? The citation to the law follows:

"(410 ILCS 130/25)

(Section scheduled to be repealed on July 1, 2020)

Sec. 25. Immunities and presumptions related to the medical use of cannabis.'..."

"(n) Nothing in this Act shall preclude local or state law enforcement agencies from searching a registered dispensing organization where there is probable cause to believe that the

criminal laws of this State have been violated and the search is conducted in conformity with the Illinois Constitution, the Constitution of the United States, and all State statutes.

(o) No individual employed by the State of Illinois shall be subject to criminal or civil penalties for taking any action in accordance with the provisions of this Act, when the actions are within the scope of his or her employment. Representation and indemnification of State employees shall be provided to State employees as set forth in Section 2 of the State Employee Indemnification Act.'..."

(Source: P.A. 98-122, eff. 1-1-14; 99-96, eff. 7-22-15.) '..."

[http://www.ilga.gov/legislation/ilcs/ilcs3.asp?ActID=3503&Cha pterID=35&Print=True]

Did the police search the detective's sole-assigned medical marijuana dispensary for patient records? The Illinois State Police would need to provide a *'chain-of-custody'* affidavit to determine how they came into possession of the *"Lawful"* and compliant detective's medical records in violation of the laws on the books (and their website).

Another law allows police to target those they choose. An *"anonymous tip"* can provide for *'probable cause'* to exist when they stop a medical marijuana cardholder and request to perform a sobriety test. Marijuana's effects are said to last only hours, yet traces can stay in the body for months. A portion of the law is cited as follows:

"(410 ILCS 130/30.) Limitations and penalties.'...' (f) Any registered qualifying patient who...' refuses a properly requested test related to operating a motor vehicle while under the influence of cannabis shall have his or her registry identification card revoked."

[http://www.ilga.gov/legislation/ilcs/ilcs3.asp?ActID=3503&Cha pterID=35&Print=True]

=== February 14, 2014 ===

Valentine's Day - 2014

"Memorandum for All United States Attorneys

Subject: Guidance Regarding Marijuana Related Financial Crimes"

[https://dfi.wa.gov/documents/banks/dept-of-justice-memo.pdf]

Barack Obama's DOJ released another *'executive order'* memo. This particular memo did not address medical marijuana but was guidance on general marijuana enforcement to be used against recreational marijuana users. The detective would later, in March 2017, have a family-business bank account closed when speaking on the phone with the bank president to determine why his ATM never worked for the withdrawing of cash. The bank president mysteriously claimed they could no longer provide banking services to the detective's family business and their 24-hour ATM checking account. The last Obama marijuana *'order'* references the *'BSA'*, *"money laundering' drug cartels"* and a *"Suspicious Activity Report"* (SAR). Does this mean banks have access to America's private medical records too?

=== May 07, 2014 ===

On this day in US History, Obama's Unites States Department of Agriculture (USDA) was looking for ambidextrous .40 caliber submachine guns (I copied and pasted – these spelling errors are not of my making):

"USDA" "Added: May 07, 2014 2:03 pm"

"The U.S. Department of Agriculture, Office of Inspector General, located in Washington, DC, pursuant to the authority of FAR

[Federal Acquisition Requirements] Part 13 [Simple Aquistions], has a requirement for the commerical acquisition of submachine guns, .40 Cal. S&W, ambidextrous safety, semi-automatic or 2 shot bursts trigger group, Tritium night sights for front and rear, rails for attachment of flashlight (front under fore grip) and scope (top rear), stock-collapsilbe or folding, magazine - 30 rd. capacity, sling, light weight, and oversized trigger guard for gloved operation. NO SOLICITATION DOCUMENT EXISTS. All responsible and/or interested sources may submit their company name, point of contact, and telephone. If received timely, shall be considered by the agency for contact to determine weapon suitability."

[https://www.fbo.gov/index?s=opportunity&mode=form&id=9fc 3a01217d03b0354e1e18b69aa7bad&tab=core&tabmode=list&=]

As one might assume, or pray to assume, these weapons will be used for perhaps, government oversight of agricultural medical marijuana crops to protect our medicine from those who mean to steal or destroy it? That is some very serious firepower for any Department of Agriculture. I guess farming has changed a bunch since I was a kid milking cows, riding tractors and chasing dinner across a chicken-coop.

A copy of the, *'Federal Acquisition Requirements – Part 13 'Simple Acquisitions'* is available at the following:

https://www.acquisition.gov/far/html/FARTOCP13.html

It seems to me that decriminalization and legalization of marijuana would require as many sub-machine guns needed to currently guard the liquor aisle of your local grocer. Legalizing removes criminal elements. This draws us to an even more astounding scientific revelation; years of research and scientific data with cross-referenced studies have amassed libraries full of information which can prove the claims of Nobel Peace Prize winning researchers and world renown scientists who all agree: *"Marijuana is a plant."*

=== July 2014 ===

State of Illinois
Illinois Department of Public Health

Illinois Medical Cannabis Pilot Program
Frequently Asked Questions (FAQs)

Are registry identification cards from other state medical cannabis programs valid in Illinois?
No. Only registry identification cards issued through the Illinois Department of Public Health Division of Medical Cannabis are valid in Illinois.

Am I protected under Illinois law if I'm visiting another state and using my medical cannabis?
No. The Compassionate Use of Medical Cannabis Pilot Program Act only applies in Illinois.

I live in another state and have one of the eligible debilitating medical conditions. May I apply?
No. Only Illinois residents can apply for the Compassionate Use of Medical Cannabis Program.

Is my confidentiality protected when I apply and if I am approved for the use of medical cannabis?
Yes. The following information received and records kept by the Illinois Department of Public Health Division of Medical Cannabis are subject to all applicable federal privacy laws, are confidential, are exempt from the Freedom of Information Act and are not subject to disclosure to any individual or public or private entity, except as necessary for authorized employees of the Department to perform official duties for the medical cannabis program:

1. applications, or renewals, their contents and supporting information submitted by qualifying patients and designated caregivers, including information regarding designated caregivers and physicians;

2. the individual name and other information identifying the person to whom the Illinois Department of Public Health Division of Medical Cannabis has issued registry identification cards; and

3. all medical records provided to the Department in connection with an application for a registry identification card.

Can I use medical cannabis anywhere in Illinois?
No. Using medical cannabis is prohibited in a school bus, on the grounds of any preschool or primary or secondary school, in any correctional facility, in any motor vehicle, in a private residence used at any time to provide licensed child care or other similar social service care on the premises and in any public place where an individual could reasonably be expected to be observed by others. A public place includes all parts of buildings owned in a whole or in part, or leased, by the state or local unit of government. A public place does not include a private residence unless the private residence is used to provide licensed child care, foster care or other similar social service care on the premises. Using medical cannabis is also prohibited in a health care facility or any other place where smoking is prohibited by the Smoke-free Illinois Act and knowingly in close physical proximity to anyone under the age of 18.

Page 13

[July 2014 – page 13 – 'IDPH Medical Cannabis FAQs' formerly located at the Illinois Department of Public Health' website – but it has since been more difficult to locate.]

The Illinois Department of Public Health *"Illinois Compassionate Use of Medical Cannabis Pilot Program Act – Frequently Asked Questions (FAQs)"* publication was made available by the IDPH in July 2014. If you want to find a copy of the *'FAQ'* IDPH document on medical marijuana in Illinois now, it isn't going to be easy without some effort. I went to great lengths to find an online *'public domain'* copy still in existence for those concerned for our Constitutional Rights (URL redacted from the book).

As far as medical marijuana patients in Illinois can determine, the document the detective had saved from the IDPH, was no longer available to the American public on the Illinois Department of Public Health's website by the time President Donald Trump was inaugurated. But as one can determine by its publication date of *'July 2014'*, the Illinois medical marijuana *'FAQs'* document was available much after Obama's DOJ released *'executive orders'* on October 19, 2009, another on September 21, 2011 and another on August 29, 2013.

The State of Illinois doesn't infringe upon Americans' Constitutional Rights according to the Illinois State Police website and the State of Illinois Department of Public Health; no Americans should lose their Constitutional Rights is their failed claim. According to Obama's DOJ 2009 *'executive order'*, the feds won't prosecute *'Lawful'* medical marijuana patients or commercial growers, and distributors. Without a criminal conviction, there's no evidence outside of unlawfully seized medical records which constitutes a *'Class B misdemeanor'*, in Illinois.

The *"State of Illinois – Illinois Department of Public Health – Illinois Medical Cannabis Pilot Program – Frequently Asked Questions (FAQs)"* document was released after 2013 when the medical marijuana pilot program was passed by the Illinois State Congress and signed into State Law. How can Illinois now claim it is Obama's previous *'orders'*?

Co-sponsor of the Illinois law, Congressman Lou Lang had stated to me on January 3, 2018 during a phone conversation I had with him, the Illinois State Police Director didn't answer his questions either. Hmmm?

=== November 2015 ===

Governor Bruce Rauner of Illinois authorized sales to begin for the state's medical marijuana program seeing that all dispensaries and grow facilities were in compliance. Illinois patients and their families began to see the needless suffering end for our fellow Americans.

The relief would soon be disrupted by the actions of the Illinois State Police, enforcing un-Constitutional federal *'orders'* in violation of America's Constitutional Rights, state laws and federal protections. Patients who once thought they were compliant would begin to learn how sinister the actions were to seize their Rights and *'Grab their Guns'*.

=== December 4, 2015 ===

Congress passed the *'FAST Act'* *(Fixing America's Surface Transportation Act)* for the federal government's funding of surface transportation spending through Obama's Federal Highway Administration (FHWA) on December 3rd; Barack Obama signed it into law the following day on December 4, 2015.

Open opponents of medical and recreational marijuana in the alcohol industry immediately lobbied congress in reference to the *'FAST Act'*, encouraging stricter enforcement of safety regulations to suppress the emerging market of legal medical cannabis as a *"Schedule 1 controlled substance"*. The *'FAST Act'* would allow Obama's Federal Highway Administration (FHWA) to fund anti-medical-marijuana law enforcement despite his 2009 DOJ executive order denying federal funds and his DOJ prosecutors from going after compliant American medical marijuana patients. Obama's *'FAST Act'* can be found at the Federal Highway Administration website: *https://www.fhwa.dot.gov/fastact/*

=== December 4, 2015 ===

(later that same day...)

'Illinois State Police are reported to have erroneously seized guns and gun cards from law-abiding medical marijuana cardholders.'

An established and well-recognized mainstream media newspaper from Chicago, Illinois published, on its online website, a story of Illinois State Police admitting error for infringing on the Rights of medical marijuana cardholders as they seized guns and FOID cards. The un-Constitutional infringements began just weeks after the medical program started sales. It was only after their seizure and the press getting ahold of the information that the Illinois State Police admitted it was just an un-Constitutional error on the part of their department. Woops?

The year 2015 saw the new Illinois governor, Bruce Rauner, authorize sales under the state's stringent medical marijuana law; Rauner's name also appears on the top left corner of the Illinois State Police *"federally prohibited"* 2nd Amendment infringement letter sent to the detective, dated January 10, 2017 before Obama's un-Constitutional ATF *'changes'* to *'Form 4473'* were to take effect on January 16, 2017.

An Illinois State Police spokesman made a statement for the mainstream media's online report from December 4, 2015 that they were working to address future issues with the medical marijuana cards. Illinois lawmakers under *'Administrative Code, Title 77: Public Health, Chapter I: Department of Public Health, Subchapter u: Miscellaneous Programs and Services, 946 Compassionate Use of Medical Cannabis Patient Registry Section 946.40 Limitations and Penalties, part k.'* now defines the State government violations of medical records as a *"Class B misdemeanor'.* It's not understood why, at this time the IDFPR decided to jump in on *'The Ex Post Facto Government Gun Grab',* but *'We the People'* are determined to find out. Will any explanation be accepted in lieu of our *'Bill of Rights'?*

=== June 30, 2016 ===

The State of Illinois updated their medical marijuana law from 2013 adding more protections further clarifying its section *5'*, in its new *'section 7'*, underscored by the elected state lawmakers of the People. Further definitions were made, and qualifying conditions were added. The State of Illinois again stipulates with the original law and new updates, that *"Lawful"* medical marijuana cardholders have nothing to worry about and their Rights are protected. The quotations from Illinois' medical marijuana law clearly states medical marijuana users are not *"unlawful users of a controlled substance"*, as a patient is defined as a *"Lawful user"*. A citation from the Illinois medical marijuana law follows:

> *"Public Act 099-0159' '(410 ILCS 130/5) '*

> *'Compassionate Use of Medical Cannabis Pilot Program Act'*

> *"...'(f) States are not required to enforce federal law or prosecute people for engaging in activities prohibited by federal law. Therefore, compliance with this Act does not put the State of Illinois in violation of federal law.*

> *(g) State law should make a distinction between the medical and non-medical uses of cannabis. Hence, the purpose of this Act is to protect patients with debilitating medical conditions, as well as their physicians and providers, from arrest and prosecution, criminal and other penalties, and property forfeiture if the patients engage in the medical use of cannabis.*

> *(Source: P.A. 98-122, eff. 1-1-14.)"*

> *" (410 ILCS 130/7 new)"*

> *"Sec. 7. Lawful user and lawful products. For the purposes of this Act and to clarify the legislative findings on the lawful use of cannabis:*

(1) A cardholder under this Act shall not be considered an unlawful user or addicted to narcotics solely as a result of his or her qualifying patient or designated caregiver status.

(2) All medical cannabis products purchased by a qualifying patient at a licensed dispensing organization shall be lawful products and a distinction shall be made between medical and non-medical uses of cannabis as a result of the qualifying patient's cardholder status under the authorized use granted under State law....”

[http://www.ilga.gov/legislation/publicacts/fulltext.asp?Name= 099-0519]

The Illinois medical marijuana law is in compliance with all federal laws established after December 15, 1791, the beginning of our *'Bill of Rights'*. The *"controlled substance"* medical marijuana, falls under our 10th Amendment and is exempted from enforcement under the CSA according to Illinois State law and our American *'Bill of Rights'*.

Amendment X

The powers not delegated to the United States by the Constitution, nor prohibited by it to the States, are reserved to the States respectively, or to the people.

Therefore, the Illinois State Police are in violation of the Illinois law and our Constitution's 10th Amendment by citing federal law to infringe a medical marijuana patient's firearm purchase. The Illinois State Police do work for the People of the State of Illinois. For the detective, who had celebrated a career without disciplinary action, the firearm denial was quite an alarming surprise.

Again, this presentation is not intended to single out any one person, but instead a systemic problem which appears to be created by design at the upper levels of enforcement. America's enemies agree with those who infringe upon the 2nd Amendment of law-abiding Americans.

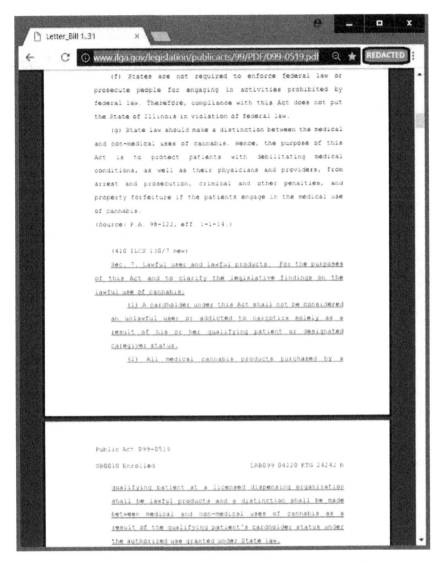

[Sections '5.f.,g.' through '7., 7.1.,7.2' of the Illinois 'medical marijuana law'; found in its entirety at the following:
http://www.ilga.gov/legislation/publicacts/99/PDF/099-0519.pdf]

=== August 01, 2016 ===

"Illinois Department of Public Health"

"Note: Effective August 1, 2016, Medical Cannabis Patient Registry Cards issued by IDPH are valid for three years. Please see the fees page for information on the cost of applying for a card.'…"

[http://www.dph.illinois.gov/topics-services/prevention-wellness/medical-cannabis/medical-cannabis-registry-application]

The State of Illinois directed law-abiding residents to pay fees for what was being classified by Obama as a felonious *'Controlled Substance'*, denying Rights to Americans falsely invited into their trap.

=== July 29, 2016 ===

"DARK Act - Denying Americans the Right to Know."

Obama got the nicknamed *'DARK Act'*, passed and signed it into law. The actual title is the *"Safe and Accurate Food Labeling Act of 2015"*. One of the things this law originally did was to invalidate Vermont's *"GMO"* labeling laws requiring food producers to notify Americans of *"genetically modified organisms"* in consumables. Denying knowledge of what we feed our families can hardly be called *"Safe and Accurate"*.

We are told *"GMO's"* are needed, partly to protect crops against increased pesticide usage due to greater insect consumption caused by *"global warming"*. Nevertheless, Obama's un-Constitutional actions cannot supersede the 10th Amendment for Americans. The link follows:

https://www.congress.gov/bill/114th-congress/house-bill/1599/text#toc-H19A6B11002B542FBB84E49D2B35479B9

=== August 10, 2016 ===

"Obama's DEA re-reclassifies marijuana as felonious 'Schedule 1'."

Barack Obama's DEA announced the re-reclassification of marijuana, including medical marijuana as a felonious *'Schedule 1 controlled substance'.* But the DEA would allow for new regulations to open up research opportunities for those with financial means to invest. This re-reclassification came one day after Obama's daughter was photographed smoking hand-rolled cigarettes of some type at the rock concert festival in Chicago's *'Smoke-Free'* Grant Park off Lake Shore Drive.

But all Americans, including the detective's medical records are still secure and protected under our state and federal laws, right? The 4th Amendment and the aforementioned Illinois Department of Public Health *"FAQ"* July 2014 publication on medical marijuana assures patients' medical records will only be used for their health department and no one else's without *'Warrants'.* Not the feds, nor the Illinois State Police would be allowed to keep or use any American's medical records, including those of the detective's, for any reason whatsoever. They aren't doctors – they are cops.

Obama's re-reclassification of marijuana as felonious came just weeks before the US 9th Circuit Court of Appeals decision from *'Wilson vs [Obama Attorney General] Lynch',* which didn't turn out with high opinions for medical marijuana patients or their Constitutional Rights. Obama's DEA is quoted as follows:

> *"DEA Announces Actions Related to Marijuana and Industrial Hemp - AUG 11 (WASHINGTON) - The Drug Enforcement Administration (DEA) announced several marijuana-related actions, including actions regarding scientific research and scheduling of marijuana, as well as principles on the cultivation of industrial hemp under the Agricultural Act of 2014."*

"DEA Publishes Responses to Two Pending Petitions to Reschedule Marijuana"

"DEA has denied two petitions to reschedule marijuana under the Controlled Substances Act (CSA). In response to the petitions, DEA requested a scientific and medical evaluation and scheduling recommendation from the Department of Health and Human Services (HHS), which was conducted by the U.S. Food and Drug Administration (FDA) in consultation with the National Institute on Drug Abuse (NIDA). Based on the legal standards in the CSA, marijuana remains a schedule I controlled substance because it does not meet the criteria for currently accepted medical use in treatment in the United States, there is a lack of accepted safety for its use under medical supervision, and it has a high potential for abuse.'…"

[*https://www.dea.gov/divisions/hq/2016/hq081116.shtml*]

Obama's DEA continued to ignore US Patent 6,630,507 for the medical use of cannabis as a treatment for diseases. The US Patent is owned by our US government. Also, the statement from his DEA said a request for a study was made but never referenced the *'study'*. Instead, the DEA referenced the controversial *'Controlled Substance Act of 1970'*, which actually conducted the study for the CSA and found marijuana should be regulated similar to alcohol as it was not dangerous.

=== August 31, 2016 ===

The US 9th Circuit gave *"opinions"* on the appeal of *'Wilson Vs. Lynch [Obama's AG]'*. Not many heard of this *"appeal dismissal"* affecting millions of Americans' *'Bill of Rights'*. Now the decision can only be appealed to the Supreme Court of the United States (SCOTUS). During the detective's January 4, 2016 phone conversation, the Illinois State Police

Firearms Service Bureau had affirmed it was this case that rapidly changed Illinois law, bypassing elected representatives of *'We the People'*. Though, it seems their jurisdiction is only for the nine Western States where the court presides, any court in the United States can use the 9th Circuit's *'opinions'* as reference. Perhaps they can set precedent with similar circumstances, even if they are inorganic circumstances?

The *'US 9th Circuit Court of Appeals August 31st, 2016 decision'* to uphold a dismissal of a civil suit trying to sue after being denied a firearm purchase by a gun-shop which somehow knew the customer had a medical marijuana card, didn't give Obama or police in every state the right to conduct UN disarmament treaties on Americans. What that means is, the gun-shop owner was correct that his knowledge of a medical-marijuana patient's seized medical records was ample means for any gun-shop owner to deny the firearm sale as Obama's DEA had just re-reclassified marijuana as a *"Schedule 1"* felony on August 10, 2016. But it was not for the gun-shop owner to know about a medical card unless the patient shared their protected medical records publicly.

But without evidence of criminal conviction on the record, why would a gun-shop owner be burdened with private and *"Lawful"* medical patient status if the police were going to eventually deny the sale after a violation of America's medical records? Would it seem as if someone besides the plaintiff was trying to get this case into a courtroom to set some precedents? Doesn't it beg the question? Or should I say, *"lobby"* the question? We know mainstream media is not asking the questions.

The original cited article claims the attorney would appeal. So, the detective researched online seeing if he could get legal counseling or perhaps even assist the plaintiff's attorney with evidence the detective had. The detective found a lawyer online with a similar spelled name and with associates named on the website in *"Moscow, Russia"* and *"Istanbul, Turkey"* as well as various other countries around the world – even *'Malta' (smh)*. The website named another attorney with a law degree in the US identifying as a transgender woman. The detective kept searching.

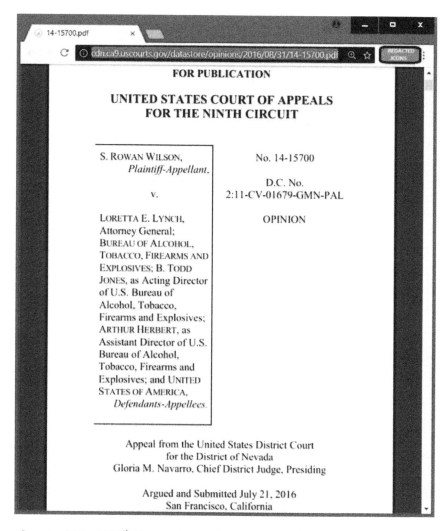

[pg. 1 of 30 - US 9ᵗʰ Circuit Court of Appeals, 'Wilson vs. Lynch' opinions at: http://cdn.ca9.uscourts.gov/datastore/opinions/2016/08/31/14-15700.pdf]

=== November 8, 2016 ===

'Donald J. Trump was elected as the 45th President of the United States.'

Some called President Trump's victory over mainstream media's globalist favorite, Hillary Rodham Clinton, a surprise; but those folks were relying on *"Fake News"* and foreign-financed political rhetoric. Savvy Americans rely on exit polls and un-bias registered-voter surveys before the *'Fake Stream Media'*.

I can attest from traveling all over the Midwestern United States, the vast majority of front lawn signs were for Bernie Sanders and Donald J. Trump – not for Hillary Clinton. Some lawn signs did exist for her, but not like the oceans of signs blanketing the Midwest for Trump and Sanders. I did see some *'Hillary Clinton'* bumper stickers; but People can park cars in a garage; and the numbers of Trump and Sanders bumper stickers again far outweighed the ones spotted for Clinton (even in cities).

Prior to the election Barack Obama claimed the government was not using federal resources to spy on Donald Trump, despite Trump's claims. Obama made it clear there was no evidence anyone could tamper with an American election in the past or present. Hillary Rodham Clinton, during a debate, demanded Donald Trump accept the results of the upcoming election – which seemed odd. Donald Trump won, and the Democrats changed their tune. Democrats and some mainstream media began to claim Clinton won the popular vote and there must've been election tampering. These outlandish claims damaged internal affairs as well as international relations. America saw what happened to the Bernie Sanders campaign; yet I suppose some figured she would accept her loss.

" 'Thou art weighed in the balances, and art found wanting."

Book of Daniel – Chapter 5: Verse 27

King James Version

=== November 16, 2016 ===

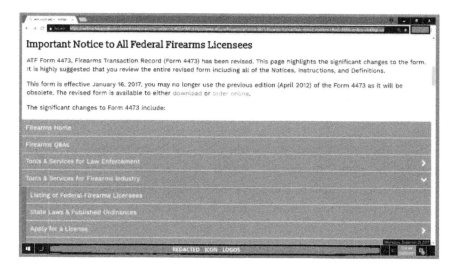

Important Notice to All Federal Firearms Licensees

ATF Form 4473, Firearms Transaction Record (Form 4473) has been revised. This page highlights the significant changes to the form. It is highly suggested that you review the entire revised form including all of the Notices, Instructions, and Definitions.

This form is effective January 16, 2017, you may no longer use the previous edition (April 2012) of the Form 4473 as it will be obsolete. The revised form is available to either download or order online.

The significant changes to Form 4473 include:

Firearms Home

Firearms Q&As

Tools & Services for Law Enforcement

Tools & Services for Firearms Industry

Listing of Federal Firearms Licensees

State Laws & Published Ordinances

Apply for a License

REDACTED ICON LOGOS

[ATF – January 16, 2017 launch of 'Revised form 4473']

"This form is effective <u>January 16, 2017</u>, you may no longer use the previous edition (April 2012) of Form 4473 as it will be obsolete. '...'"

[<u>https://www.atf.gov/firearms/atf-form-4473-firearms-transaction-record-revisions</u>]

The ATF website announcement of changes to use *'Revised form 4473 – federal background check for firearm purchases'* beginning during Obama's last days in office on January 16, 2017, would precede President Donald J. Trump's inauguration by a little more than 100 hours. Why not make the change instantaneous? Why try to sneak them in last minute?

Why did Barack Obama's Federal Bureau of Alcohol Tobacco and Firearms announce this on a website hardly anyone follows? How did the mainstream media miss publicizing this one? Many bloggers nowadays seem much more beholden to the truth and Edward R. Murrow's understanding of integrity in journalism than the mainstream media.

==== December 2016 ===

During the month of December, the Illinois Department of Financial and Professional Regulation (IDFPR), the same state licensing department that issues the medical marijuana cards, renewed the detective's Firearm Control Card (FCC) via a private email with a link sent only to the detective licensee to access, where his licenses could be printed.

The IDFPR sent no notifications of infringement, or license seizure, or status change, or issuing of new licenses for which the detective never applied. The state was still honoring their commitment to the People though it was obvious to the detective, his state, federal and ultimately 4th Amendment protected medical records had already become available to municipal police departments and their radio-dispatchers earlier in the year.

The detective continued to search for answers. Many police officers around the country moonlight in the detective's same profession; the information the police had was damaging to their competitor, though obtained in violation of our state, federal and Constitutional Law.

=== December 9, 2016 ===

Barack Obama sent a public message to the Senate as he continued to push for the United Nations Arms Trade Treaty.

John Robert Bolton, former United States Ambassador to the United Nations had, in the past, warned Americans of this international deal designed to strip us of our Constitutional *'Bill of Rights'*. A screenshot of the Obama White House website, quote and link follows:

[*screenshot from:* *https://obamawhitehouse.archives.gov/the-press-office/2016/12/09/message-senate-arms-trade-treaty*]

I have underlined certain sections to hi-lite items of concern:

"The White House - Office of the Press Secretary"

"For Immediate Release December 09, 2016

Message to the Senate -- Arms Trade Treaty

TO THE SENATE OF THE UNITED STATES:

With a view to receiving the advice and consent of the Senate to ratification, subject to certain declarations and understandings set forth in the enclosed report, I transmit herewith the Arms Trade Treaty, done at New York on April 2, 2013, and signed by the United States on September 25, 2013. I also transmit, for the information of the Senate, the report of the Secretary of State with respect to the Treaty, which contains a detailed article-by-article analysis of the Treaty.

The Treaty is designed to regulate the international trade in conventional arms -- including small arms, tanks, combat aircraft, *[continued from previous page] and warships -- and to reduce the risk that international arms transfers will be used to commit atrocities, without impeding the legitimate arms trade. It will contribute to international peace and security, <u>will strengthen the legitimate international trade in conventional arms, and is fully consistent with rights of U.S. citizens (including those secured by the Second Amendment to the U.S. Constitution). United States national control systems and practices to regulate the international transfer of conventional arms already meet or exceed the requirements of the Treaty, and no further legislation is necessary to comply with the Treaty.</u> A key goal of the Treaty is to persuade other States to adopt national control systems for the international transfer of conventional arms that are closer to our own high standards.*

By providing a basis for insisting that other countries improve national control systems for the international transfer of conventional arms, the Treaty will help reduce the risk that international transfers of specific conventional arms and items will be abused to carry out the world's worst crimes, including genocide, crimes against humanity, and war crimes. It will be an important foundational tool in ongoing efforts to prevent the illicit proliferation of conventional weapons around the world, which creates instability and supports some of the world's most violent regimes, terrorists, and criminals. The Treaty commits States Parties to establish and maintain a national system for the international transfer of conventional arms and to implement provisions of the Treaty that establish common international standards for conducting the international trade in conventional arms in a responsible manner. The Treaty is an important first step in bringing other countries up towards our own high national standards that already meet or exceed those of the Treaty.

The Treaty will strengthen our security without undermining legitimate international trade in conventional arms. The Treaty [continued from previous page] reflects the realities of the global nature of the defense supply chain in today's world. It will benefit U.S. companies by requiring States Parties to apply a common set of standards in regulating the defense trade, which establishes a more level playing field for U.S. industry. Industry also will benefit from the international transparency required by the Treaty, allowing U.S. industry to be better informed in advance of the national regulations of countries with which it is engaged in trade. This will provide U.S. industry with a clearer view of the international trading arena, fostering its ability to make more competitive and responsible business decisions based on more refined strategic analyses of the risks, including risks of possible diversion or potential gaps in accountability for international arms transfers, and the associated mitigation measures to reduce such risks in a given market.

The Treaty explicitly reaffirms the sovereign right of each country to decide for itself, pursuant to its own constitutional and legal system, how to deal with conventional arms that are traded exclusively within its borders. It also recognizes that legitimate purposes and interests exist for both individuals and governments to own, transfer, and use conventional arms. <u>The Treaty is fully consistent with the domestic rights of U.S. citizens, including those guaranteed under the U.S. Constitution.</u>

I recommend that the Senate give early and favorable consideration to the Treaty, and that it give its advice and consent to ratification of the Treaty, subject to the understandings and declarations set forth in the accompanying report.

BARACK OBAMA '...THE WHITE HOUSE, December 9, 2016."
[https://obamawhitehouse.archives.gov/the-press-office/2016/12/09/message-senate-arms-trade-treaty]

I have underlined certain phrases in the previous citation that were not originally underlined by Obama's White House. I did so to illustrate the concerns that came to fruition as President Donald Trump was left to preserve, protect and defend our United States of America, our Constitution and our citizenry while he was attacked from the press with unfounded claims lacking sufficient evidence.

Barack Obama, believing his endorsement of Hillary would have assured their UN Arms Trade Treaty, was faced with a new President who has a reputation of standing against the globalist's *'New World Order'*. Obama desperately desired to get his promises to the UN accomplished. The UN Small Arms Treaty can be viewed at the following UNODA (UN Office of Disarmament Affairs) link:

http://undocs.org/A/Res/71/50

=== December 15, 2016 ===

By December 15, 2016 the Illinois laws were updated and in place that provided Illinois residents, including the detective, safe treatments for their qualifying medical conditions. Government review brought the Illinois Administrative Code; it can be found under the heading as follows:

"TITLE 77: PUBLIC HEALTH

CHAPTER I: DEPARTMENT OF PUBLIC HEALTH

SUBCHAPTER u: MISCELLANEOUS PROGRAMS AND SERVICES

PART 946 COMPASSIONATE USE OF MEDICAL CANNABIS PATIENT REGISTRY"

[*ftp://www.ilga.gov/jcar/admincode/077/07700946sections.html*]

The law speaks to *"Confidentiality"* in section 946.60 cited as follows:

"Section 946.60 Confidentiality"

" a) The following information received and records kept by the Department for purposes of administering this Part are subject to all applicable federal privacy laws, are confidential, are exempt from the Illinois Freedom of Information Act, and are not subject to disclosure to any individual or public or private entity, except as necessary for authorized employees of the Department to perform official duties of the Department pursuant to this Part:

1) Applications or renewals, their contents and supporting information submitted by qualifying patients and designated caregivers, including information regarding designated caregivers and physicians;

2) The individual names and other information identifying persons to whom the Department has issued registry identification cards; and

3) All medical records provided to the Department in connection with an application for a registry identification card.'…"

"…' e) The Department of Agriculture, the Department of Financial and Professional Regulation and the Illinois State Police may verify registry identification cards. Law enforcement personnel shall have access to the Department's on-line verification system to verify application date and application status of qualifying patients who have submitted an application for a registry identification card.'…"

[http://www.ilga.gov/commission/jcar/admincode/077/077009 460A00600R.html]

Section 946.40 of the Illinois law describes the penalties for government employees who violate a patient's confidentiality by exposing their state and federally protected private medical records; the citation follows:

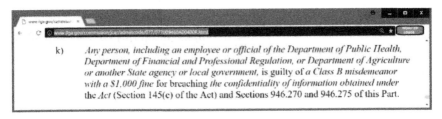

k) *Any person, including an employee or official of the Department of Public Health, Department of Financial and Professional Regulation, or Department of Agriculture or another State agency or local government, is guilty of a Class B misdemeanor with a $1,000 fine for breaching the confidentiality of information obtained under the Act* (Section 145(e) of the Act) and Sections 946.270 and 946.275 of this Part.

[http://www.ilga.gov/commission/jcar/admincode/077/077009460A00 400R.html]

==== December 27, 2016 ===

After learning of Obama's ATF announcement to soon make effective the *'new'* federal firearm transfer *'Form 4473 - Revised October 2016',* the detective visited a gun-shop before these un-Constitutional *'changes'* created havoc within our legal system, our Constitutional Rights and for his family business and personal safety.

The detective's receipt was dated *"12-27-16"*. His firearms purchase would be un-Constitutionally infringed the following year, beyond the legally required *'72-hours'* police are granted, despite the detective explaining to state police he had filled out the proper *'Form 4473 Revised April 2012'*. 9th Circuit court decisions do not affect Illinois law regarding medical marijuana according to our 10th Amendment and the *'Illinois Compassionate Use of Medical Cannabis Pilot Program Act'* (or even the Illinois State Police - Firearms Service Bureau website).

The detective filled out the proper federal background check *'Form 4473 Revised April 2012'* as it was before Obama's un-Constitutional change set to take place on January 16, 2017 according to the ATF website. *"What Happened?"*

Some have titled books to address the questions; but those books sucked more than a vacuum. This presentation is better. Accurate.

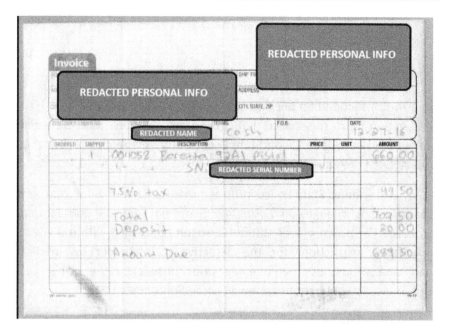

[Author-Redacted copy of Lawful firearm down-payment – 12/27/2016]

"Are you an unlawful user of, or addicted to marijuana or any depressant, stimulant, narcotic drug, or any other controlled substance? Yes [or] No"

The detective answered, *"NO"* as the Illinois State laws continue to indicate medical marijuana users are *"Lawful"*. The detective then made a down-payment on one firearm at a local, family-owned gun-shop.

December 27, 2016 – Firearm down-payment receipt date.

January 04, 2017 – infringed by Illinois State Police over the phone.

January 10, 2017 – Illinois State Police dated the infringement letter.

January 16, 2017 – 'Form 4473 Revised October 2016' takes effect.

January 20, 2017 – Donald J. Trump is inaugurated as the 45th President.

February 14, 2017 – Illinois State Police denial letter is postdated by USPS.

=== January 04, 2017 ===

The detective received a voicemail from the gun-shop stating his firearm transaction had been denied by the Illinois State Police without explanation; but the police left a contact number. The detective immediately called the Illinois State Police at the telephone number they provided for the gun-shop to forward.

The Illinois State Police informed the detective it didn't matter if Obama's *'new'* changes on *'Form 4473'* were not effective until January 16, 2017. The police officer stated he wasn't concerned with the law as he offered instructions for the detective to surrender his medical marijuana card no less than one year prior to the expiration of his FOID card or else it would not be renewed come September 1, 2019.

This didn't make sense to the detective. During my research for this presentation, I was able to identify a similar reference in our laws not applying to medical marijuana users. It referenced those *"addicted to narcotics"* for FOID card revocation and firearm ownership. I find it personally offensive that anyone would refer to medical marijuana patients, including President Jimmy Carter, as *"addicted to narcotics"*.

==== January 10, 2017 ===

The Illinois State Police dated the detective's notification of infringement on our 2nd, 4th and 5th Amendment Rights with Obama's *"Bill of Attainder'* and *'ex post facto Law"*, six days prior to the effective rule change, several days after the initial infringement and weeks after the attempted purchase. Donald J. Trump's Presidential inauguration was quickly approaching, as most of America remained in the dark about Obama's un-Constitutional changes to our *'Bill of Rights'.*

=== January 16, 2017 ===

On December 27, 2016, when the detective attempted his firearm purchases, a different *'Form 4473'* was being used by the government for gun purchases. Yet, on January 16, 2017, Obama's changes took effect on Americans, bypassing our elected congress.

" 11., e. – Are you an unlawful user of, or addicted to, marijuana or any depressant, stimulant, narcotic drug, or any other controlled substance? Warning: The use or possession of marijuana remains unlawful under Federal law regardless of whether it has been legalized or decriminalized for medicinal or recreational purposes in the state where you reside.

Yes [or] No ?"

The form the detective filled out on his December 27th, 2016 attempted firearm purchases was the form the gun-shop was supposed to be using and did use according to Obama's ATF cited below with underscores made by myself:

"ATF Form 4473, Firearms Transaction Record (Form 4473) has been revised. This page highlights the significant changes to the form. It is highly suggested that you review the entire revised form including all of the Notices, Instructions, and Definitions.

This form is effective January 16, 2017, you may no longer use the previous edition (April 2012) of the Form 4473 as it will be obsolete. The revised form is available to either download or order online."

"ATF – Bureau of Alcohol Tobacco and Firearms"

[https://www.atf.gov/firearms/atf-form-4473-firearms-transaction-record-revisions]

The Illinois State Police have 72 hours, by law, to approve or deny all firearm transfers; the police took much, much longer spilling their infringement into President Trump's first term. As one can determine, the Illinois State Police took their time with America's precious 2nd Amendment Right, *'being necessary to the security of a free State'*.

The *'Countdown-Clock'* continues for all Americans, set into motion by Barack Obama's *'Ex-Post-Facto Government Gun Grab'*. As the Illinois State Police *'jumped-the-gun'* for unlawful enforcement on the detective, the rest of America will find a sunset-date for our *'Bill of Rights'* expiring deep inside President Trump's first term.

=== January 20, 2017 ===

'President Donald John Trump is inaugurated as the 45th President of the United States.'

President Donald John Trump, entered the Oval Office with chaos left behind by the previous Obama administration. He was instantly attacked with unsubstantiated charges of *"Russian collusion"* in the election. Apparently, the Democrats don't like *'freedom of the press'?*

=== February 2, 2017 ===

Groundhog Day - 2017

The Center for Disease Control (CDC) released a publication referencing headlines on the Native American federal authority granted by Obama to grow, possess and distribute marijuana on Reservations. However, the headlines covered the continued battle over *"Lawful"* medical marijuana as Obama failed his promises to Native American Tribal Chiefs - yet not the UN. The CDC link follows:

https://www.cdc.gov/phlp/docs/resources-marijuana.pdf

=== February 14, 2017 ===

Valentine's Day

[Firearm purchase 12/27/2016 – infringement postdated 2/14/2017]

[Letter dated January 10th, 2017 – postdated February 14th, 2017]

Following is the attachment made special for Obama's *'Ex-Post-Facto Government Gun Grab'* included in the 2/14/17 postdated envelope:

Illinois State Police – Firearms Services Bureau
Request for Appeal
DENIAL OF A FIREARM TRANSFER

I, _____, am requesting an appeal of the denial of my firearm transfer.

By completing and signing this form, I am appealing to the Director of the Illinois State Police the denial of my firearm transfer. I understand my review will not occur until all requested documentation is received by the Illinois State Police, Firearms Services Bureau, Appeals Section.

☐ The decision to deny my firearm transfer was made in error. I am challenging the record used to determine my eligibility to purchase a firearm. I do not currently possess or have never possessed a medical marijuana license.

☐ I am appealing the decision to deny my firearm transfer. I no longer possess a medical marijuana license. I have enclosed supporting documents.

Printed Name: _____ Date of Birth: _____

Signature _____ Date: _____

ADDITIONAL COMMENTS:

This form must be completed, signed, dated, and returned to: Illinois State Police
Firearms Services Bureau -- ATTN: APPEALS
801 South 7th Street, Suite 400-M
Springfield, IL 62703

Page 1 of 1

[IL State Police - no legal refence on 'Medical Marijuana' Request for Appeal – DENIAL OF FIREARM TRANSFER –USPS postdated 2/14/2017]

=== February 27, 2017 ===

H.R. 1227 *'Ending Federal Marijuana Prohibition Act of 2017'* was introduced into congress. The bill was strife with federal oversight and didn't play into our Freedom very well. The Senate would have their own bill introduced in the coming months. House Resolution 1227 can be viewed at the following link:

https://www.congress.gov/bill/115th-congress/house-bill/1227

=== March 30, 2017 ===

The detective's new business 24-hour-ATM/checking account was closed after the detective inquired for a sixth time why their 24-hour ATM card never worked. At first the bank said they would fix the problem. Then the bank president stated in a later phone conversation the same day, his bank would no longer be able to accommodate their family business needs and would close their bank account.

Obama's 4th *'executive order'* on marijuana speaks to the *'Bank Secrecy Act'* (BSA), *"money laundering, drug cartels,"* and a *"Suspicious Activity Report'*. The detective's business income is provided by checks and credit card payments from other licensed detective agencies. The income he received was only as much as his sole proprietorship could handle. Nothing was suspicious about the $1800 dollars he deposited over the course of six weeks into his family's new business checking account. The letter sent to the detective by the bank to close his account references an *'FDIC' (Federal Deposit Insurance Corporation)* logo in the lower corner. Does this mean banks also have access to America's medical records via Obama's *'executive orders'* and previous laws like the *'Bank Secrecy Act'* and other anti-money laundering banking measures?

=== April 24, 2017 ===

In his first public appearance after leaving the White House, visiting his several homes across the United States and vacationing with billionaires, Barack Obama sat on stage at the University of Chicago where he spoke to students as he claimed:

> *"... The single most important thing I can do is to help, in any way I can, prepare the next generation of leadership to take up the baton.'..., I would advise all of you to be a little more circumspect about your selfies. If you had pictures of everything I'd done when I was in high school, I probably wouldn't have been president of the United States." – Barack Obama*

This poses a question many Americans have as the Obama's have chosen to use their Washington D.C. address as their primary residence out of as many as five reported homes spread out across our United States. Washington D.C. legalized the recreational use of marijuana with no medical paper-trail. Wasn't Obama photographed as a youngster posing with a self-rolled cigarette which looked like a marijuana joint?

=== April 24 – 27, 2017 ===

"Obama makes $800,000 in two canter speeches on Wall Street."

Barack Obama took the cash from Wall Street within weeks of leaving the White House. Obama prosecuted zero bankers on Wall Street during his tenure. *'Wall Street'* is the key phrase. After the *'housing-bubble crash'* Obama did go after one banker of Middle-Eastern ancestry, working in New York who was a citizen of France. I doubt highly that the single Frenchman was to blame for the bulk of the housing market crash happening when Obama first took office.

=== June 15, 2017 ===

*"The Compassionate Access, Research Expansion and Respect States
(CARERS) Act is introduced into Congress."*

Senators Lisa Murkowski (R-AK), Corey Booker (D-NJ), Rand Paul
(R-KY), Kirsten Gillibrand (D-NY), Mike Lee (R-UT), and Al Franken (D-MN)
joined together to introduce legislation to protect medical marijuana and
its users from federal interference. A link to the *'CARERS Act'* follows:

https://www.congress.gov/bill/114th-congress/senate-bill/683

=== August 01, 2017 ===

Senator Cory Booker (D-NJ) introduced *'S. 1689 – Marijuana
Justice Act of 2017'* into the Senate. The *'Act'* proposes fragmented
grammatical addendums to the *'Controlled Substance Act of 1970'* and
other laws. All the laws would need to be compared side-by-side to see
exactly what Booker's proposing; it's a very convoluted and fragmented
bill. Or, we just trust Congress, the Senator from New Jersey and his
lobbyist campaign supporters?

Booker did gain notoriety from voting down former Presidential
candidate, Senator Bernie Sanders's Canadian prescription drug bill
which claimed to save substantial costs for every American household.
Though Senator Booker's intentions may be what he considers in our
America's best interest, it seems Congress is divided with Americans who
recognize the dangers of a globalist economy infringing unto our
American *'Free Market'*. The *'Marijuana Justice Act of 2017'* can be
viewed at the following Congressional webpage link:

https://www.congress.gov/bill/115th-congress/senate-bill/1689/text

=== November 2, 2017 ===

"Look, this is a real problem. But what we've got to do as Democrats, now, is we've got to hold this [Democratic] party accountable..."

Senator Elizabeth Warren calls on Democrats to hold the Democratic Party accountable for rigging the 2016 Democratic Primary against Bernie Sanders voters.

The next morning, President Donald J. Trump publicly called upon the DOJ and FBI to investigate the DNC. America waited... And waited...

==== November 28, 2017 ===

United States Attorney General Jeff Sessions publicly indicated in statements to the press, he may be supporting a congressional change to Obama's *"dangerous as heroin"* federal *"Schedule 1 controlled substance"* classification of America's medical marijuana healthcare. Yet the Attorney General's statement did indicate marijuana remains illegal. Former President Jimmy Carter, our American veterans, American police officers, law-abiding citizens and their families who choose to treat their cancer, Post Traumatic Stress Disorder (PTSD), epilepsy or any other qualifying conditions with medical marijuana will now be registered at the FBI's NCIS (National Criminal Investigative Service) as felonious drug users prohibited from their 2nd Amendment Right, without *'due process' just compensation' Habeas Corpus'* and a myriad of other Rights.

The numbers of legal firearms Obama's ongoing *'Bill of Attainder'* targets from law-abiding American households through the state's legal marijuana industries is estimated in the tens of millions if not hundreds of millions. That number makes America's enemies drool with a hunger for tyranny. Evil dictators appreciate Obama's disarmament efforts.

Will Obama's ongoing *'Bill of Attainder'* holding law-abiding Americans under an impossible *'time-travel'* compliance *'ex post fact Law'* prohibited by our US Constitution decide to utilize surveillance footage to target recreational marijuana patrons? Remember, the US 9th Circuit Court of Appeals in August of 2016 had ruled Americans need not use marijuana; simply having *'access'* to marijuana is enough to seize an American's *'Bill of Rights'.* That's why a non-user mother of a sick child is suing Attorney General Jeff Sessions for her 2nd Amendment Right back. The mother was fortunate to find an attorney. The law firm representing her told the detective to appeal to the police without legal representation and thanked him for calling – then abruptly hung-up. Click. *[dial tone....]*

If the number of firearms decreases to an acceptable number possessed by the citizenry of a country, tyrannical threats outside the USA begin to recalculate invasion strategies, factoring in the country's own misguided law enforcement working in congruence with their sinister agendas. AG Sessions' statement follows:

> *"Our policy is the same, really, fundamentally as the [Obama] Holder-Lynch policy, which is that the federal law remains in effect and a state can legalize marijuana for its law enforcement purposes but it still remains illegal with regard to federal purposes."* United States Attorney General Jeff Sessions

=== December 14, 2017 ===

'Cook County's Commissioner suggests United Nations troops be utilized in Chicago, Illinois and surrounding suburbs to combat gun-violence.'

Local television affiliates of mainstream media reported that the Commissioner of the largest populated county in the Midwestern USA had suggested to bring UN troops into town to combat the gun-violence from criminals illegally possessing firearms.

An independent radio station in Chicago, Illinois mysteriously went silent when trying to report a story of UN trucks carried on the back of a freight train into Chicago during the wee-morning hours not long after the Cook County Commissioner's call for UN assistance.

=== January 01, 2018 ===

Happy New Year?

The number of US States selling *"recreational"* marijuana grows.

=== January 04, 2018 ===

United States Attorney General Jeff Sessions released a memo to his US Attorneys reminding prosecution of America's marijuana industry is the law. The memo speaks to *"money laundering"*, as it reminds prosecutors of the crimes used to identify criminal threats. Attorney General Sessions had publicly stated he is enforcing the Obama-era laws.

In my non-lawyerly, noon-medical opinion, paraphrasing, I would tell a client, this memo speaks to the continued enforcement of laws under the guidance and precedents of the previous Obama administration. As one reads Sessions' DOJ memo, it is quickly determined no new guidelines exist. Attorney General Jeff Sessions has made a career out of being a hardliner on the laws of our United States.

Obama knew how closely Sessions followed laws and chose to announce the changes to his federal firearm transfer *'Form 4473'* days after Trump won, allowing legally permitted medical marijuana to advance his UN disarmament treaty.

Office of the Attorney General
Washington, D. C. 20530

January 4, 2018

MEMORANDUM FOR ALL UNITED STATES ATTORNEYS

FROM: Jefferson B. Sessions, III
          Attorney General

SUBJECT: Marijuana Enforcement

     In the Controlled Substances Act, Congress has generally prohibited the cultivation, distribution, and possession of marijuana. 21 U.S.C. § 801 *et seq.* It has established significant penalties for these crimes. 21 U.S.C. § 841 *et seq.* These activities also may serve as the basis for the prosecution of other crimes, such as those prohibited by the money laundering statutes, the unlicensed money transmitter statute, and the Bank Secrecy Act. 18 U.S.C. §§ 1956-57, 1960; 31 U.S.C. § 5318. These statutes reflect Congress's determination that marijuana is a dangerous drug and that marijuana activity is a serious crime.

     In deciding which marijuana activities to prosecute under these laws with the Department's finite resources, prosecutors should follow the well-established principles that govern all federal prosecutions. Attorney General Benjamin Civiletti originally set forth these principles in 1980, and they have been refined over time, as reflected in chapter 9-27.000 of the U.S. Attorneys' Manual. These principles require federal prosecutors deciding which cases to prosecute to weigh all relevant considerations, including federal law enforcement priorities set by the Attorney General, the seriousness of the crime, the deterrent effect of criminal prosecution, and the cumulative impact of particular crimes on the community.

     Given the Department's well-established general principles, previous nationwide guidance specific to marijuana enforcement is unnecessary and is rescinded, effective immediately.[1] This memorandum is intended solely as a guide to the exercise of investigative and prosecutorial discretion in accordance with all applicable laws, regulations, and appropriations. It is not intended to, does not, and may not be relied upon to create any rights, substantive or procedural, enforceable at law by any party in any matter civil or criminal.

---

[1] Previous guidance includes: David W. Ogden, Deputy Att'y Gen., Memorandum for Selected United States Attorneys: Investigations and Prosecutions in States Authorizing the Medical Use of Marijuana (Oct. 19, 2009); James M. Cole, Deputy Att'y Gen., Memorandum for United States Attorneys: Guidance Regarding the Ogden Memo in Jurisdictions Seeking to Authorize Marijuana for Medical Use (June 29, 2011); James M. Cole, Deputy Att'y Gen., Memorandum for All United States Attorneys: Guidance Regarding Marijuana Enforcement (Aug. 29, 2013); James M. Cole, Deputy Att'y Gen., Memorandum for All United States Attorneys: Guidance Regarding Marijuana Related Financial Crimes (Feb. 14, 2014); and Monty Wilkinson, Director of the Executive Office for U.S. Att'ys, Policy Statement Regarding Marijuana Issues in Indian Country (Oct. 28, 2014).

[January 04,2018 – AG Sessions memo on marijuana enforcement – located at: https://www.justice.gov/opa/press-release/file/1022196/download]

=======

This timeline is only a portion of the news that affected our American laws and our American way of life in *'The Modus Operandi'* of Obama's ongoing *'Ex Post Facto Government Gun Grab'*.

Obama ended his tenure at America's White House with a long list of pardons and commutations. Mainstream media published a list of the final pardons, but it was updated quickly. Perhaps to deemphasize the details of the amounts of guns, rifles, submachine-guns, cocaine, heroin and pharmaceuticals that some individuals were convicted of possessing in our American towns, cities and quiet countryside?

A list of the Barack Obama pardons can be viewed at the following link:

https://www.justice.gov/pardon/obama-pardons

Barack Obama's commutations of sentences are listed at the following:

https://www.justice.gov/pardon/obama-commutations

Some continue to criticize President Donald J. Trump's slogan to, *"Make America Great Again"*. We pray all Americans can do as much as *'We'* can for one another, United, to *"Make America Great Again"* and to *"Keep America Great"*. The mainstream media keeps getting stories wrong, consistently, in-favor of a *'Globalist New World Agenda'*, stripping Freedoms, Liberty and National Sovereignty from every inch of our world.

I understand how things like the United Nations *'Agenda 21'*, their plan for *"Sustainable Development"* in the 21st Century, has a nice ring to it; but once the plans are examined up-close, we can see a darker, more sinister agenda emerges over the masses.

Since President Trump has taken office it seems political operatives have been working double-time against him to disrupt America's *"… unalienable Rights, that among these are Life, Liberty and the pursuit of Happiness….".*

=======

Some maintain, this Obama-era infringement on our American Constitutional Rights is isolated to only a few, select Americans who have unfortunately experienced a clerical error, like the one the Illinois State Police already used as an excuse to perform Obama's *'Gun Grab'*, reported in mainstream media's online article from December 4, 2015.

Others contend the numbers of law-abiding Americans experiencing this Obama-era attack on our *'Bill of Rights',* are far greater than the few Patriots kept in online obscurity at MSM back channels. Law-abiding Americans like the detective and his family and millions of families, are reluctant to step forward because of legal implications and costs, not to mention the stereotyping and public backlash that comes with speaking a politically inconvenient truth.

Maybe Obama's infringement is only targeting a select few Americans and their small businesses? Though I am not a betting man, I would say it could be a smart wager of a *'Buffalo Nickel'* that every law-abiding medical marijuana cardholder, if not also every other American, has already had their medical records *'seized'* under the Obama-era *'changes'* in law enforcement's interpretations of our Congressional Laws and *'The Constitution of the United States'*.

Amendment IV

The right of the people to be secure in their persons, houses, papers, and effects, against unreasonable searches and seizures, shall not be violated, and no Warrants shall issue, but upon probable cause, supported by Oath or affirmation, and particularly describing the place to be searched, and the persons or things to be seized.

=======

Have you ever spoken to your doctor about medical marijuana? Have you researched medical marijuana on the internet? Have you ever told your doctor you are depressed or feeling a *'little blue'*?

Will the police decide you are mentally unstable without your doctor involved? In Illinois they can. Have you ever told your doctor things about yourself or your children's medical history you may not want law enforcement to know about? Are you certain your *'Bill of Rights'* and 2nd Amendment are still intact? Even if you still have your Rights, will police hold your family to Obama's ongoing *'Bill of Attainder'* next?

If the Obama-era FBI NCIS and state police departments did take a peek at all of America's private medical records to share with municipal police departments, as they did the detective's medical records in violation of our own laws, does this mean this the Obama-era law enforcement measure is still waiting in the shadows for a reason to rear its ugly head and snatch your Rights along with your 2nd Amendment and medical treatments anytime they deem necessary for sake of *'National Security'?* Will law enforcement share with the UN? Even if it is during someone else's tenure as the Chief Executive at the White House?

The infringements of the 2nd Amendment on law-abiding Americans is something our enemies dream of. Many Americans claim the firearm-gun-lobbies are to blame for gun-violence as they see a healthy profit from the sales of firearms to those law-abiding Americans. Yet, many never consider the profits that can be gained through the mass disarmament of a state, a country, a continent or even our whole world.

=======

'The Facts, The Evidence' and *'The Modus Operandi'* have been covered, or un-covered as it were, thus far.

Now, are invited to examine *'The Remedies'* Americans have offered to preserve, protect and defend our Freedoms, and our Liberty from foreign and domestic tyrannical powers continuing to operate against *'We the People of the United States of America'.*

Chapter 4

The Remedies.

"The people of these United States are the rightful masters of both congresses and courts, not to over-throw the Constitution, but to over-throw the men who pervert that Constitution."

Abraham Lincoln

=== February 2, 2018 ===

Groundhog Day

Congressman Devon Nunes, Chairman of the House Permanent Select Intelligence Committee, presented a memo that was declassified by the federal government illustrating a paper-trail of abuses under the previous executive administration.

The Obama DOJ appears to have weaponized the government, the FBI and the FISA court against their political adversary, Donald J. Trump. Then Obama's administration testified under oath to Congress it never happened. They got caught. The trail of evidence is certain to begin a series of investigations and possible prosecutions for those charged.

"... They never thought they were going to get caught...

We caught 'em. We are like the Great Sleuth."

President Donald J. Trump

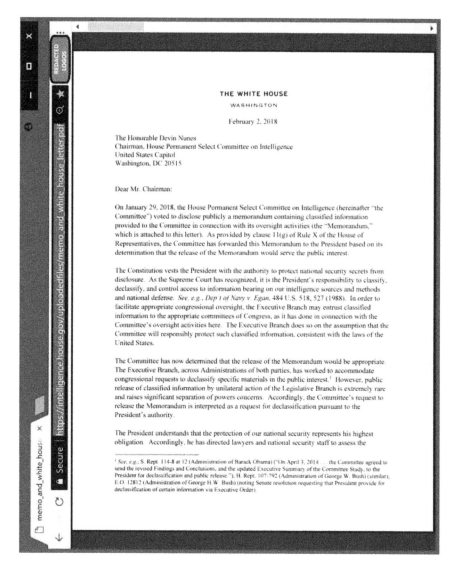

[Page 1 of 6 White House & House of Representatives declassification of the Nunes Memo located at:
https://intelligence.house.gov/uploadedfiles/memo_and_white_house_l etter.pdf]

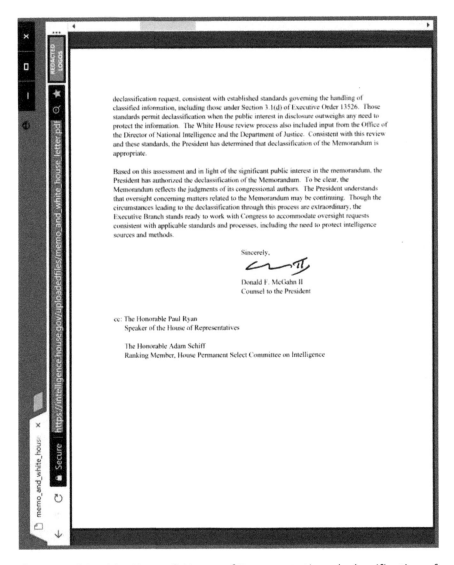

declassification request, consistent with established standards governing the handling of classified information, including those under Section 3.1(d) of Executive Order 13526. Those standards permit declassification when the public interest in disclosure outweighs any need to protect the information. The White House review process also included input from the Office of the Director of National Intelligence and the Department of Justice. Consistent with this review and these standards, the President has determined that declassification of the Memorandum is appropriate.

Based on this assessment and in light of the significant public interest in the memorandum, the President has authorized the declassification of the Memorandum. To be clear, the Memorandum reflects the judgments of its congressional authors. The President understands that oversight concerning matters related to the Memorandum may be continuing. Though the circumstances leading to the declassification through this process are extraordinary, the Executive Branch stands ready to work with Congress to accommodate oversight requests consistent with applicable standards and processes, including the need to protect intelligence sources and methods.

Sincerely,

Donald F. McGahn II
Counsel to the President

cc: The Honorable Paul Ryan
Speaker of the House of Representatives

The Honorable Adam Schiff
Ranking Member, House Permanent Select Committee on Intelligence

[Page 2 of 6 White House & House of Representatives declassification of the Nunes Memo located at:
https://intelligence.house.gov/uploadedfiles/memo_and_white_house_l etter.pdf]

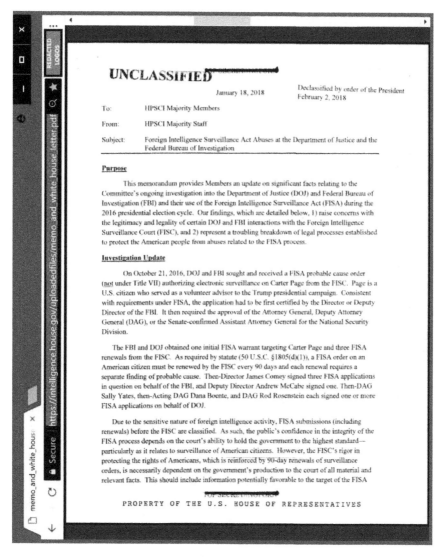

UNCLASSIFIED

January 18, 2018

Declassified by order of the President
February 2, 2018

To: HPSCI Majority Members

From: HPSCI Majority Staff

Subject: Foreign Intelligence Surveillance Act Abuses at the Department of Justice and the
Federal Bureau of Investigation

Purpose

This memorandum provides Members an update on significant facts relating to the
Committee's ongoing investigation into the Department of Justice (DOJ) and Federal Bureau of
Investigation (FBI) and their use of the Foreign Intelligence Surveillance Act (FISA) during the
2016 presidential election cycle. Our findings, which are detailed below, 1) raise concerns with
the legitimacy and legality of certain DOJ and FBI interactions with the Foreign Intelligence
Surveillance Court (FISC), and 2) represent a troubling breakdown of legal processes established
to protect the American people from abuses related to the FISA process.

Investigation Update

On October 21, 2016, DOJ and FBI sought and received a FISA probable cause order
(not under Title VII) authorizing electronic surveillance on Carter Page from the FISC. Page is a
U.S. citizen who served as a volunteer advisor to the Trump presidential campaign. Consistent
with requirements under FISA, the application had to be first certified by the Director or Deputy
Director of the FBI. It then required the approval of the Attorney General, Deputy Attorney
General (DAG), or the Senate-confirmed Assistant Attorney General for the National Security
Division.

The FBI and DOJ obtained one initial FISA warrant targeting Carter Page and three FISA
renewals from the FISC. As required by statute (50 U.S.C. §1805(d)(1)), a FISA order on an
American citizen must be renewed by the FISC every 90 days and each renewal requires a
separate finding of probable cause. Then-Director James Comey signed three FISA applications
in question on behalf of the FBI, and Deputy Director Andrew McCabe signed one. Then-DAG
Sally Yates, then-Acting DAG Dana Boente, and DAG Rod Rosenstein each signed one or more
FISA applications on behalf of DOJ.

Due to the sensitive nature of foreign intelligence activity, FISA submissions (including
renewals) before the FISC are classified. As such, the public's confidence in the integrity of the
FISA process depends on the court's ability to hold the government to the highest standard—
particularly as it relates to surveillance of American citizens. However, the FISC's rigor in
protecting the rights of Americans, which is reinforced by 90-day renewals of surveillance
orders, is necessarily dependent on the government's production to the court of all material and
relevant facts. This should include information potentially favorable to the target of the FISA

PROPERTY OF THE U.S. HOUSE OF REPRESENTATIVES

*[Page 3 of 6 White House & House of Representatives declassification of
the Nunes Memo located at:
https://intelligence.house.gov/uploadedfiles/memo_and_white_house_l
etter.pdf]*

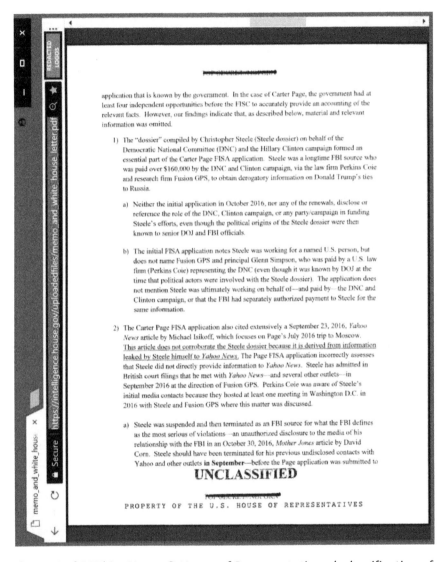

application that is known by the government. In the case of Carter Page, the government had at least four independent opportunities before the FISC to accurately provide an accounting of the relevant facts. However, our findings indicate that, as described below, material and relevant information was omitted.

1) The "dossier" compiled by Christopher Steele (Steele dossier) on behalf of the Democratic National Committee (DNC) and the Hillary Clinton campaign formed an essential part of the Carter Page FISA application. Steele was a longtime FBI source who was paid over $160,000 by the DNC and Clinton campaign, via the law firm Perkins Coie and research firm Fusion GPS, to obtain derogatory information on Donald Trump's ties to Russia.

   a) Neither the initial application in October 2016, nor any of the renewals, disclose or reference the role of the DNC, Clinton campaign, or any party/campaign in funding Steele's efforts, even though the political origins of the Steele dossier were then known to senior DOJ and FBI officials.

   b) The initial FISA application notes Steele was working for a named U.S. person, but does not name Fusion GPS and principal Glenn Simpson, who was paid by a U.S. law firm (Perkins Coie) representing the DNC (even though it was known by DOJ at the time that political actors were involved with the Steele dossier). The application does not mention Steele was ultimately working on behalf of—and paid by—the DNC and Clinton campaign, or that the FBI had separately authorized payment to Steele for the same information.

2) The Carter Page FISA application also cited extensively a September 23, 2016, *Yahoo News* article by Michael Isikoff, which focuses on Page's July 2016 trip to Moscow. This article does not corroborate the Steele dossier because it is derived from information leaked by Steele himself to *Yahoo News*. The Page FISA application incorrectly assesses that Steele did not directly provide information to *Yahoo News*. Steele has admitted in British court filings that he met with *Yahoo News*—and several other outlets—in September 2016 at the direction of Fusion GPS. Perkins Coie was aware of Steele's initial media contacts because they hosted at least one meeting in Washington D.C. in 2016 with Steele and Fusion GPS where this matter was discussed.

   a) Steele was suspended and then terminated as an FBI source for what the FBI defines as the most serious of violations—an unauthorized disclosure to the media of his relationship with the FBI in an October 30, 2016, *Mother Jones* article by David Corn. Steele should have been terminated for his previous undisclosed contacts with Yahoo and other outlets **in September**—before the Page application was submitted to

UNCLASSIFIED

[Page 4 of 6 White House & House of Representatives declassification of the Nunes Memo located at:
https://intelligence.house.gov/uploadedfiles/memo_and_white_house_l
etter.pdf]

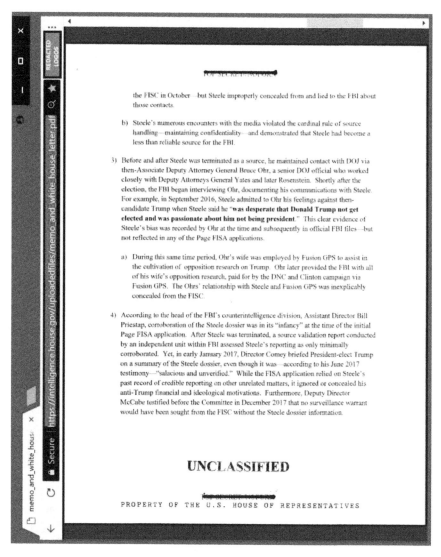

the FISC in October—but Steele improperly concealed from and lied to the FBI about those contacts.

b) Steele's numerous encounters with the media violated the cardinal rule of source handling—maintaining confidentiality—and demonstrated that Steele had become a less than reliable source for the FBI.

3) Before and after Steele was terminated as a source, he maintained contact with DOJ via then-Associate Deputy Attorney General Bruce Ohr, a senior DOJ official who worked closely with Deputy Attorneys General Yates and later Rosenstein. Shortly after the election, the FBI began interviewing Ohr, documenting his communications with Steele. For example, in September 2016, Steele admitted to Ohr his feelings against then-candidate Trump when Steele said he **"was desperate that Donald Trump not get elected and was passionate about him not being president."** This clear evidence of Steele's bias was recorded by Ohr at the time and subsequently in official FBI files—but not reflected in any of the Page FISA applications.

a) During this same time period, Ohr's wife was employed by Fusion GPS to assist in the cultivation of opposition research on Trump. Ohr later provided the FBI with all of his wife's opposition research, paid for by the DNC and Clinton campaign via Fusion GPS. The Ohrs' relationship with Steele and Fusion GPS was inexplicably concealed from the FISC.

4) According to the head of the FBI's counterintelligence division, Assistant Director Bill Priestap, corroboration of the Steele dossier was in its "infancy" at the time of the initial Page FISA application. After Steele was terminated, a source validation report conducted by an independent unit within FBI assessed Steele's reporting as only minimally corroborated. Yet, in early January 2017, Director Comey briefed President-elect Trump on a summary of the Steele dossier, even though it was—according to his June 2017 testimony—"salacious and unverified." While the FISA application relied on Steele's past record of credible reporting on other unrelated matters, it ignored or concealed his anti-Trump financial and ideological motivations. Furthermore, Deputy Director McCabe testified before the Committee in December 2017 that no surveillance warrant would have been sought from the FISC without the Steele dossier information.

UNCLASSIFIED

PROPERTY OF THE U.S. HOUSE OF REPRESENTATIVES

[Page 5 of 6 White House & House of Representatives declassification of the Nunes Memo located at:
https://intelligence.house.gov/uploadedfiles/memo_and_white_house_letter.pdf]

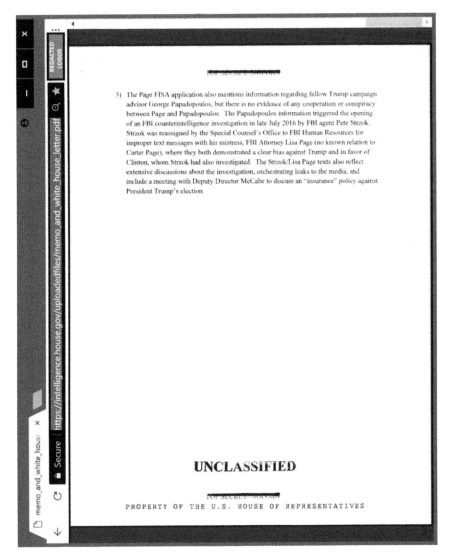

5) The Page FISA application also mentions information regarding fellow Trump campaign advisor George Papadopoulos, but there is no evidence of any cooperation or conspiracy between Page and Papadopoulos. The Papadopoulos information triggered the opening of an FBI counterintelligence investigation in late July 2016 by FBI agent Pete Strzok. Strzok was reassigned by the Special Counsel's Office to FBI Human Resources for improper text messages with his mistress, FBI Attorney Lisa Page (no known relation to Carter Page), where they both demonstrated a clear bias against Trump and in favor of Clinton, whom Strzok had also investigated. The Strzok/Lisa Page texts also reflect extensive discussions about the investigation, orchestrating leaks to the media, and include a meeting with Deputy Director McCabe to discuss an "insurance" policy against President Trump's election.

UNCLASSIFIED

PROPERTY OF THE U.S. HOUSE OF REPRESENTATIVES

[Page 6 of 6 White House & House of Representatives declassification of the Nunes Memo located at:
https://intelligence.house.gov/uploadedfiles/memo_and_white_house_l etter.pdf]

The un-Constitutional *'Bill of Attainder'* and *'ex post facto Law'* were implemented by Barack Obama's DOJ and law enforcement agencies, from state to federal, outside of elected representatives of *'We the People'*, approximately 100 hours before President Donald J. Trump was inaugurated as America's 45th President of the United States, changing every American's access to our *'Bill of Rights'*.

We can no longer expect law-abiding Americans to be held to double standards under Barack Obama's ongoing *'Bill of Attainder'*, punished for crimes they have not committed nor been charged with, as our streets are filled with violence. Leaving folks in this *'New Dodge City'* unable to protect their families, homes and businesses is endangering American lives. The detective and his family face even greater challenges after the lifetime he spent working as a professional detective, protecting American families, businesses and communities from criminal elements.

A dismissed civil case appeal in the US 9th Circuit isn't enough to instantly change Constitutional Law for millions of law-abiding Americans. These un-Constitutional attacks must not be allowed to further infect President Trump's administration. The court decision does not affect our American Constitutional Rights as we are protected by our 4th, 10th and even our 5th Amendment.

An *'executive order'* does not change America's Constitutional Rights. The confusion and chaos Obama's *'Ex-Post-Facto Government Gun Grab'* has caused for Americans, their families, their businesses and our elected representatives, appears to be by a specific *'Modus Operandi'* or method of operation.

It is a method that can be reversed by any American President with a reversion back to the previous *'Form 4473'* for firearm transfers. President Donald J. Trump holds the *'executive pen'* which can defend Americans and our *'Bill of Rights'* from this treasonous presence which continues to slash its cutting edge through America's supreme law of our land, *'The Constitution of the United States'*.

Though the detective and all the medical marijuana patients approved by states were verified through police background checks as being legally complaint and *"Lawful"*, they were never told in a court, nor provided a jury to decide if they were *"unlawful users"* of a *"controlled substance"*. To punish without conviction is a *'Bill of Attainder'*.

President Jimmy Carter became a medical marijuana cardholder during Barack Obama's tenure. Do Illinois State Police feel that Jimmy Carter is a threat because the US 9th Circuit Court of Appeals says that marijuana can cause Americans to become *"unpredictable"*? Really? Or will the ATF continue to push Obama's un-Constitutional *'Ex-Post-Facto Government Gun Grab'* onto unsuspecting, law-abiding Americans because there are no more tyrants left in the world threatening our democracy? *H. G. Wells' 'Time-Machine'* certainly could come in handy with Obama's new *'rules'* for Donald Trump's Presidency. Do these government bodies under Obama's *'rules'* suggest *'We the People'* should, *'citizens-arrest'* Jimmy Carter, because his medical marijuana *"...raises the risk of irrational or unpredictable behavior with which gun use should not be associated.'..."*, as the US 9th Circuit Court of Appeals included in their opinions made public to the American People? Please don't arrest Carter; he's not a threat to America. I can't make the same claim for the US 9th Circuit Court of Appeals.

Obama's *'rules'* classifying Jimmy Carter as a felonious narcotic user in the FBI's National Criminal Investigative Service (NCIS) seems a bit extreme to most all Americans - but not for Barack Obama or the US 9th Circuit Court of Appeals, or the Illinois State Police who would infringe upon Jimmy Carter's Constitutional Rights. That is, unless there's a separate set of laws for working-class Americans, and different laws enforced for others, like a former President's access to effective and safe cancer treatments?

Will only working-class Americans without Secret Service protection need to build *'time-machines'* to meet the impossible standards of Obama's *'ex post facto Law'* and *'Bill of Attainder'*?

President Donald Trump holds the power in his *'Executive'* pen to declassify marijuana from a *"Schedule 1 controlled substance"*. Or he can completely remove it from any scheduling and allow our 50 United States to decide for themselves with laws already in place at state levels – lest Illinois and Hawaii's confusion left in the wake of Obama's un-Constitutional, *'Ex-Post-Facto Government Gun Grab'*. Congress may not approve but *'We the People'* are in the majority on the issue.

Decriminalization of marijuana will allow research to progress medical advances as well as providing safe and reliable tested products for the American public. Or Americans could organically grow the plant themselves as several states already allow – lest places like Illinois and its all-cash cartel. President Donald J. Trump, with his signature, can undo the chaos set into motion by Barack Hussein Obama. The question is: Will the President continue his progress in protecting America from those who pervert our US Constitution?

The questions that arise from Barack Obama's *'Ex-Post-Facto Government Gun Grab'* are plentiful. Someone could write a book (ha ha). But it is important *'We the People'* examine some of the questions, so we may collectively formulate an educated debate and informed decisions on the subject of *"Lawful"* marijuana. The following questions arise for all Americans:

- <u>Public Office:</u> In the State of Illinois, convicted felons found to be in violation of the *'Controlled Substance Act'* cannot purchase a firearm nor can they run for office. So, Jimmy Carter is disqualified for public office in Illinois under Obama's *'Bill of Attainder'*, though no conviction exists?
- <u>Child Custody:</u> Do parents, grandparents, etcetera, become criminals in Obama's ongoing enforcement if they are medical marijuana cardholders and are left alone in the presence of a child? The Department of Children and Family Services (DCFS), I believe forbids felonious drug users to babysit kids. Could a parent lose custody of their own child?

- <u>The Draft:</u> Obama supported registering women for the draft while American men already are required by law to register at 18 years of age. But aren't medical marijuana users too dangerous for firearms according to the US 9th Circuit and Obama? So, then there's no draft for pot smokers either?
- <u>Welfare:</u> Cash payments are made to poverty-stricken parents in need as long as they are not found to be users of a felonious *'Schedule 1 controlled substance'* like marijuana. Will Jimmy Carter have his Presidential pension stopped too under Obama's ongoing *'rules'?* Will seniors who partake eventually lose their social security income benefits too?
- <u>Insurance Policies:</u> They're often nullified for anyone found to knowingly engage in felonious behavior - like perhaps being *"an unlawful user of a controlled substance"?* Will lawyers mitigate insurance claims based upon someone's private medicine cabinet at home? The detective, and assumingly Jimmy Carter, use medical marijuana as directed and never while at work or operating heavy machinery like an automobile. Does Jimmy Carter have auto insurance? Is our former President a threat to our highways? *'Just Say No'*.
- <u>Prescription Drugs:</u> Will the controlled substance opiate painkillers which are to be taken under a doctor's direction become *'unlawful'* if an old bottle expires in an American's medicine cabinet at home? Will that American no longer be *"in clear and unambiguous compliance with state law"* as Obama's *'orders'* seem to indicate? Will they lose their *'Bill of Rights'* too according to the protected medical records the state police and FBI NCIS already seized under Obama?
- <u>Police officers:</u> Will cops be infringed from their 2nd Amendment if they are living in a house with a sick family member who is medicinally taking the *'Controlled Substance'*, medical marijuana? Why punish a parent helping their child? And we need law enforcement officers serving America, unless you are looking to create chaos.

- <u>Foreign Aid:</u> It is handed out in buckets from American taxpayers to countries who have decriminalized marijuana for their citizens well-being. Will Obama's ongoing *'rules'* end funding to our ally Israel as they have already added cannabis products to their pharmacies, paid for by their single-payer national healthcare system when prescribed by their doctors.
- <u>Employment:</u> Many Americans are not self-employed and employers can still fire law-abiding Americans for testing positive for marijuana - Jimmy Carter's anti-cancer medicine. Foreign companies who lobby American lawmakers and employ American workers in the United States can fire them based upon the current *'rules'* invented by Barack Obama, even if those countries have decriminalized marijuana.
- <u>Recreational Marijuana Users:</u> The American People are told by courts and our CSA that users of *"Schedule 1 controlled substances"* can display *"irrational and unpredictable behavior"*. Should concerned citizens begin surveilling marijuana dispensaries to see who the threats are in our communities? Is the FBI already doing so? Again, I just don't feel as threatened by Jimmy Carter as Obama or cops do.
- <u>Voting:</u> Felons in Illinois cannot buy guns or vote. Will their plans include to invalidate recreational users' ballots next?

These are just some of the many questions raised in the wake of Obama's chaos. A vast, overwhelming majority of Americans are in favor of decriminalizing, taxing and regulating recreational and medicinal marijuana. For those who feel the plant is dangerous, perhaps they should compare what else is dangerous. Opiates? Alcohol? Lack of sleep?

Current lawsuits already aimed to go after President Trump and his US Attorney General for (Obama's) discrimination against medical marijuana patients. As the documentation contained in this presentation demonstrates, the actions began under Barack Obama's executive administration and the havoc caused by his un-Constitutional actions.

Obama's January 16, 2017 *'Form 4473'* changes to America's access to our *'Bill of Rights',* is auspiciously timed for those wanting to forward disarmament treaties with the United Nations - exactly like Obama pushed in the US Senate on his way out of our White House.

It's the wrong lawsuit folks - not to say discriminating against medical marijuana patients, or any patients is legal. It's just plain wrong. That lawsuit will bring the issues to a courtroom for the lucky few who didn't have their attorneys decline to accept the cases among the millions of Americans instantly affected by Obama's *'new rules'.* The decision affects everyone. But at the very least, it is progress to get testimony on the record. And a favorable decision works for all Americans. A non-favorable decision is likely to be appealed to the Supreme Court of the United States if necessary. But the real crime is being overlooked. The impossible retroactive *'time-travel'* compliance enforced onto law-abiding Americans is what makes this un-Constitutional from the get-go with its *'ex post facto Law'* holding America to Obama's *'Bill of Attainder'.*

A Congressional bill may solve things, but it's tough to get anything accomplished in such a big room – especially when this needs to be done retroactively in the past. *'Time-Travel',* again, seems a bit extreme for Obama to demand from Americans who require access to their *'Bill of Rights'.* Where's Herbert George Wells *'when'* he's needed?

All the President need do is to sign an *'executive order'* which doesn't trample on our US Constitution. Amending the *'Form 4473'* back to what is was takes the teeth out of Obama's *'Gun Grab'* while restoring Constitutional Law. Nixon's *'Shafer Commission Report'* already spoke favorably to marijuana decriminalization despite lobbyist influence on government to ignore the report's findings. It is no secret *'Big Pharma'* drugs earning the industry hundreds of billions of dollars per year, will be threatened when facing a safer alternative to doctor prescribed medicine. Marijuana can grow in a planter on a window-sill. America can become self-sustainable. We can *'Make America Great Again'* and then *'Keep America Great'* in the upcoming elections.

Furthermore, US Patent No. 6,630,507 is already owned by our United States government claiming the legal rights to the medicinal qualities of the plant. If the government doesn't want it, does that mean it is up for grabs? Or is that just our 2nd Amendment Right that is up for *'The Ex-Post-Facto' Government Gun Grab'*?

If Obama has his way, and his ongoing un-Constitutional infringement on our Rights continues under President Trump, will medical marijuana cardholders be able to *'Lawfully'* surrender their firearms to the state police who, similar to drug cartels, oversee the production of a felonious *"controlled substance"* for distribution to customers only they approve in their *'all-cash'* cartel that currently can't use our American banking system because it remains a *"felony"?* Or will those medical marijuana cardholders be charged with aiding and abetting those who run a felonious *"Schedule 1 controlled substance"* production and distribution *'cartel?* Or will those Americans be told it's okay only to learn later they need to build another *"time-machine"* to stay out of for-profit prisons Obama and his cops are encouraged to invest in?

In addition to our existing *'Bill of Rights'*, many American's shared their beliefs on how *'We the People'* should preserve, protect and defend our individuals Freedoms, Liberties and Independence with our American Constitutional Rights from those who are bent on profiting from their demise. The following, in no particular order, are the thoughts and beliefs of Patriotic Americans, past and present, on our *'Inalienable Rights'*...

=======

"There exists a shadowy government with its own Air Force, its own Navy, its own fundraising-mechanism, and the ability to pursue its own ideas of national interest, free from all checks and balances, and free from the law itself."

Senator Daniel Ken Inouye

Senate Hearing on Secret Military Assistance to Iran and Nicaragua – 1987 Iran-Contra hearings.

"So, I am concerned, and I'm speaking for a lot of people in my state who are worried about the inconsistency between the state marijuana laws as well as the federal policy. The Department of Justice has not taken the position thus far that state marijuana laws are completely preempted by the Controlled Substances Act – I don't know if you are headed in that direction – the Cole Memorandum suggests deference to strong state laws but we're not seeing the federal government doing much to ensure that those strong state laws are enforceable. So, the bigger question is, where are we heading with marijuana?"

Senator Lisa Murkowski

Appropriations Subcommittee SD-192 – June 2017.

=======

"With officers laid-off and furloughed, simply calling 911 and waiting is no longer your best option. You can beg for mercy from a violent criminal, hide under the bed, or you can fight back, but are you prepared? Consider taking a certified safety course 'n handling a firearm, so you can defend yourself until we get there. You have a duty to protect yourself and your family. We're partners now. Can I count on you?"

Sheriff David Clarke

A public message to Milwaukee County, Wisconsin – 01/25/2013.

=======

"I'm all for gun control, I just define it a little differently. If you can put 2 rounds into the same hole from 25 meters, that's gun control! If you're going to own a gun, you have an obligation to know what you're doing with it. When the Constitution gave us the right to bear arms, it also made us responsible for using them properly. It's not fair of us as citizens to lean more heavily on one side of that equation than on the other."

Jesse Ventura – former Minnesota Governor and US Navy (ret.).

"Those who would give up essential Liberty, to purchase a little temporary Safety, deserve neither Liberty nor Safety."

Benjamin Franklin -Founding Father.

=======

"That no man should scruple, or hesitate a moment, to use arms in defence of so valuable a blessing, on which all the good and evil of life depends, is clearly my opinion."

George Washington - in a letter to George Mason - April 5, 1769.

=======

"Besides the advantage of being armed, which the Americans possess over the people of almost every other nation, the existence of subordinate governments, to which the people are attached, and by which the militia officers are appointed, forms a barrier against the enterprises of ambition, more insurmountable than any which a simple government of any form can admit of."

James Madison - Federalist No. 46 - January 29, 1788.

=======

"...the ultimate authority, wherever the derivative may be found, resides in the people alone..."

James Madison - Federalist No. 46 - January 29, 1788.

=======

"The right of the people to keep and bear arms shall not be infringed. A well regulated Militia, composed of the body of the people, trained to arms, is the best and most natural defense of a free country."

James Madison - Annals of Congress 434 - June 8, 1789.

=======

"That a well-regulated militia, composed of the body of the people, trained to arms, is the proper, natural and safe defense of a free state; that standing armies, in time of peace, should be avoided as dangerous to liberty; and that, in all cases, the military should be under strict subordination to, and governed by, the civil power."

George Mason - Virginia Declaration of Rights - June 12, 1776.

=======

"Before a standing army can rule, the people must be disarmed, as they are in almost every country in Europe. The supreme power in America cannot enforce unjust laws by the sword; because the whole body of the people are armed, and constitute a force superior to any band of regular troops."

Noah Webster - An Examination of the Leading Principles of the Federal Constitution - October 10, 1787.

=======

"A militia when properly formed are in fact the people themselves...and include, according to the past and general usage of the states, all men capable of bearing arms... To preserve liberty, it is essential that the whole body of the people always possess arms, and be taught alike, especially when young, how to use them."

Richard Henry Lee - Federal Farmer Number 18 - January 25, 1788.

=======

"No free government was ever founded, or ever preserved its liberty, without uniting the characters of the citizen and soldier in those destined for the defense of the state...such area well-regulated militia, composed of the freeholders, citizen and husbandman, who take up arms to preserve their property, as individuals, and their rights as freemen."

Richard Henry Lee - Charleston Gazette - September 8, 1788.

"Guard with jealous attention the public liberty. Suspect everyone who approaches that jewel. Unfortunately, nothing will preserve it but downright force. Whenever you give up that force, you are ruined.... The great object is that every man be armed. Everyone who is able might have a gun."

Patrick Henry - in a speech at the Virginia Ratifying Convention - June 5, 1778.

=======

"Are we at last brought to such humiliating and debasing degradation that we cannot be trusted with arms for our defense? Where is the difference between having our arms in possession and under our direction, and having them under the management of Congress? If our defense be the real object of having those arms, in whose hands can they be trusted with more propriety, or equal safety to us, as in our own hands?"

Patrick Henry - at the debates on the adoption of our US Constitution.

=======

"The supposed quietude of a good man allures the ruffian; while on the other hand, arms, like law, discourage and keep the invader and the plunderer in awe, and preserve order in the world as well as property. The balance of power is the scale of peace. The same balance would be preserved were all the world destitute of arms, for all would be alike; but since some will not, others dare not lay them aside. And while a single nation refuses to lay them down, it is proper that all should keep them up. Horrid mischief would ensue were one-half the world deprived of the use of them; for while avarice and ambition have a place in the heart of man, the weak will become a prey to the strong. The history of every age and nation establishes these truths, and facts need but little arguments when they prove themselves."

Thomas Paine - article entitled "Thoughts on Defensive War", Pennsylvania Magazine - July 1775.

"And that the said Constitution be never construed to authorize Congress to infringe the just liberty of the press, or the rights of conscience; or to prevent the people of the United States, who are peaceable citizens, from keeping their own arms; or to raise standing armies, unless necessary for the defense of the United States, or of some one or more of them; or to prevent the people from petitioning, in a peaceable and orderly manner, the federal legislature, for a redress of grievances; or to subject the people to unreasonable searches and seizures of their persons, papers or possessions."

Samuel Adams, Massachusetts convention to ratify our US Constitution - 1788.

=======

"The right of the citizens to keep and bear arms has justly been considered, as the palladium of the liberties of a republic; since it offers a strong moral check against the usurpation and arbitrary power of rulers; and will generally, even if these are successful in the first instance, enable the people to resist and triumph over them."

Joseph Story - Commentaries on the US Constitution – 1833.

=======

"What, Sir, is the use of a militia? It is to prevent the establishment of a standing army, the bane of liberty …. Whenever Governments mean to invade the rights and liberties of the people, they always attempt to destroy the militia, in order to raise an army upon their ruins."

Representative Elbridge Gerry of Massachusetts - I Annals of Congress 750 - August 17, 1789.

=======

"To disarm the people…[i]s the most effectual way to enslave them."

George Mason - referencing advice Pennsylvania Governor, Sir William Keith gave to British Parliament - June 14, 1788.

"When the people fear the government you have tyranny. Where the government fears the people you have liberty."

John Basil Barnhill - writer & publisher, 'Indictment of Socialism'

=======

"Some are whigs, liberals, democrats, call them what you please. Others are tories, serviles, aristocrats,'. The latter fear the people, and wish to transfer all power to the higher classes of society; the former consider the people as the safest depository of power in the last resort; they cherish them therefore, and wish to leave in them all the powers to the exercise of which they are competent."

Thomas Jefferson - in an 1825 letter to William Short.

========

"An elective despotism was not the government we fought for, but one which should not only be founded on true free principles, but in which the powers of government should be so divided and balanced among general bodies of magistracy, as that no one could transcend their legal limits without being effectually checked and restrained by the others."

Thomas Jefferson

=======

"[The People] are the ultimate, guardians of their own liberty."

Thomas Jefferson

=======

"No free man shall ever be debarred the use of arms'... "

Thomas Jefferson - Virginia Constitution - First Draft – 1776.

=======

"I prefer dangerous freedom over peaceful slavery."

Thomas Jefferson - in a letter to James Madison, January 20, 1787.

=======

"What country can preserve its liberties if their rulers are not warned from time to time that their people preserve the spirit of resistance. Let them take arms."

Thomas Jefferson - in a letter to James Madison, December 20, 1787.

=======

"Rightful liberty is unobstructed action according to our will within limits drawn around us by the equal rights of others. I do not add 'within the limits of the law,' because law is often but the tyrant's will, and always so when it violates the rights of the individual."

Thomas Jefferson - in a letter to Isaac H. Tiffany, April 4, 1819.

=======

"The laws that forbid the carrying of arms are laws of such a nature. They disarm only those who are neither inclined nor determined to commit crimes.... Such laws make things worse for the assaulted and better for the assailants; they serve rather to encourage than to prevent homicides, for an unarmed man may be attacked with greater confidence than an armed man."

Thomas Jefferson - Commonplace Book 'quoting 18th century criminologist Cesare Beccaria' – 1774 to 1776.

=======

"The Constitution of most of our states (and of the United States) assert that all power is inherent in the people; that they may exercise it by themselves; that it is their right and duty to be at all times armed."

Thomas Jefferson - in a letter to John Cartwright – June 5, 1824.

"A strong body makes the mind strong. As to the species of exercises, I advise the gun. While this gives moderate exercise to the body, it gives boldness, enterprise and independence to the mind. Games played with the ball, and others of that nature, are too violent for the body and stamp no character on the mind. Let your gun therefore be your constant companion of your walks."

Thomas Jefferson - in a letter to Peter Carr - August 19, 1785.

=======

"On every occasion [of Constitutional interpretation] let us carry ourselves back to the time when the Constitution was adopted, recollect the spirit manifested in the debates, and instead of trying [to force] what meaning may be squeezed out of the text, or invented against it, [instead let us] conform to the probable one in which it was passed."

Thomas Jefferson - in a letter to William Johnson – June 12, 1823.

=======

"I enclose you a list of the killed, wounded, and captives of the enemy from the commencement of hostilities at Lexington in April, 1775, until November, 1777, since which there has been no event of any consequence … I think that upon the whole it has been about one half the number lost by them, in some instances more, but in others less. This difference is ascribed to our superiority in taking aim when we fire; every soldier in our army having been intimate with his gun from his infancy."

Thomas Jefferson - in a letter to Giovanni Fabbroni - June 8, 1778.

=======

" 'When once a republic is corrupted, there is no possibility of remedying any of the growing evils but by removing the corruption and restoring its lost principles; every other correction is either useless or a new evil.' "

Thomas Jefferson recited Montesquieu in 'Spirit of the Laws'.

=======

"For it is a truth, which the experience of ages has attested, that the people are always most in danger when the means of injuring their rights are in the possession of those of whom they entertain the least suspicion."

Alexander Hamilton - Federalist Number 25 - December 21, 1787.

=======

"If the representatives of the people betray their constituents, there is then no resource left but in the exertion of that original right of self-defense which is paramount to all positive forms of government, and which against the usurpations of the national rulers, may be exerted with infinitely better prospect of success than against those of the rulers of an individual state. In a single state, if the persons intrusted with supreme power become usurpers, the different parcels, subdivisions, or districts of which it consists, having no distinct government in each, can take no regular measures for defense. The citizens must rush tumultuously to arms, without concert, without system, without resource; except in their courage and despair."

Alexander Hamilton - Federalist Number 28.

=======

"[I]f circumstances should at any time oblige the government to form an army of any magnitude that army can never be formidable to the liberties of the people while there is a large body of citizens, little, if at all, inferior to them in discipline and the use of arms, who stand ready to defend their own rights and those of their fellow-citizens. This appears to me the only substitute that can be devised for a standing army, and the best possible security against it, if it should exist."

Alexander Hamilton - Federalist Number 28 - January 10, 1788.

=======

"Little more can reasonably be aimed at, with respect to the people at large, than to have them properly armed and equipped; and in order to see that this be not neglected, it will be necessary to assemble them once or twice in the course of a year."

Alexander Hamilton - Federalist Number 29 - January 9, 1788.

=======

"As civil rulers, not having their duty to the people before them, may attempt to tyrannize, and as the military forces which must be occasionally raised to defend our country, might pervert their power to the injury of their fellow citizens, the people are confirmed by the article in their right to keep and bear their private arms."

Tench Coxe - Philadelphia Federal Gazette - June 18, 1789.

=======

"The militia of these free commonwealths, entitled and accustomed to their arms, when compared with any possible army, must be tremendous and irresistible. Who are the militia? Are they not ourselves? Is it feared, then, that we shall turn our arms each man against his own bosom. Congress have no power to disarm the militia. Their swords, and every other terrible implement of the soldier, are the birth-right of an American ... the unlimited power of the sword is not in the hands of either the federal or state governments, but, where I trust in God it will ever remain, in the hands of the people."

Tenche Coxe -The Pennsylvania Gazette - February 20, 1788.

=======

"The people are not to be disarmed of their weapons. They are left in full possession of them."

Zachariah Johnson

Virginia convention to ratify the US Constitution - June 25, 1788.

=======

"With hearts fortified with these animating reflections, we most solemnly, before God and the world, declare, that, exerting the utmost energy of those powers, which our beneficent Creator hath graciously bestowed upon us, the arms we have compelled by our enemies to assume, we will, in defiance of every hazard, with unabating firmness and perseverance employ for the preservation of our liberties; being with one mind resolved to die freemen rather than to live as slaves."

John Dickinson - July 6, 1775.

=======

"(C)onceived it to be the privilege of every citizen, and one of his most essential rights, to bear arms, and to resist every attack upon his liberty or property, by whomsoever made. The particular States, like private citizens, have a right to be armed, and to defend by force of arms, their rights, when invaded."

Roger Sherman - Debates on 1790 Militia Act.

=======

"Speak softly and carry a big stick."

President Theodore Roosevelt

=======

(Part IV excerpt from President Eisenhower's farewell speech)

"... A vital element in keeping the peace is our military establishment. Our arms must be mighty, ready for instant action, so that no potential aggressor may be tempted to risk his own destruction.

Our military organization today bears little relation to that known by any of my predecessors in peace time, or indeed by the fighting men of World War II or Korea.

Until the latest of our world conflicts, the United States had no armaments industry. American makers of plowshares could, with time and as required, make swords as well. But now we can no longer risk emergency improvisation of national defense; we have been compelled to create a permanent armaments industry of vast proportions. Added to this, three and a half million men and women are directly engaged in the defense establishment. We annually spend on military security more than the net income of all United State corporations.

This conjunction of an immense military establishment and a large arms industry is new in the American experience. The total influence-economic, political, even spiritual-is felt in every city, every state house, every office of the Federal government. We recognize the imperative need for this development. Yet we must not fail to comprehend its grave implications. Our toil, resources and livelihood are all involved; so is the very structure of our society.

In the councils of government, we must guard against the acquisition of unwarranted influence, whether sought or unsought, by the military-industrial complex. The potential for the disastrous rise of misplaced power exists and will persist.

We must never let the weight of this combination endanger our liberties or democratic processes. We should take nothing for granted only an alert and knowledgeable citizenry can compel the proper meshing of huge industrial and military machinery of defense with our peaceful methods and goals, so that security and liberty may prosper together.

Akin to, and largely responsible for the sweeping changes in our industrial-military posture, has been the technological revolution during recent decades.

In this revolution, research has become central; it also becomes more formalized, complex, and costly. A steadily increasing share is conducted for, by, or at the direction of, the Federal government.

Today, the solitary inventor, tinkering in his shop, has been over shadowed by task forces of scientists in laboratories and testing fields. In the same fashion, the free university, historically the fountainhead of free ideas and scientific discovery, has experienced a revolution in the conduct of research. Partly because of the huge costs involved, a government contract becomes virtually a substitute for intellectual curiosity. For every old blackboard there are now hundreds of new electronic computers.

The prospect of domination of the nation's scholars by Federal employment, project allocations, and the power of money is ever present and is gravely to be regarded.

Yet, in holding scientific research and discovery in respect, as we should, we must also be alert to the equal and opposite danger that public policy could itself become the captive of a scientific-technological elite.

It is the task of statesmanship to mold, to balance, and to integrate these and other forces, new and old, within the principles of our democratic system-ever aiming toward the supreme goals of our free society.'..."

President Dwight D. Eisenhower - Farewell Address – Part IV.

January 17, 1961

[Eisenhower's full speech 'public domain' transcripts can be accessed at the following link:
https://www.ourdocuments.gov/print_friendly.php?flash=false&page=t ranscript&doc=90&title=Transcript+of+President+Dwight+D.+Eisenhow ers+Farewell+Address+%281961%29]

=======

President Eisenhower warned of dangers, lurking in the shadows, threatened by America's *'Bill of Rights'*. President Donald J. Trump holds the power of the pen to instantly end this siege against our Constitution. But it may be up to Congress as the President faces staunch criticism at every turn, regardless of Donald Trump's history of Patriotism.

The *'Problem-Reaction-Solution'*, *'Hegelian-Dialectic'* being played over and over by powerful forces upon our government continues to destroy the trust the People once held for law enforcement. If Obama's ongoing *'executive' 'Ordo ad Chao' (Latin: 'Order out of Chaos')* can snatch a business from a law-abiding American family who made a career out of lawful compliance and service to the People, what chance do any law-abiding Americans have to access healthcare or our *'Bill of Rights'*?

Action must be taken by Americans before *'We the People'* are victimized further by the tyranny persisting beyond Obama's tenure. As a Patriotic American, I stand United with the American People and our President Donald J. Trump as our nation faces these insurmountable attacks from those wanting to harm our United States.

More Americans are affected each day in growing numbers yet are hesitant to step forward for fear of government reprisals. Americans ask, what laws can stop such fraudulent government behavior enforcing Obama's, *'Ex Post Facto Government Gun Grab'*? There are *'Remedies'*.

'The False Claims Act of 1863', enacted by President Abraham Lincoln, was in response to Civil War contractors stuffing sawdust into the gunpowder they sold to the Union Army to turnover a corrupt-buck. Whistleblowing for corrupt governmental systems began. Our Department of Justice makes information available on Lincoln's Act:

[https://www.justice.gov/sites/default/files/civil/legacy/2011/04/22/C-FRAUDS_FCA_Primer.pdf]

In 1986, President Ronald Reagan signed *'The False Claims Reform Act'*, further strengthening America's battle against tyrannical practices within our governmental systems. Will Americans speak-up if there is no accountability to crimes for those working for our American government? A link to the law follows:

[https://www.justice.gov/jmd/false-claims-amendments-act-1986-pl-99-562]

In 1991 *'The Illinois Whistleblower Reward and Protection Act, 740 ILCS 175/1',* was enacted to expose the fraudulent actions of state employees, politicians, and contractors. Later, in 1995, the Act was amended to make the Act's provisions applicable to local public bodies. The Act encourages Americans to monitor our government and report the fraudulent behavior of elected officials, government employees and even government contractors doing business with the government. Up to triple damages can be recovered from the wrongdoers. But, our detective already reported the police to the police on 01/04/2017. Nevertheless, the Illinois law and updates can be viewed at the following:

[http://www.ilga.gov/legislation/ilcs/ilcs3.asp?ActID=2058&ChapterID= 57]

As the information herein demonstrates a need for transparency, I, Matthew P. Kulesza, Illinois resident, and Patriotic natural born citizen of the United States of America, officially in writing, notify the People of the United States and our President Donald J. Trump of the ongoing cover-up to conceal the truth from the American People at state and federal levels in violation of *'The Constitution of the United States'.*

=======

'The Evidence, The Facts, The Modus Operandi' & The Remedies' demonstrate *'The Ex-Post-Facto Government Gun Grab'.* Born of the Obama administration, yet sunsetting deep inside Donald Trump's Presidency, this siege on our Liberty will reach every American Family.

As I cannot speak to the confidentiality of our investigations, nor anyone's Constitutionally protected medical records, including the detective's, in the next section we will learn about my family's heritage, our detective agency, and the measures all Patriotic Americans can take to preserve, protect and defend our businesses, homes, families and our best *'Remedy'* against tyranny, *'The Constitution of the United States'.* Now, let's meet, *'America's Private Eyes'.*

Chapter 5

America's Private Eyes.

Our mother, Roberta *'Bobbie'* Kulesza, circa 1953.

Our mother was the best. I'm sure most Americans feel the exact same of their mothers. We wouldn't be here without them. I would not have been able to start my detective agency without my family, and especially my mother and father. In addition to all Mom taught us of Christianity, she instilled in our souls our Patriotic Duty to uphold *'The Constitution of the United States';* for it is our Nation's *'Equal Justice',* which allows for America to progress with safeguards for a greater future.

In this section I will introduce the private detective's *'Remedy',* our agency, *Stonehenge Ventures, llc [IL Detective Agency # 117-001584]* can provide for Americans to assure future safeguards to our Families, our Freedoms and our *'Bill of Rights'.* But first, we will discover how my family owned and operated detective agency came into existence. To do so, I will begin with a brief history of our Christian-American Heritage. You are invited to meet, *'America's Private Eyes'.*

=======

My Great-Great-Grandparents, Anton and Marie Koss, immigrated from Hamburg, Germany aboard the *'Moravia',* with their children Auguste (age 8), Mathilde (6), Franz (age 2 - or *'Frank'* as he was later known) and my Great Grandmother Martha (4) in 1890.

Great Grandpa (Elmer) Chester is of 100% German ancestry; he was born in the United States a few years before Martha was born in Germany; Chester's mother and father may have also been born in the United States. Nevertheless, Martha and Chester's hearts met in the Great State of Michigan. Great Grandma Martha and our Great Grandpa Chester fell in love. They were married in no time.

Martha and Chester moved across the shores of Lake Michigan to the Windy City of Chicago, Illinois. They got a place with storefronts off Diversy with living quarters attached where they could raise their family. Martha ran the Candy-Shop/Toy-Store on one side of the building. Chester worked only a few feet away as he ran their other family-owned emerging hi-tech business, *'Chicago Radio Service'.*

[My Maternal Great Grandmother Martha – 1886 to 1971.]

Great Grandma Martha was my only great grandparent I met, though I was too young to remember. I really wish I could have met them all. Such wonderful People with so much to pass on to the next generations. Until we meet again Great-Grandma…, Love You.

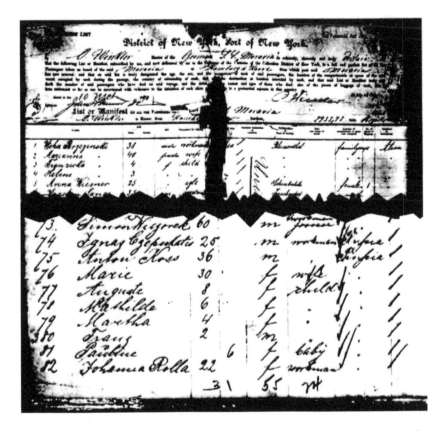

[Great-Grandma Martha, 4 years old - immigrated March 10, 1890.]

Our Great-Grandparents, Martha and Chester's first born was my Grandpa Albert, though he was called *"Elmer"* by everyone who knew him. Grandpa was the oldest of five kids. He helped with his family as all sons and daughters did back in the day.

Grandpa immediately grew an interest in his father's profession; radios. He tinkered with them when he could and repaired them as he grew older. But that wasn't the only task for Grandpa. America wasn't the high-tech world it is now. And Americans were more self-sustainable in our proud past. The cost of sustainability was time and labor.

Chores needed to be accomplished and the animals needed to be tended to. Of course, Grandpa Elmer's brothers and one sister would always help, but Grandpa was great with animals. Being the oldest can be tough, yet he still got to have some fun as a kid. Here's Grandpa Elmer making his way through Chicago with his goat in the early part of the Twentieth Century. Automobiles, once, were not common in America.

[Grandpa Elmer and his goat, 'Billy' patrolling Chicago – circa 1915.]

Our Grandpa Elmer joined the Unites States Army Air Force in the 1920's and became a *'US Army Air Force Radio Operator',* putting his nepotistic skills in service for America. His daughter, my Aunt Kay (Katheryn) joined the US Air Force in years to follow; not long after, his son, my Uncle Kenny (Kenneth), enlisted in the US Navy. The odd thing is, neither Mom nor Dad or even Grandma spoke of Grandpa's service in the US Army Air Force. It made us kids ponder why? Conspiracy theories began to spin around our heads. Grandpa knew how to intercept and transmit radio communications, often traveled, knew lots of prominent folks and worked for the mainstream media... CIA? Naw, can't be?

Our Grandpa Elmer - US Army Air Force - circa 1927.

Grandpa Elmer, after returning from his US Army Air Force service, took over his parent's shop. The Candy-Store/Toy-Shop closed to provide expansion for the new emerging *'Television Service'* industry. The new family business name became *'Chicago Television & Radio Service'*.

[Grandpa Elmer at our *'Chicago Television & Radio Service Shop'*.]

My maternal Grandma Mary was 100% of Irish ancestry, born in America circa 1910 just before her younger sister Harriette. I believe her older siblings were born in Ireland and immigrated to America with her folks. Grandma Mary and her siblings lost their loving mother when she was only five years old. By the time Grandma was 13, her father had passed away too. I can only imagine how tough it was for Grandma Mary and her siblings to be raised in orphanages; I heard stories. My Grandmother's strong Christian values never withered; her and her siblings stuck together through thick and thin. My Great Grandparents must have made quite an impression on them. I wish I could have known my Great Grandparents, Edward and Hattie Walsh. Good Christian Folks.

[Our Maternal Great Grandparents Edward & Harriette 'Hattie' Walsh.]

Our maternal Grandparents, Elmer and Mary instantly fell in love when they first met; marriage soon followed. They raised a family and ran their family business. Years later, our Grandmother went on to work for a legal publication still in business in Chicago, Illinois. My Grandma stirred my interest in American Civics and our legal system... and how to bake chocolate chips cookies too.

Elmer and Mary were always together. Years after Grandpa passed on, my Grandmother told me a story. She had been baking Grandpa his *"favorite dessert"*, pumpkin pie for special occasions since they first met. After a lifetime in love with each other, our Grandfather fessed-up and admitted, though he didn't mind his wife's pumpkin pie, he just told our Grandmother it was his *"favorite"* so he would get a chance to see her again when they first began courting. He was in love and didn't want her to get away. My Grandmother and I laughed at the sweet gesture of deception my Grandfather had carried for so many years. Grandpa Elmer was a kind, caring man. Though young, I remember him. He took us to my first Cubs game at Wrigley Field in '73. Cubs won!

Grandpa Elmer & Grandma Mary at their family-owned business, the *'Chicago Television & Radio Repair Shop'*.

[Our Maternal Grandparents, Elmer & Mary - circa 1929.]

Grandpa was invited to join the *'Free Masons'.* Though he never spoke poorly of them, I don't think *'secret societies'* were for Grandpa. He didn't attend many of the *'Free Mason'* meetings and just stopped going altogether after a while. Or maybe he was just keeping it secret? Grandpa's membership did lead to new work and income opportunities.

Grandpa eventually went to work for a mainstream media network affiliate (there was only three) in Chicago as their *'in-studio'* news camera-operator. His son, my Uncle Kenny would join him at the studio in the years to come. The television cameras were being pointed at the anchors on the nightly network news by my Grandpa and my Uncle Kenny. I thought it was neat as a kid. Mom would show me the TV screen and say, *"Grandpa and Uncle Kenny are broadcasting this."*

While going through old papers, I found a sketch I made which Mom had saved from when I was a kid; it was drawn on back of one of Grandpa's old television news program schedules. I remember Grandma kept the scratch paper in the buffet cabinet. Reduce, Reuse, Recycle.

TV CHICAGO	PROGRAM SCHEDULE & LOG FRIDAY 9/1/1972							PAGE
			FACILITY		PGM SOURCE AND TYPE	SPOT CLASS		
TIME BEGIN END	TITLE ** STUDIO CC **	DUR	VIDEO	AUD				SPONS IDENT
	1972 XXTH OLYMPIAD (CONTD)		AVC	Ø Ø	S			
	15A. PROD LINE	:30						
	15B.	:30						
	16A. RAZOR	:30						
	LCL CUT IN							
	16B. #2312-30	:30	F16- 13B	Ø				(
	17. TV SET/SLACKS							
	:33 LCL STN BRK FLWS :03 NET ID)							
	Ogilvie T#XGOT 0211	:10	TAPE	Ø		CM		Comm. for
	T#KOFR 2038	:10	TAPE	Ø		CM		
	au T#XMRB 0005	:10	TAPE	Ø		CM		
	F) (Video ID)	:03	F16-11A	X		PSA		U.S.O.

[Remnants of Grandpa Elmer's in-studio program schedule - 9/01/1972.]

Grandma and Grandpa traveled the world more than a few times over. It seemed our Grandfather never stopped flying around the world since his days as a US Army Air Force Radio Operator. They loved traveling and got to see it all. Asia, Africa and Europe were regular stops for our world-traveling Grandparents.

Our Grandparents went everywhere together. Paris, London, Athens, Rome, Beijing, Jerusalem and Sydney were just a few cities around the world that saw our grandparents. Promenades on the Great Wall of China, cruises throughout the shores of the Mediterranean Sea, Mass at Notre Dame, attendance at the Colosseum in Rome, hiking the Swiss Alps, visiting the Holy Land and even exploring the Great Pyramid on the Giza Plateau were all part of our grandparents' American romance.

All of my Grandparents have since passed on. We lost both our grandfathers in 1974 when I was still just a toddler, though I remember the times we spent with one another and their infinite kindness. Grandpa Elmer succumbed to heart-disease. 'Tetrahydrocannabinol' (THC), found in marijuana claims to treat many illnesses from which our families suffer.

Grandpa told me he got the camel from a *"tentmaker"* named *"Omar"*.

Grandpa Elmer atop his camel on the Giza Plateau, circa 1959.

Grandma Mary seeing me off before my 'Junior-Year-High School-Prom', Spring 1986.

[Our Grandmother Mary aboard the *'Statue of Liberty Ferry'* traveling in New York with 48 Stars adorning our American Flag, circa 1957.]

Grandma Mary loved to play tennis with us. Doubles was always fun. I don't think Grandma and I ever lost a match. Of course, we were not playing in competitions. We only played tennis with family and friends - but it was a blast. Grandma always spoke about the next time we would play. She was even up for tennis the last day I saw her.

Grandma Mary passed away peacefully in her sleep at home one night in 1989. Her heart couldn't go another day without him. She had joined Grandpa, her true love, reunited once again, to be together for all eternity.

[Our Grandma Marie and Grandpa Michael Kulesza, circa 1927.]

My Fraternal Grandparents were both born in the United States. They fell in love and kept falling in love. They had a huge family with nine kids giving me a total eight aunts and uncles, sixteen total through marriage, with 27 cousins just on my dad's side alone! I find that number amazing. I had 33 first cousins total; with their spouses, kids, grandkids and great grandkids, and all our aunts, uncles, grandparents, great-grandparents and great-great-grandparents, our family *'get-togethers'* look like a parade has come to town.

Today, large families are far and few between. Population control has become all too common. I would guess mainly due to suppressed economies in an over-regulated *'Free Market'*. My Grandfather worked as a carpenter providing for his big family through the *'Great Depression'*, while Grandma Marie did a divine job raising Dad and his siblings, all with our Christian Faith and a Patriotic sense of duty to America.

My Grandmother, Marie, was born in Joliet, Illinois. She was born in her home as many Americans chose a more natural environment for birth back in the day. Plus, hospitals were mostly for sick, contagious people during the turn of the century. My father tells me his grandparents had cows, goats, pigs and chickens at their property. All the neighbors had some livestock back then. It sounds like our government promoted self-sustainability more so at times throughout our US History than at others.

Another interesting thing Dad told me was his grandparent's home where my grandmother was born was located across the street from Joliet State Prison in Illinois. An iconic American Musical Film begins its opening music at a point when one brother awaits the release of his sibling outside the prison gates. That was right across where our Great Grandparents lived. Dad wasn't sure, but thought their property was exactly where the actors were standing. The camera was likely on my Great-Grandparents' former front yard.

My Grandma Marie's mother, my Great Grandmother Stefanek spoke nine languages fluently. When I discovered that, I asked Dad if she was a college professor. He smiled and said she was not. Dad explained, my Great Grandma was from Eastern Europe during a time of warlords. Staying in a village under siege meant the men would be killed and horrible things for the women – so people often moved. And as we all know, unlike most America, moving a few hundred miles away in Europe can place one in a different dialect. My Great Grandmother Stefanek needed to learn the languages so they could survive in a war-torn Europe.

The violence is what prompted my Great Grandma Stefanek to become a United States Citizens, where the Rights of the People are safeguarded by our US Constitution. Today, immigration is a hot-topic. Some residents of America are here illegally but refuse to ask for asylum or refuge from whatever they are escaping. Legal immigration was the only way for my ancestors. Thanks, Great Grandma Stefanek. Though we never met, I owe you everything as we do all our ancestors. Thank you.

My Grandfather Michael M. Kulesza was a great man. He was well respected in their Chicago neighborhood. A self-employed carpenter running his own business since he was a young man, Grandpa provided for a huge family through the lean years of World War II. His neighbors appreciated his generosity in always lending his helping-hand.

Grandpa Kulesza was born in Chicago after the turn of the century. His mother and father were married in Europe. His mother was German, and his father was from Prussia. Some in my family say different places, but perhaps it was because they feared being called *"Russians"* during our *'Cold War'*. Some also claim Poland as the country of Poland makes up a large portion of what was formerly known as Prussia. But my fraternal ancestors sharing my surname were from the area of the borderland near Poland and Belarus, just east of the Baltic Sea. The land was known as *'White Russia'*. It was a province of the United Soviet Socialist Republic (USSR) for many years and later became the countries we know today as Latvia, Lithuania and Belarus. In my understanding, *'Bela"* can be translated as *"inside, pure"* or *"white"*; *'Bela-Rus'* basically means, *'White Russian'* or *'White Ruski'* after the ancient land of Ruthenia. The name likely derived from when our European ancestors stopped the *'Mongol Onslaught'* and preserved their purity threatened by warlords trying to disrupt the gene-pool. Tyrants wanted our woman.

Grandpa Michael had suffered a stroke and was partially disabled in his 60's. Not too long after, he suffered another stroke and didn't survive our mortal realm. Grandpa Kulesza passed on in 1974, the same year as our other Grandpa Elmer was taken by heart disease. Grandma Marie walked everywhere in Chicago and didn't own a car. I don't believe she even had a driver's license in her later years. It kept her healthy. She lived 96 years on Earth and was able to hold her Great-Great-Grand Daughter in her arms. But eventually Grandma Marie began to rapidly decline from *'Alzheimer's Disease'*. First the disease affected her memory. Eventually her whole body was shut down by the de-habilitating condition. In 2008 Grandma joined her eternal love, Grandpa. After 34 long years apart, they were together again. Marijuana treats Alzheimer's.

Our Dad, Ralph M. Kulesza with sister, 'Bunny' and parents, circa 1935.

Our father, Ralph M. Kulesza was the oldest son of nine children. As a young man, my father studied hard and worked hard as was taught to him by his devout Christian parents.

[Our Dad, Ralph M. Kulesza – circa 1942 & September 1953.]

Our father received top grades at his Chicago schools where he became a letterman in track and other sports activities. After high school classes, Dad was a lifeguard at Chicago's Oak Street Beach where he earned money to help-out his huge family while saving some for college. Saving others from drowning was something our Dad did on a regular basis. He was quite the swimmer. One of my uncles said he once saw our Dad sleeping on the water as if he was atop a floatation device. As it turned out, Dad wasn't on anything except the waves ~ catching a nap.

Dad went on to serve in the US Army from the early 1950's to 1961. As a *'Scout Patrol'*, Dad defended and patrolled our borders with German shepherds. Dad hunted spies and enemy combatants trying to cross into US Army held territory. For a short spell Dad also put his wrestling skills to work as a self-defense instructor for our US Army.

[Our Dad, Ralph M. Kulesza, 33rd Light Infantry Scout Patrol, 1953-1961.]

The genes passed down from Grandpa and Grandma to our Dad gave him blonde hair, blues eyes and a height of over six feet, three inches tall. This classical Germanic-look prompted our US Government to offer jobs to our father when he was in the service, to work under-cover posing as a corporate electronics salesman to gather intelligence throughout Eastern Europe for the Central Intelligence Agency (CIA). Our father told us he kindly declined the multiple offers. Dad chose to return home where he could help-out his folks, open a business and start a family of his own. Thank you, Dad.

[Our father, Ralph M. Kulesza – US Army - circa 1954.]

Our father officially departed from the US Army with an Honorable Discharge at the end of 1961 after suffering partial hearing loss along with injuries to his knees and back during his service.

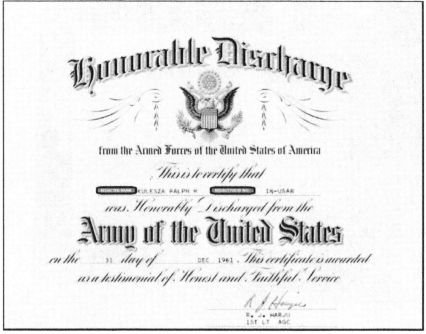

[Our Dad, Ralph M. Kulesza's Honorable Discharge, December 31, 1961.]

The crazy thing was, the military lost our father's, and several other service members' military records in a big fire at an Army storage warehouse in the early 1960's when JFK was making headlines. I believe the fire was in the Great State of Missouri if my memory serves? Many vets, just like Dad, were also denied their United States military service *'just compensation'* for their disabilities.

Mom and Dad fell in love upon our father's return from his service to our country. Not long after that, they were married. They were terrific parents. Dad attended Northwestern University and worked at a few companies in the Chicagoland area, while mom prepared our home for the family they were about to build upon.

My oldest sibling was born just days before Dad graduated from Northwestern in Evanston, Illinois.

[Ralph M. Kulesza, Northwestern University Graduate, June 15, 1963.]

After graduation, Dad landed a great job involving his two passions: literature and finance. He was hired by the largest media distribution company in the central United States. It's distribution hub, located in the Chicagoland area, was strategically located in the Midwest, extending its influence for publishing houses from coast to coast. Our father's title at the media company, ultimately, was as their *'Publishers Financial Manager',* where he helped close book deals with some of the world's biggest authors and most recognizable names.

Dad made a decent living. We were proud of him. Mom and Dad were able to save money and invest in businesses. First, our parents bought a tavern in Chicago on Milwaukee Avenue just after we had moved to the suburbs. Dad kept his job and worked the late shift and weekends at the tavern. Our Mom convinced Dad to sell our share to his brothers. Our folks reinvested in a store nearer our new suburban home.

[Our Dad's, Ralph M. Kulesza – Press Passes 1963 to 1992.]

I looked up to my father, as most folks do theirs. Yet when it came to his work, I envied him. Our dad worked with famous people and celebrities just about every day. Big names like First Lady Betty Ford, George Burns, Jim Brown, Lady Colin Campbell, Ali MacGraw, Martha Stewart, Tony Randall, Shirley MacClaine and even controversial publisher Larry Flynt were just some of the celebrities he worked closely with that sit on the forefront of my thoughts.

And then there were the recognizable authors our father worked with, of the likes of John Grisham, Stephen King, Catherine Coulter, Norman Mailer and many more, including famed *'Private Eye'* novelist, Mickey Spillane (one of my favorites).

Our father, Ralph M. Kulesza, worked close with both fiction and non-fiction authors like American iconic automaker, Lee Iacocca.

[Our father, Ralph M. Kulesza with American Industrialist-Automaker, Lee Iacocca - May 1991.]

Back in the day, I once remember Dad finishing an editor's copy of a book, still in the works I believe, from a relatively unknown author at that time. Dad rarely spoke about the thousands of books he read for work; but he knew I would like the one he just finished. Dad said the book was so good they would instantly make it into a movie. I asked him what the book was about. Dad told me a fantastical story of an unbelievable wildlife attraction on a tropical island. He said the attractions at the park were genetically engineered dinosaurs from prehistoric blood found inside mosquitos preserved within fossilized tree amber. He was right. Hollywood made a classic monster flick we all know.

Dad was a fan of Charlton *'Chuck'* Heston. Heston and our Dad became friends in the months they worked together during the publishing of Heston's journals. I still have his autograph; Charlton Heston's autograph, not my Dad's - lol. As many know, Charlton Heston was also a spokesman for one of the largest national firearm lobbies. It was cool to be at home watching *"The Ten Commandments"* on television and then Dad walks in telling us who he just had dinner with. I saved the photo from the last time Dad saw his old friend Chuck.

[Our father, Ralph M. Kulesza – publisher's party with former NRA head and American Film Legend, Charlton Heston - circa 1979.]

Our father, Ralph M. Kulesza with General H. Norman Schwarzkopf -
May 1992.

Though our father only knew General H. Norman Schwarzkopf for a brief time, they became immediate friends sharing their old war stories. Our father, Ralph Kulesza helped closed the book deal for the General's autobiography in the early 1990's. Some may remember General H. Norman Schwarzkopf as Commander of *'Operation Desert Storm'*, the most successful military campaign in recorded history. Our father retired from the publishing industry by the mid 1990's, not long after meeting his new friend, the General.

=======

For a brief history on myself: I am an American Patriot and Christian who loves his family and our country. I was born in the late 1960's in Chicago. Our family went to church every week. My older siblings taught me algebra before I learned to read the alphabet in kindergarten. I learned the words to *'The Star-Spangled Banner'* in Cub Scouts. I received good grades in school until we moved to the suburbs and found their public-school district didn't always have enough seats for all the new students. Some claimed it was a good thing because the school also saw an increase in the number of troublemakers matching exactly the rate of extra-student seat shortages. Isn't that convenient?

Years later, as an adult I became friends with a public high school teacher. The way my teacher friend explained things to me was the teacher's union contracted teachers to be paid for students that receive passing grades in a contractually-set classroom size. If the classroom size increases due to population growth, the teacher would get a substantial pay-bonus for any additional students who received a passing grade beyond the contracted number of students allowed in a normal size classroom. My friend explained for teachers who are not tenured, nor guaranteed a job, it is in their best interest to appease the school district's wishes (even if their wishes are not spoken aloud). The bonus money paid to a teacher for passing additional students would need to come from the school's budget. My public-school district's budget paid for carpeted hallways, a professional-drainage-tiled baseball diamond (most colleges couldn't afford), lights on the football field (rarely did a high school have lights on the field), several tennis courts (now at least double that), three indoor gymnasiums, two weight-rooms (one just for the athletes), an Olympic-sized indoor heated swimming pool and an indoor planetarium at the largest of the middle schools. Nice, huh? Expensive? You bet.

[Author/Detective Matthew P. Kulesza – Chicago Shoreline, circa 1974.]

Toward the end of high school, I went to the US Navy recruiter and took the test. The Navy recruiter said he had never seen such a high score on an entrance exam in all his military career; he was being flattering I suppose. The recruiter said he would like me to join our United States Navy and drive nuclear submarines. That sounded perfect to me. But before I could enlist I needed to speak with my parents as I was still only 17 years old. School was over in a few weeks and I would be back.

Then tragedy struck me. Playing sports after getting home from the last day of high school, I twisted my knee 180 degrees backwards. When I hit the ground the first pain I felt was in my backend; then I saw my left foot was turned backwards and pain streaked through me. Dad was home, and he pulled my leg straight, popping my knee back where it was supposed to be. Mom and Dad drove me to the emergency room. By the next day I had a cast on my left leg for several weeks.

After getting my cast off, I worked hard to rebuild the strength in my leg. Before I was totally back to 100%, tragedy struck again. A popular kid everyone knew from town got a bit rowdy while he randomly wrestled folks walking about, without their consent. He was a real nice guy but, my good right knee was folded backward 90 degrees, my hamstring was torn and my anterior cruciate ligament (ACL) snapped. I knew the ER would only offer a brace; I already had one. So, I wore my knee-brace until the knee began to feel stronger, then I folded it backwards again. Pain subsided after months; then I dislocated it again, and again, and again. Each time I dislocated it I did more damage to the surrounding tissue and needed more time for the pain to subside. Clearly, I needed surgery.

At the beginning of the 1990's I had complete reconstructive ACL surgery. The doctor drilled holes though the bottom of my femur (thigh bone) and the top of my tibia (shin bone). Then the doctor threaded a graft of my patellar tendon through the holes in my knee bones, securing it into both bones with titanium screws, thereby simulating the anterior cruciate ligament that was snapped. I don't think the insurance covered the torn hamstring; so, I have only one and the other leg now shares.

I asked the doc if I would be able to engage in heavy physical activity like playing sports. He explained my knees had dislocated when I was perfectly healthy. Now that I was injured with a reconstructed knee and a missing hamstring, he stated competitive sports would not be recommended. I had to try and get my leg stronger than the doctor thought it would become. Muscles can strengthen, but joints are only as strong as the ligaments and tendons with which we were born.

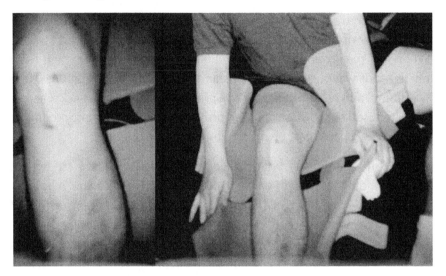

[ACL reconstructive surgery staples - circa 1991]

After a year of allowing my knee to heal while working feverishly on my leg strength, I went back to the recruiters, now in my early twenties. At first, the recruiter didn't remember me, but he remembered my test score. The Navy recruiter asked where I had been. I avoided talking of the knee problems the best I could, but *'truth will out'*.

I down-played my injury to the recruiter and explained I would be very willing to sign a waiver for my reconstructed knee and bad hamstring as I saw a change in the sailor's demeanor looking down to my legs. The US Naval recruiter was very kind. But he said the US Navy was not going to happen in my future.

My hopes and dreams of following in my grandfather's and my father's footsteps were shattered. I held my head high and tried to hide my disappointment, though the recruiter could see I was troubled by the revelation. He said, *"I'm sorry, son,"* as I shook his hand and thanked him for taking the time to speak with me again.

I considered, at one time, becoming a police officer to serve our country, but I could see how a few cops in our town treated good folks, neighbors, seniors and even kids. It wasn't something I could be a part of. Please don't misunderstand, law enforcement is absolutely necessary. And all law enforcement officers put their life on the line daily. But a few bad apples can spoil the bunch in the eyes of public opinion.

I needed something else where I could apply my skills more effectively and still serve *'We the People'*. I was tackling the crippling effects from dislocated knees and a snapped hamstring when I learned how expensive life could become as I tried to pay my own way through community colleges.

Once out of the stifling environment of union-regulated classrooms of high school, I was back to receiving top grades (when work wasn't getting in the way). Once virtual-distance-learning classrooms and telecourses became more prevalent, I made a push to finish college – but never quite made it to graduation. It was rough paying for school. I worked and was forced to attend only part-time. I took a few semesters off here and there to help-out my folks. By my mid-twenties, I was running out of 200 level courses to take at the community colleges. For my family, I needed to contribute something more than student debt.

===

In the late 1990's, as I was still attempting to work my way through college, our father felt ill one afternoon, home alone, and thought he would drive himself to the hospital. After driving the distance to the hospital, our father was stopped just before the hospital's driveway entrance by a police officer who noticed him swerve slightly.

My father attempted to explain to the officer he was trying to reach the hospital as he was becoming more ill; cell phones were not a common thing back in the 1990's. But as my father started to have a stroke, his words began to slur. The officer mistook the warning-signs of a stroke as our father being drunk; but dad wasn't a drinker and tried to explain to the officer. The policeman wouldn't listen as he pulled our father from the driver's seat. Dad's stroke caused his heart to stop there on the roadside in front of the hospital as he was detained by the police officer for a search and sobriety test. Our US Army veteran was down.

According to what we were told, the police officer, out of protocol, finally realizing our father was seizing from a stroke, at some point called for an ambulance to drive Dad the few hundred feet to the ER entrance doors. Several minutes passed before the doctors were able to get our father's heart started again. Oxygen had been deprived to his brain for too long. Our father spent three days in a coma in the hospital's ICU (Intensive Care Unit). Doctors didn't know if he would survive. After waking, it took him a couple of days to begin to speak clearly and almost a week before Dad was able to recognize all his family and friends.

Our veteran father spent the next three months in a Christian rehabilitation hospital where he learned to walk and perform daily tasks again. The left side of his body, and some of his right side, had suffered paralysis; some paralysis would be permanent leaving crippling effects beyond his already injured knees from his service in the US Army. The police? I asked for a dashcam video, but it seems to have been misplaced or deleted? I never heard back from the police department. Dad needed my help. With his military disability papers still missing for decades, I didn't hold out much hope for the dashcam video.

When my father was able to return home from the Christian rehabilitation hospital he needed full-time help. Our senior mother wasn't in a position to do it alone. I became my father's primary caregiver from that point on. I had to find a job and forget about getting a college degree (that was burying most all of America's students in debt anyways).

Knee injuries and reconstructive surgery kept the US Navy from accepting me. Retail couldn't cover the bills and executive jobs were for college grads. Of course, my family helped-out a bunch, but more was needed.

I needed a career. Follow your passions, I was once told, and success will follow. Mom and I loved to go to the movies together; suspense, comedy, sci-fi, action flicks and detective movies would occupy our free time. Dad would bring home detective novels and I'd tear through them. Dad and I always watched detective shows on the tube. Our weekends saw maybe even an old *'Sherlock Holmes'* flick. It made sense when I saw in the classifieds a detective agency hiring and willing to train motivated people. My parents needed my support more than ever. Dad's savings weren't lasting after his stroke as healthcare costs kept increasing; we could all see that. This was my new career. I began working as a private investigator with an Illinois PERC card in 2003.

After several years working with an Illinois detective *'permit'* (PERC card) for good detective agencies and bad, I was able to qualify to take the Illinois detective license exam, to obtain my own license and follow our family tradition of opening my own family business. I wouldn't be surprised to learn if 99%, who take the Illinois detective exam, fail. It's a tough test; that's why the State of Illinois allows for an additional method of licensing to avoid the dreaded exam. The alternative licensing method in Illinois is called, *"Licensure by Endorsement"*; this is where one obtains a license in a state where it isn't as difficult, and then gets some noteworthy member of society, a politician or military officer, industry leader, etcetera, to *"endorse"* their application to become an Illinois private detective. *Voila.*

Fearful I too would fail the expensive detective exam, I called and asked the Illinois Department of Financial and Professional Regulation if just anyone could *'endorse'* my application. I was told, *'yes'*. But when I asked if it would better assure approval if the endorsement came from a governor or congressman instead of, say, my mom, the IDFPR representative replied, *"Probably yes"*. As Illinois allows only licensed detectives to open a business, and not PERC card holders, I had to try for our family. After years of meeting the qualifying requirements and intensive studying, I succeeded on the Illinois private detective exam and opened our detective agency, Stonehenge Ventures, llc [IL license number 117-001584] in 2011, right in our home State of Illinois.

Passing the detective exam was good news and there was more on the way. My father was a patient, two to three days every week at the VA Veteran's Hospital in North Chicago, Illinois since his stroke in the late 1990's. During that time, he met many veterans on his regular visits. My father became friends with a Colonel he met at the VA Hospital. After the Colonel heard our Dad was one of the many veterans who had their military disability papers burned during the early 1960's in a huge fire at an Army storage warehouse, the Colonel made some phone calls. My dad's new friend, the Colonel, was able to locate some salvaged copies of my father's partially-burned military disability papers. Thanks Colonel.

Dad was soon getting a little extra money every month for his disabilities from injuries suffered during his service in the United States Army. Dad, in good spirits, sarcastically joked with the Colonel if he thought the Army would reimburse the lost interest over almost 50 years; our Dad's passion for finance calculated the interest at well over $2,500,000.00. The Colonel and Dad broke into laughter knowing the US Army rarely pays such claims. If the US Army did pay, they could owe the same to the thousands, maybe even hundreds of thousands of others who were robbed of their military disability *'just compensation'*.

I had the great honor of caring for our father until the day he passed. My father died in our home under hospice care at midnight on December 30, 2013. Dad's health took a downward turn at the beginning of that year; he began losing balance and falling. The civilian hospital he was taken to explained he had congestive heart failure for *"at least six years"* as it was in *"end-stage"*. I guess Dad's VA missed it? The People at the VA are terrific; but the system seemed to be very slow and a bit out of sorts. Our veterans could sure use our prayers and our assistance.

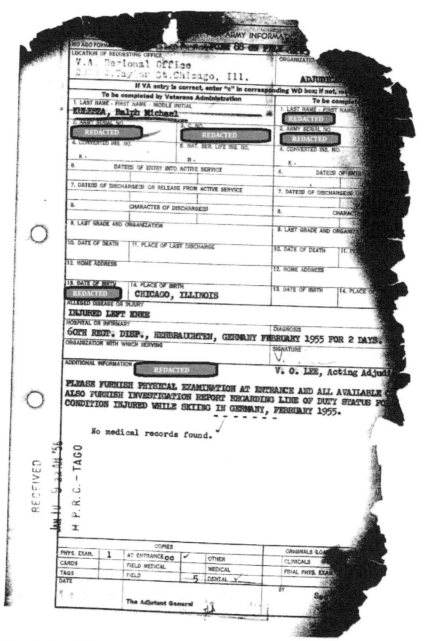

[Our Dad, Ralph M. Kulesza's found military disability papers; pg. 1 of 6.]

REQUEST FOR MEDICAL/DENTAL RECORDS

1. TO: Commanding Officer 34th ISDP APO 176, New York, New York	**2. FROM:** ☐ The Adjutant General Washington 25, D. C. ATTN: AGPI- ☒ CO. Military Personnel Re 4700 Goodfellow Boulevard St. Louis 20, Missouri ATTN: AGBC-D
3. PATIENT (*Last Name – First Name – Middle Initial*) Kulesza, Ralph M.	**4. SERVICE NUMBER (S)** REDACTED
	5. VIA CLAIM NUMBER REDACTED

6. ORGANIZATION AND PLACE OF TREATMENT	7. DATES OF TREATMENT (*Incl*)	8. DISEASE OR INJURY
REDACTED	Feb 1955	Left knee inju

9. RECORDS REQUESTED

☐ CLINICAL
☐ OUT-PATIENT
☐ DENTAL REGISTER
☐ X-RAY
☐ MEDICAL REPORT CARDS. EMERGENCY TAGS. FIELD MEDICAL CARDS
☐ OTHERS (*See remarks*)
☒ ALL AVAILABLE RECORDS (*Search will include all hospital, dispensary, clinics, or other medical facilities*)

10. REMARKS
** Also furnish investigation r garding Line of Duty Status

11. SIGNATURE
By Order of Wilber M. Brucker, Secretary of t

NOTE: *Records described above should be forwarded, if available, or negative reply furnished direct to the address shown under item 12 below.*

Adjutant Gen

FIRST INDORSEMENT (*See instructions on reverse side*)

12. TO: Veterans Administration Regional Office 2030 W. Taylor St. Chicago, Ill.	13. ACTION TAKEN ☐ AVAILABLE RECORDS INCLOSED ☐ NO RECORDS ON FILE
14. ____ INCLOSURES (*Number of*) ____ CLINICAL ____ OUT-PATIENT ____ DENTAL REGISTER ____ X-RAY ____ MEDICAL REPORT CARDS. EMERGENCY MEDICAL TAGS. FIELD MEDICAL CARDS ____ OTHER	15. REMARKS
	16. SIGNATURE
DATE	

TAGO FORM 104
1 MAR 54

[Our Dad, Ralph M. Kulesza's found military disability papers; pg. 2 of 6.]

REPORT OF MEDICAL HISTORY

THIS INFORMATION IS FOR OFFICIAL USE ONLY AND WILL NOT BE RELEASED TO UNAUTHORIZED

REDACTED

REDACTED

Separation

U S Army

REDACTED

REDACTED

15. EXAMINING FACILITY OR EXAMINER AND ADDRESS
US Army Infirmary, Ft. Sheridan, Ill.

[Our Dad, Ralph M. Kulesza's found military disability papers; pg. 3 of 6.]

	52. WEIGHT	53. COLOR HAIR	54. COLOR EYES	55.
HEIGHT	171½	Blonde	Hazel	

57. BLOOD PRESSURE (Arm at heart level) | **58. PULSE (Arm at heart level)**

	SYS.	RECUM.	SYS.	STANDING (3 min.)	SYS.	SITTING	AFTER EXERCISE
SITTING	126	BENT				96	104
	DIAS. 80		DIAS.		DIAS.		

59. DISTANT VISION		60.		REFRACTION		61.
RIGHT 20/ 20	CORR. TO 20/		BY	S.	CR	
LEFT 20/ 20	CORR. TO 20/		BY	S.	CX	

62. HETEROPHORIA (Specify distance)	ES°	EX°	R. H.	L. H.	PRISM DIV.	PRISM CONV.

63. ACCOMMODATION		64. COLOR VISION (Test used and result)	65. DEPTH PERCEPTION (Test used and score)	UNCORRECTED
RIGHT	LEFT			CORRECTED
66. FIELD OF VISION		67. NIGHT VISION (Test used and score)	68. RED LENS	

70. HEARING	71.	AUDIOMETER							72. PSYCHOLOGICAL
		250	500	1000	2000	3000	4000	6000	
RIGHT WV 15 /15 SV 15/15	RIGHT								
LEFT WV 15 /15 SV 15/15	LEFT								

73. NOTES (Continued) AND SIGNIFICANT OR INTERVAL HISTORY

Heat, overwork, stuffiness always give him dizzy spells- Fell over only
Burning pain or pulling in chest - following cold or swimming in cold
Cramp in stomach relieved by vomiting- may occur weekly at times or on
Coughed up blood(on field problem bad cold) as blood streaked mucous
Back sore- 2 months spring 55. No trouble since June 55
Left knee requires wrapping occasionally "torn cartilage"-injured while

(Use additional sheets of plain paper if necessary)

74. SUMMARY OF DEFECTS AND DIAGNOSES (List diagnoses with item numbers)

75. RECOMMENDATIONS—FURTHER SPECIALIST EXAMINATIONS INDICATED (Specify) | 76. | P U
| | 1

77. EXAMINEE (Check) IS QUALIFIED FOR — IS NOT QUALIFIED FOR

78. IF NOT QUALIFIED, LIST DISQUALIFYING DEFECTS BY ITEM NUMBER | A B

79. TYPED OR PRINTED NAME OF PHYSICIAN | SIGNATURE

80. TYPED OR PRINTED NAME OF PHYSICIAN | SIGNATURE

81. TYPED OR PRINTED NAME OF DENTIST OR PHYSICIAN (Indicate which) | SIGNATURE

TYPED OR PRINTED NAME OF REVIEWING OFFICER OR APPROVING AUTHORITY | SIGNATURE

U. S. GOVERNMENT PRINTING OFFICE   16—02288—1

[Our Dad, Ralph M. Kulesza's found military disability papers; pg. 4 of 6.]

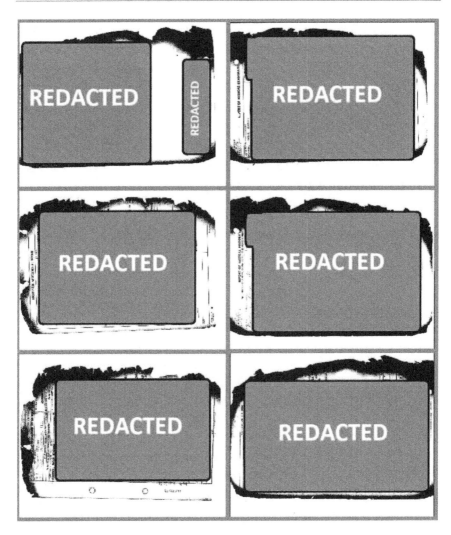

[Pgs. 1 thru 6 of our Dad's, Ralph M. Kulesza's found disability papers, missing almost 50 years after Army fire - $2,500,000 in lost interest.]

Neither Dad, nor mom or I ever held a grudge toward the VA; we only wished we could've assisted them to help more veterans. What the Veteran's Administration needs, in my humble opinion, is more medical staff and less wounded vets. Easier said than done, I am sure. I'm still praying for miracles. I believe in America.

But it is important for the People to understand, World Peace is profitable for those outside the *'Military Industrial Complex'*, but rarely within it. As campaign dollars come pouring in from industrial leaders and corporate banks, the American People are placed in greater danger by a globalist agenda to destroy individual Freedoms and national sovereignty. Our Grandparents traveled the world over and national sovereignty was celebrated by each country welcoming the tourism. Things have changed. And it is certainly never a good time to infringe upon any American Rights, especially in a world full of tyrannical desires.

Our mother, who was also suffering from a weak heart, fell ill while home alone, after a family celebration breakfast at one of our favorite restaurants. Though mom had a *'DNR'* – *"Do Not Resuscitate"* healthcare directive for emergency workers, the paramedics my mother was able to call before losing consciousness, ignored her DNR while police kept our arriving family out of the home as they began CPR inside. After at least 12 minutes without oxygen, the paramedics restarted our mother's heart. It may have been 18 minutes or longer; we're not sure.

Our mother never woke from her coma. For six days we stayed with Mom in the Intensive Care Unit as she suffered wincing, back-arching seizures every few minutes. We listened to an ICU doctor, who's native language was not English, mispronounce the word *"there"* as the word *"dead"* might be phonetically pronounced, over and over again, confusing our family and the hospital staff who was hearing the same phonetic pronunciation as we heard from the doctor's broken English.

Our family and the ICU staff couldn't understand why the ICU doctor after making his examination was saying our mother's brain was *"not dead"* when actually, the foreign-born doctor was failing to inform us, *"Your mother's brain is not THERE."*

Lost in translation, we were done watching our mother wince in pain, arching her back from the hospital bed as she suffered seizure after seizure. Mom never wanted to be on life support machines in a hospital.

On the sixth day, we brought Mom back home in hospice care. Our mother passed away at our family home, just about 11 minutes after she arrived on March 11, 2016, with her children at her side. She survived cancer surgery in 1977, 1987, and 2007. We miss you dearly, Mom. Our world misses all our mothers and fathers, grandmothers and grandfathers we've lost. It pains Americans to consider the squandering of our Rights and healthcare for which we all continue to pay so dearly.

=======

We have a very large family of aunts and uncles, cousins and new generations of family too. Many of our cousins, male and female, as well as our uncles and even my Aunt Kay joined the US Armed Forces. But I want to speak of one cousin in particular; our Cousin Craig.

Craig was older than I by a few years, but that didn't matter because our family is very close. I grew up just around the corner from his home. He joined the US Navy in the late 70's as a high school graduate. Craig never intended to make a career out of the military. Instead, he too wanted to start his own family business – the American Dream. Craig was good with building things, mechanics, carpentry; he was a real talent.

Our cousin eventually moved out to the West Coast after the military. California had work and beautiful weather – at least milder than Chicago's. As life happens, I lost touch with our cousin as families sometimes do; but in our family, it never mattered. Whence reunited it was as if we were never apart. I always assumed I would have more time to catch-up and strengthen our already strong family ties. Plus, our family is so big, if I wasn't speaking with a cousin, I figured my other family members were. But sadly, I discovered, sometimes, that's not the case.

By the time I realized no one had heard from our Cousin Craig, our family received tragic news. Craig was working as a self-employed carpenter. A man he worked with had collected the money for a job they did together; and Craig was to stop by and pick up his payment. The man and the man's girlfriend had different ideas for our cousin and his money.

From what little information was available, it appears the female testified against her boyfriend who shot and murdered our Cousin Craig with a shotgun. According to an appeal summary, the man told her he would kill our cousin as she waited in the bedroom where they concealed the shotgun. When Craig arrived, he was murdered for his $700 dollars.

The couple were reported by MSM to have left our cousin's body to rot in their apartment for five days. Then, as they feared the stench of a corpse decomposing would expose their crime, Craig's body was driven to a field and lit on fire in an attempt to conceal forensics evidence of the murder and our cousin's identity. Craig's car, which was left at the killer's residence, was dumped along a remote highway to cover their tracks.

Eventually, through the sharing of information the dedicated police investigators were able to identify our cousin's body, notify his next of kin, and catch the couple still living in their home with the stench of death lingering in the air, I'm sure. I mention the important and crucial *'sharing of information'* as after tragedy was reported at *"Sandy Hook School in Newtown, Connecticut"* in 2012, legislators passed stifling laws to prevent the sharing of information in shootings. This makes no sense.

In my professional investigative experience, any action by legislators to suppress vital and critical information only helps criminal killers regardless of what their *"professional investigators"* may say. Identifying information can be redacted to protect family identities from leaking to the press - which has never been a problem in the past. There's no reason to suppress information of a killer's *'modus operandi';* and there's every reason to share the information crucial to prevent further tragedy as *'We the People'* protect our country, our families, our children.

When NASA, America's *'National Aeronautical Space Administration',* believes an asteroid, meteor or comet may collide with our planet threatening all existence, NASA doesn't tell everyone not to look up because that's NASA's job. No. NASA pleads with the public to assist in protecting our planet, our home, our families, our children, our future as we are invited to search the skies for threats. But in Newtown, Connecticut, only their professional investigators are worthy of investigating to prevent further shootings? How's that working?

Our Cousin Craig – 1962 to 2011

Our Cousin Craig's killer was convicted of murder and imprisoned after the killer's girlfriend provided testimony against him. She was at very least a witness who failed to report the murder; it seems she may have been freed in exchange for her testimony and now living in California somewhere? Even the online mainstream media updated their stories and removed her face from their archived feature photos years after reporting on our cousin's murder. Not much can be found on either one of the two originally charged. Are they Americans? Does she still have her 2nd Amendment Right? Or is it only law-abiding American Citizens like the detective and President of the United States Jimmy Carter who lose theirs? Obviously, our country's Constitution and our Rights are under attack. These infringements cost American lives.

=======

As I started our detective agency, Stonehenge Ventures, llc, it helped to have morally supportive parents. Mom assisted whenever she could. And Dad worked as our agency's forensic investigator. Dad's military, forensic and business finance experience helped my agency immensely. Mom's infinite patience, office skills and expertise in logistics was an invaluable resource to our family's practice.

Our parents were Patriotic Americans who took us to church every Sunday, taught us to respect ourselves and others, respect our country, our Constitution, and to respect our American Flag. Our father would warn of those who want to seize our 2nd Amendment and firearms. Dad was not a huge gun-fanatic at all; but he knew world history as well as anyone. Our father understood thieves and lone-gunmen are the least of America's concerns when it comes to providing safeguards *'being necessary to the security of a free State'*. It is the tyrants who pose the greatest threat to American Freedoms, and ultimately American Families.

North Korea, Iran, the Taliban, drug cartels, terrorists and even world powers like China also all agree with the anti-2nd Amendment lobby that Americans should surrender their firearms and 2nd Amendment Rights, *'being necessary to the security of a free State.'*

Folks, *'Gun-Free-Zones'* like public schools are extremely attractive to those criminals who mean to do harm to Americans and our children. And it seems school shootings are occurring almost as regularly as anti-2nd Amendment advertisements. It makes you wonder. There is never a time for anyone to be infringing upon law-abiding Americans and their Constitutional Rights. The cost is too high.

Many Americans' firearms continue to be family-heirlooms, to be kept by their family's future generations so they may continue to protect their families, their homes, and our beloved country from ever present tyranny. No one is suggesting a sole Patriot can defend a nation. But a well-Armed populace, *'being necessary to the security of a free State'* is the best defense against tyrants of all makes and sizes. They become deterred as pause it put into the hearts and minds of America's enemies, when *'We the People'* Stand Armed and United. America's Forefathers knew it; my father knew it. I know it. *'We the People of the United States'* know and understand it better than any others.

What has happened to the detective and millions of Americans, overnight, is wrong. If this can happen to a detective who went out of his way to remain in compliance, then what chance do others have? It needs to stop before these un-Constitutional *'rules'* destroy any more of our precious Liberties. We must Unite to strengthen our American Family from *'Sea to Shining Sea'*.

I've worked with many great detectives over the years. I've personally trained dozens upon dozens of private detectives for different agencies all over our United States. They came from a variety of careers in all walks of life. From law enforcement, military, politics, business owners, retail clerks, musicians and artists, all have made for successful private detectives. Those I have worked with have always acted to the standards that make Americans proud. From police officers to the Army, Navy, Air Force, Marines and even federal agents too, it is always an honor to work among those who put forth all they could for our fellow Americans and our United States.

Personally, for myself and my family, I was planning on a humble retirement someday of hunting, fishing and gardening at a ranch. And perhaps even writing that great detective novel to inspire the next generation of young Americans. I never needed fame or notoriety. That was not the intent of this book. This book should never have needed to be written. Our American Constitution should never need lawyers or detectives for Americans to interpret our access to our *'Bill of Rights'*.

=======

'But when a long train of abuses and usurpations, pursuing invariably the same Object evinces a design to reduce them under absolute Despotism, it is their right, it is their duty, to throw off such Government, and to provide new Guards for their future security'

The Declaration of Independence

July 4, 1776

=======

I would like to invite all law-abiding Americans who wish to conduct investigations to protect their families, towns, territories, States and America to pursue a career as a private investigator. The *'Illinois Private Detective Act of 2004'* licenses detectives and agencies to make:

"... investigations for a fee or other consideration to obtain information relating to:

(1) Crimes or wrongs done or threatened against the United States, any state or territory of the United States, or any local government of a state or territory.

(2) The identity, habits, conduct, business occupation, honesty, integrity, credibility, knowledge, trustworthiness, efficiency, loyalty, activity, movements, whereabouts, affiliations, associations, transactions, acts, reputation, or character or any person, firm, or other entity, by any means manual or electronic.

(3) The location, disposition, or recovery of lost or stolen property.

(4) The cause, origin, or responsibility for fires, accidents, or injuries to individuals or real or personal property.

(5) The truth or falsity of any statement or representation.

(6) Securing evidence to be used before any court, board, or investigating body.

(7) The protection of individuals from bodily harm or death (bodyguard functions).

(8) Service of process in criminal and civil proceedings.'..."

[Source: 'Illinois Private Detective Act of 2004' (225 ILCS 447/) - 'Private Detective' definition at:
http://www.ilga.gov/legislation/ilcs/ilcs5.asp?DocName=&ActI D=2474&ChapterID=24&SeqStart=&SeqEnd=&Print=True]

Our family owned Private Detective Agency, Stonehenge Ventures, llc – Investigative Services [IL License Number 117-001584] is always looking for qualified *"independent contractors"*. Our agency can provide the necessary training that will allow those seeking to be their own boss the opportunity to generate income as either an *'independent contractor private detective"* or *"independent contractor sales affiliate"* – or both. Licensing laws vary from state to state. Our website and blog can offer details on the necessary steps to begin a new career as a private detective. Visit us at *www.AAAprivateEYE.org* for details on how to start your new career in private investigations.

Though we cannot guarantee your eligibility under the rules of the state where you reside, our training does meet the State of Illinois private detective training requirements to obtain an Illinois State-issued *"Permanent Employee Registration Card"* (PERC) which allows its holder to conduct private investigations for a licensed Illinois private detective agency. A qualified candidate can be trained in as little as one weekend.

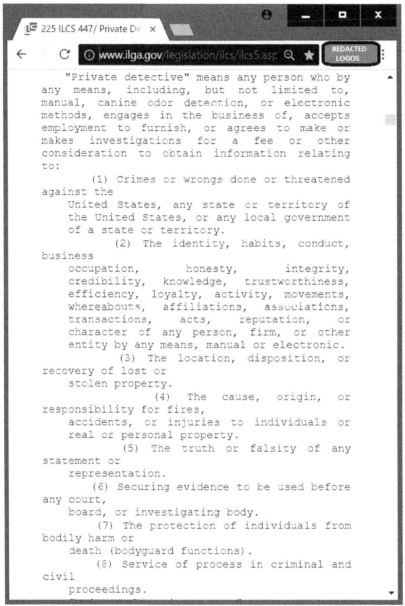

"Private detective" means any person who by any means, including, but not limited to, manual, canine odor detection, or electronic methods, engages in the business of, accepts employment to furnish, or agrees to make or makes investigations for a fee or other consideration to obtain information relating to:

(1) Crimes or wrongs done or threatened against the
United States, any state or territory of the United States, or any local government of a state or territory.

(2) The identity, habits, conduct, business
occupation, honesty, integrity, credibility, knowledge, trustworthiness, efficiency, loyalty, activity, movements, whereabouts, affiliations, associations, transactions, acts, reputation, or character of any person, firm, or other entity by any means, manual or electronic.

(3) The location, disposition, or recovery of lost or
stolen property.

(4) The cause, origin, or responsibility for fires,
accidents, or injuries to individuals or real or personal property.

(5) The truth or falsity of any statement or
representation.

(6) Securing evidence to be used before any court,
board, or investigating body.

(7) The protection of individuals from bodily harm or
death (bodyguard functions).

(8) Service of process in criminal and civil
proceedings.

['Illinois Private Detective Act of 2004' – 'Private Detective' definition at:
http://www.ilga.gov/legislation/ilcs/ilcs5.asp?DocName=&ActID=2474&
ChapterID=24&SeqStart=&SeqEnd=&Print=True]

Those wishing to operate as an *'independent contractor private detective'* in the State of Illinois will need to do so with either their own licensing or on the roster of a licensed Illinois private detective agency with a *'Permanent Employee Registration Card (PERC)",* which allows its holder to perform work on behalf of a licensed Illinois detective agency.

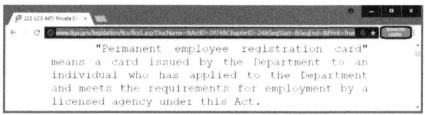

[http://www.ilga.gov/legislation/ilcs/ilcs5.asp?DocName=&ActID=2474 &ChapterID=24&SeqStart=&SeqEnd=&Print=True]

There's no need to obtain the elusive and rarely-issued Illinois State Private Detective license which requires its holder to carry $1,000,000.00 liability insurance, when you can work for our Detective Agency, Stonehenge Ventures, llc as an Illinois PERC (Permanent Employee Registration Card) *'Independent Contractor Private Detective'.*

A *'Bachelor of Science'* in Criminal Justice or operating three out of the previous five years, full-time, as a *'PERC'* detective for licensed detective agencies will qualify a candidate to apply for the Illinois Private Detective Licensing Exam. You can start earning income and gaining experience as an *'independent contractor'* private detective once on our agency's roster. An annual fee covers your continuing education and our administrative costs. But rest assured, our Illinois Licensed Private Detective Agency's training program *"meets the requirements for employment by a licensed agency under this Act'…"*

There are three ways to obtain the elusive and rarely issued *'Illinois Private Detective License'.* Applicants can apply for *"Licensure by Endorsement";* this method requires applicants to obtain licensing in a state with similar requirements to Illinois licensing requirements and, then have an endorsement of your application.

When speaking with the Illinois Department of Financial and Professional Regulations, the private detective licensing agency in Illinois, it was strongly suggested that the odds of approval were greater if the *"endorsement"* came from a prominent member of society, perhaps a politician or military officer, etcetera.

The other two methods of obtaining your own private detective license in Illinois require passing the Illinois Detective Licensing Exam. Only applicants with a BS in Criminal Justice or with work-history for three out of the past five years, full-time, with a detective agency can qualify for the exam's application process and fee schedules.

Without *'detective training'*, anyone can become an *"Independent Contractor Sales Affiliate"* with our agency. Our *'affiliates'* can promote their own investigative services through our agency to generate their own investigative assignments as one of our *'Independent Contractor Private Detectives'*, once they've completed our state-qualified private detective training course.

Bring in cases and earn a commission. Investigate the cases and earn even more, as we offer some of the highest competitive wages in the industry for our *'Independent Contractor Private Detectives'*.

There's more. Qualified out of state residents can also apply for the Illinois Conceal Carry License (CCL) as our agency encourages Americans to exercise their Rights. And qualified Illinois residents can obtain the Illinois Firearm Control Card (FCC) under our agency's licensing once they complete the state certified firearm training and obtain their *'Original Firearms Training Certificate'*.

The Illinois FCC certifies detectives for the following firearms:

- Rifle
- Shotgun
- Revolver
- Semi-Automatic

The State of Illinois also offers a *'Concealed Carry License'* issued by the Illinois State Police. The CCL doesn't allow one to offer armed protective services in the state. But a state-issued Firearm Control Card (FCC) through a licensed detective agency will allow its holder to perform armed protective services for businesses, individuals, towns and schools.

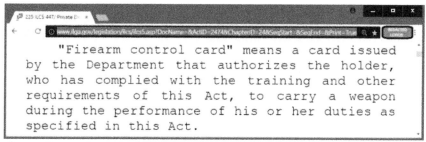

[http://www.ilga.gov/legislation/ilcs/ilcs5.asp?DocName=&ActID=2474 &ChapterID=24&SeqStart=&SeqEnd=&Print=True]

For more information on income opportunities, please visit our website and blog at: *www.AAAprivateEYE.org.*

It is always a smart idea to see the good guys able to protect our American families and our children. Never is there an advisable time to be disarming the good, Patriotic Americans like the detective who got into this business to offer armed protective services to individuals, towns, counties, states and even our United States federal government. But mostly, he acquired his Firearm Control Card to offer armed protective services to our public and private schools, daycares, colleges, universities and even churches.

We see reports of school shootings and some become lost, led down paths to disarmament of themselves and other law-abiding Americans, leaving our country open to tyrants while our American families are left vulnerable to more violent armed-attacks from those also wishing their victims to be unarmed. Attacks at public schools are in *'gun-free zones'*. It seems another name could be *'criminal-gun only zones'*?

While some inside our government's law enforcement seem to be chasing-down leads from *'fake news'*, they majority of our American law enforcement, elected lawmakers and communities work feverishly to prevent further attacks against our businesses, our country, our families. The attacks will continue to be fueled by the destruction of our best defense against tyranny, America's *'Bill of Rights'*.

My generation has witnessed our United States move from Prosperity and Greatness toward the despair of a Third-World country. We need to return to our proud past and *'Make America Great Again'.* We can peacefully *'Keep America Great',* with our Rights to always ferociously defend, *'The Constitution of the United States'.*

The Right to be active participants in our government will be returned to America's last line of defense, the caretakers of our Republic, defenders of democracy, *'We the People of the United States of America'.*

The Kulesza Family – 1970.

All the proceeds I receive from this book will go to assist the detective and his family who, in addition to having their income-source destroyed by Obama's *'ex post facto Law'* and *'Bill of Attainder',* are in need of resources to withstand the ongoing implications of the impossible *'time-travel'* measure needed to comply with Obama-era un-Constitutional *'orders'.* The detective's family requires increased security measures, including but not limited to protective services which can run over a few million dollars per year to counter the un-Constitutional endangerments imposed by Obama's *'Bill of Attainder'.*

The detective would have never entered into Illinois' *"Lawful"* medical marijuana program, placing himself, his family and their family business in jeopardy without the false assurances of lawmakers, courts, the Illinois Department of Public Health, Barack Obama's DOJ and the Illinois State Police Department's own website. Illinois requires detective agencies to have a *'brick and mortar'* in the state; so, relocation costs are extremely burdensome considerations that are approaching fast as Obama's *'Countdown-Clock'* continues to drain the sands of time for their family owned business, the detective's healthcare and his overall health.

Our agency is dedicated to offering what limited resources we have, to assist the detective and his family. We have started an ongoing public-funding-campaign through our agency, Stonehenge Ventures, llc *[IL License # 117-001584]* to raise funds for the detective and his family as they continue our defense of *'The Constitution of the United States'.*

If you would like to learn what you can do to assist the detective and his family as they face the impossible burden of the un-Constitutional *'ex post facto Law'* holding the detective to a *'Bill of Attainder',* please visit our website at: *www.AAAprivateEYE.org*

Thanks for reading. God Bless.

THE END ?

Matthew P. Kulesza

Made in the USA
Middletown, DE
17 May 2019